IMAGES of America

HELLERTOWN

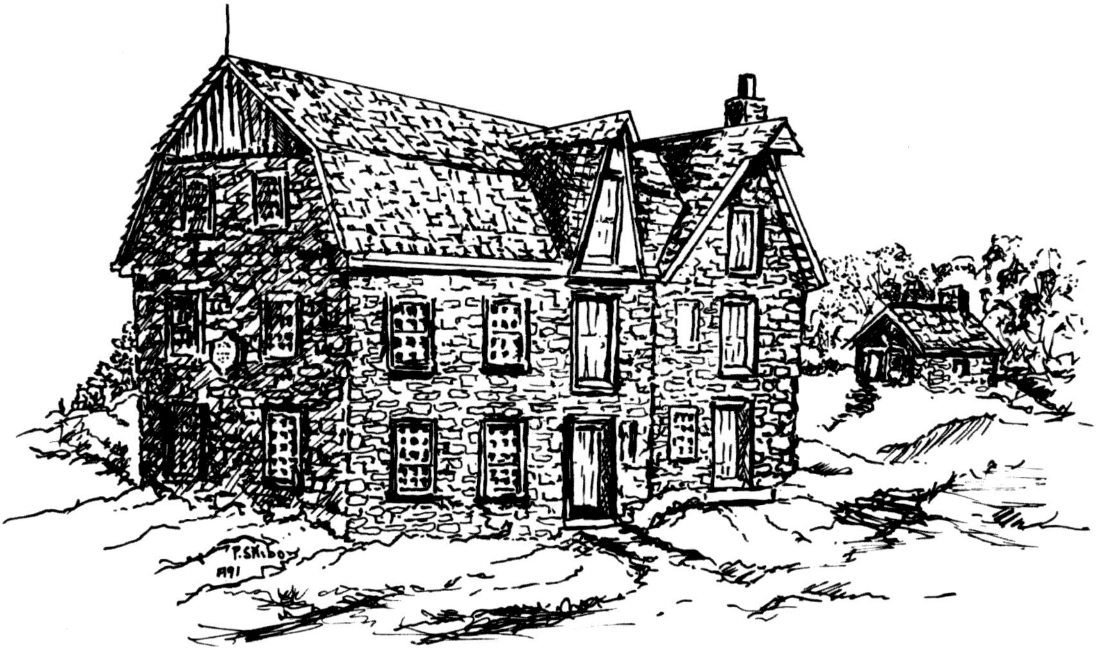

This 18th-century mill was purchased by Christopher Wagner in the 1740s. It was restored in the late 20th century and is now home to the Hellertown Historical Society.

IMAGES
of America

HELLERTOWN

Lee A. Weidner with the Hellertown Historical Society

ARCADIA
PUBLISHING

ISBN 978-0-7385-1162-7

Published by Arcadia Publishing
Charleston, South Carolina

Printed in the United States of America

Library of Congress Catalog Card Number: 2002115306

For all general information contact Arcadia Publishing at:
Telephone 843-853-2070
Fax 843-853-0044
E-mail sales@arcadiapublishing.com
For customer service and orders:
Toll-Free 1-888-313-2665

Visit us on the Internet at www.arcadiapublishing.com

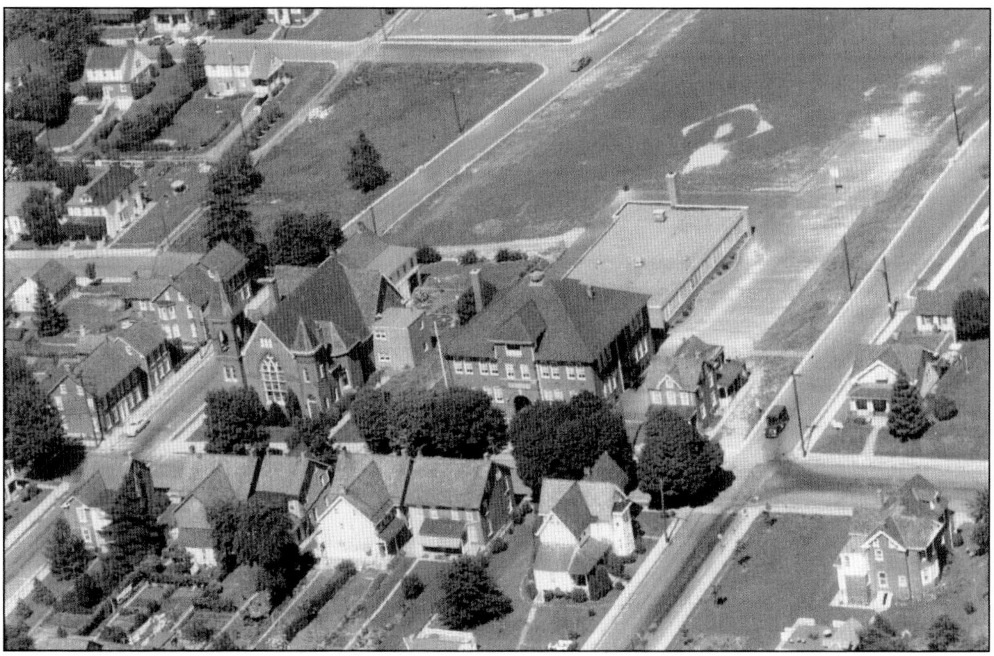

Looking east, this photograph by Stanley Keck plainly shows the Reinhard School and Christ Union Church.

Contents

ACKNOWLEDGMENTS

This book is dedicated to all past and present Hellertown Historical Society members who have helped reveal Hellertown's history to the present generation. For the donated photographs during the 20th century, special thanks are due to residents who saw fit to preserve Hellertown's heritage.

Individually, the president of the society, Albert Hoppes, has been an inspiration during the last three years. Also, Harry and Jeanette Boos have been influential by bringing Arcadia Publishing materials to my attention after one of their sojourns to New England.

Many society members stop by the Miller's House on Tuesdays and Saturdays to share stories of the early 20th century and sometimes donate family artifacts to which there are attached anecdotes.

This volume would not have been completed without the extraordinary word processing skills of my children, Lynn, Robert, and Laura.

—Lee A. Weidner

INTRODUCTION

During the latter years of the 19th century and first half of the 20th century, Hellertown resembled any small town in America with industry and small businesses on the rise. Many residents participated in two world wars and suffered through the Great Depression, yet they maintained a positive attitude toward the growth of democracy. This book records these years as a lasting tribute to the citizens who lived through them. The photographs were donated by Hellertown residents to the Hellertown Historical Society during the 20th century.

South of the cities of Allentown and Bethlehem and west of Easton, Hellertown sits securely in the Saucon Valley. The borough is bordered on its west side by the Saucon Creek for about one and one-half miles. Centuries ago, the Native Americans in the area named the creek *Sakunk*, which means "place where a small stream empties into a larger stream." During the 18th century, various businesses depended upon its waterpower to operate. One such business was the Wagner Gristmill, which since 1980 has been restored as both meeting place and as the home of the Hellertown Historical Society.

The borough derives its name from one of the first inhabitants, Christopher Heller. He and his six sons left Amsterdam in 1738 aboard the ship *Winter Galley*, arriving in Philadelphia on September 15. The Heller family originated from Petershiem, near Bingen, Germany, along the Rhine River in the province of Pfaltz. Coincidentally, aboard the *Winter Galley* on the same voyage came the Wagner family of Rotterdam, Holland. Johan Simon Heller, Christopher's second son, later purchased a 200-acre parcel of land along the Saucon Creek, where he built what by 1746 had become Wagner's Grist and Saw Mill. In Christopher Sower's *Germantown* newspaper (published between 1743 and 1762), Christopher Wagner was listed as innkeeper in this same building. Maps of the time indicate that the tavern-gristmill was located seven-tenths of a mile from the center of Hellertown. By this time, the Heller family had moved east into Plainfield Township, near Easton.

During the 1800s, many so-called Pennsylvania Dutch immigrants occupied Hellertown, although *Dutch* was a misnomer. The immigrants spoke *Deutsch* (German), which sounded like *Dutch*. Therefore, the correct name for many of Hellertown families' ancestors was Pennsylvania German. According to *The Story of the Pennsylvania Germans* (1898), by William Beidelman, the ancestors of these hearty and industrious people came from the region of the Upper Rhine and from the Valley of the Neckar in South Germany. These people had become known as German Palatines. Until the start of the 20th century, children of Pennsylvania

German extraction had a great disadvantage in area schools that were primarily conducted in English. Some texts were written so as to contain both languages side by side.

Another important early family in town was that of Anthony Boehm, who built the very first homestead on what was to be known as the King's Highway and later Main Street. Anthony was the son of the famed Rev. John Philip Boehm, the first Reformed Church minister in Pennsylvania. Born in 1818 in Hellertown, Thomas Weber was to be still another very influential resident in the town's history. Besides writing a hymnal that would reach 16 editions, he published Hellertown's first newspaper, the *Hellertown Telegraph*, in 1858. Also a surveyor and civil engineer, Weber was commissioned by the town council to survey Hellertown for a future water system in 1885.

In 1886, the Hellertown plant of the Thomas Iron Company was chartered and eventually covered 73 acres of what was then Lower Saucon (now Hellertown). Thomas Iron owned the Saucon Valley Iron and Railroad Company, a necessity for carrying materials. During the 20th century, many Hellertonians were employed by the major industry in the area, the Bethlehem Steel Company. This book chronicles primarily one generation of Hellertonians before 1900 and two in the subsequent years.

One

RESIDENTS

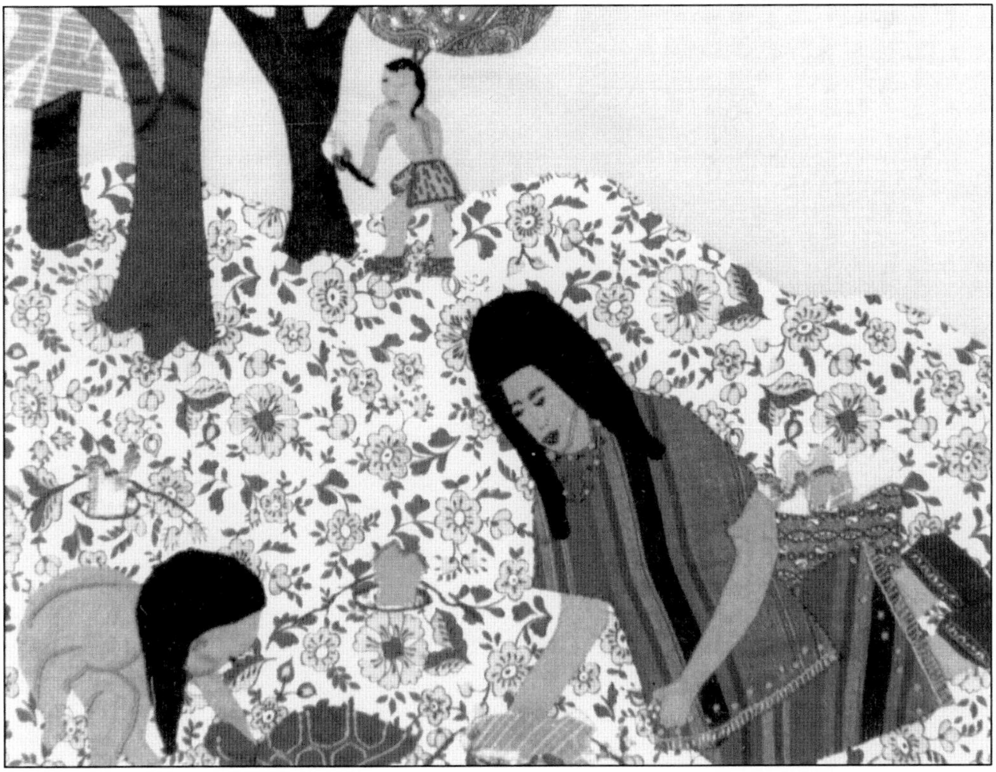

The Native Americans of the region called the Saucon Creek *Sakunk*, which denotes a place of outlet where a small stream empties into a larger stream. Today, children still swim or tube in the creek. Trout fisherman have considered the Saucon one of the best streams noted for native trout. For years, walkers at sunrise have reflected upon the natural beauty of the stream while trekking north or south along the east side of the Saucon. In 1924, the Saucon Valley Camp, No. 168 of the Hellertown group of the United Sportsmen of Pennsylvania, featured its fishing competition along the Saucon.

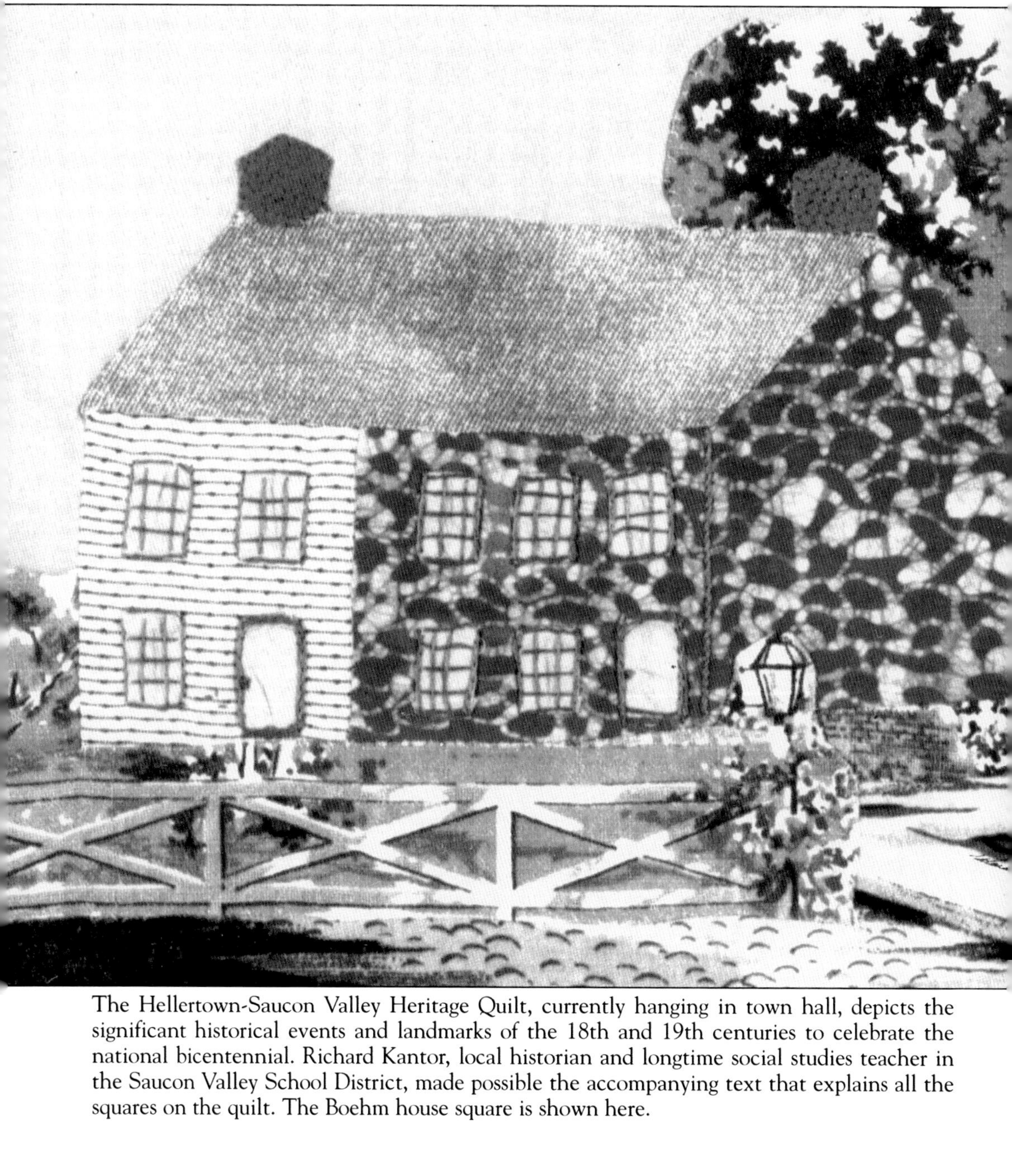

The Hellertown-Saucon Valley Heritage Quilt, currently hanging in town hall, depicts the significant historical events and landmarks of the 18th and 19th centuries to celebrate the national bicentennial. Richard Kantor, local historian and longtime social studies teacher in the Saucon Valley School District, made possible the accompanying text that explains all the squares on the quilt. The Boehm house square is shown here.

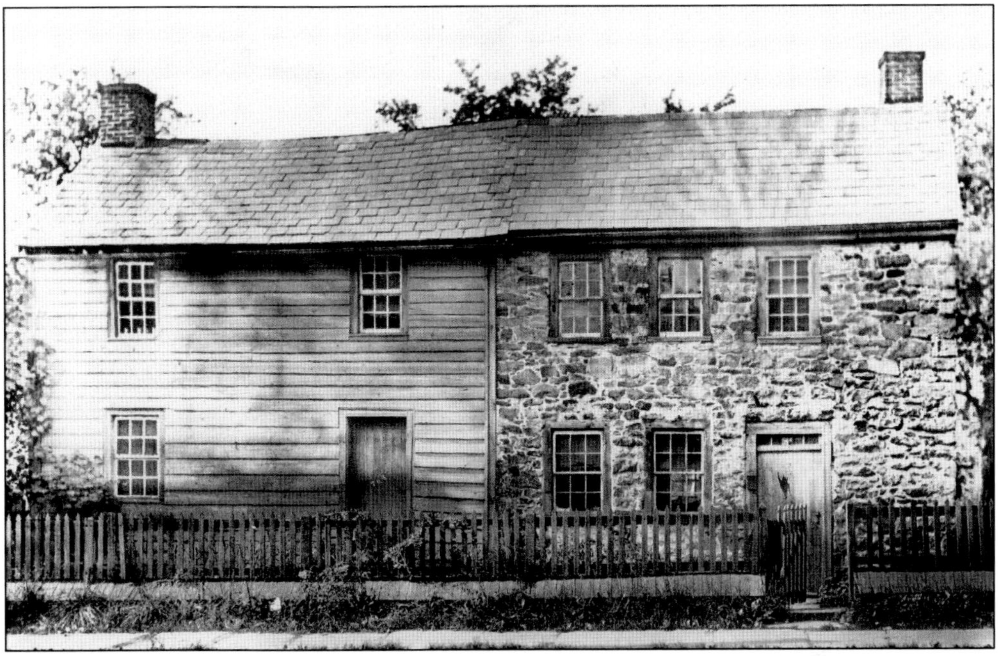

John Philip Boehm was driven from his land, the Palatinate in Germany, by fierce persecution between 1690 and 1720. He was an accomplished schoolmaster and was ordained as preacher in 1729 in New York. He preached until the day of his death, May 1, 1749. Built in 1747 of logs, the Boehm house is recognized as the first house in Hellertown.

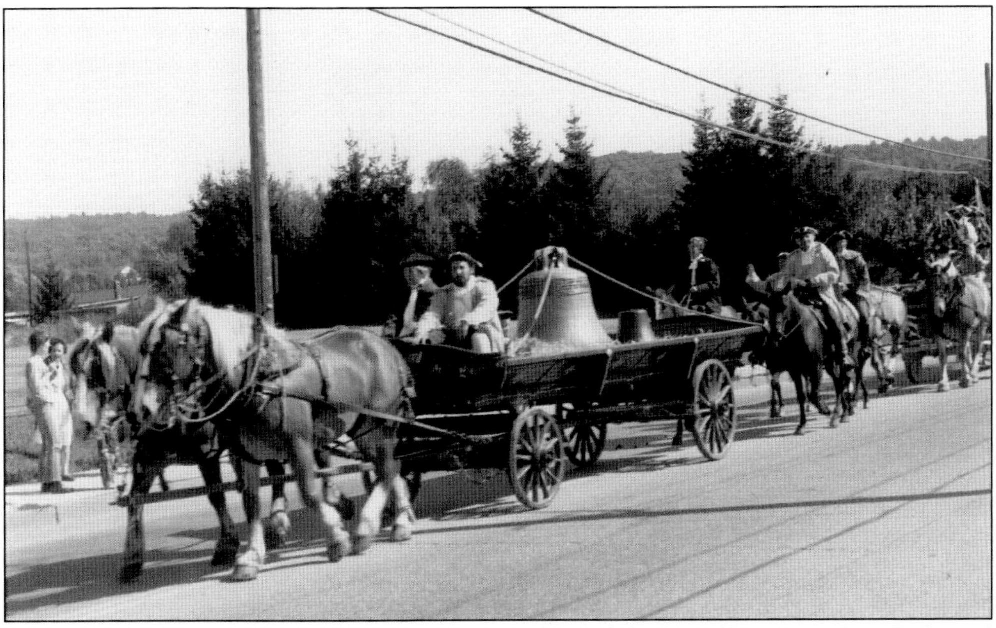

In 1777, the Liberty Bell had to be moved from Philadelphia to Allentown's Zion Reformed Church and, on its way, passed through Hellertown on the King's Highway, as shown in this photograph of a re-creation held for the national bicentennial. Meanwhile, Michael Heller, one of Christopher Heller's sons, left Saucon Valley with provisions for Washington's starving army encamped at Valley Forge.

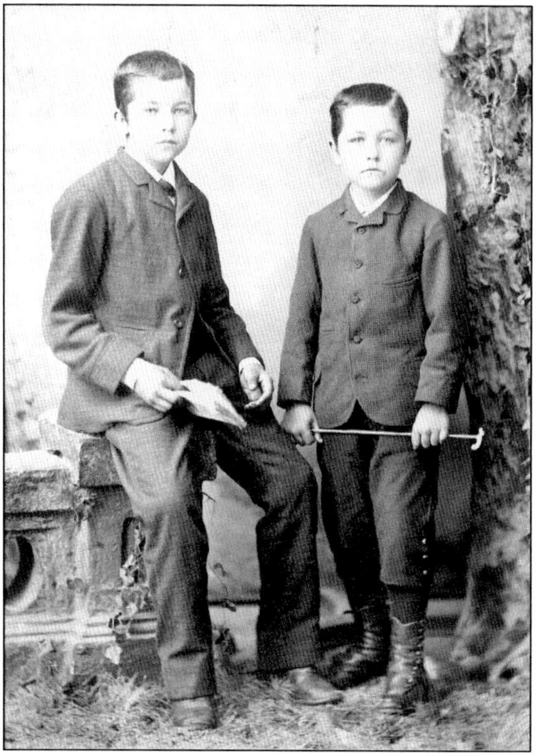

David Christopher Heller (1873–1920), left, and brother Jacob Heller Jr. were descended from the original Heller family for which Hellertown was named. The first Christopher and his six sons arrived in Philadelphia aboard the *Winter Galley* on September 15, 1738. Aboard the same ship was Christopher Wagner, ancestor of the Saucon and Hellertown Wagners. Wagner had come form Rotterdam, Holland, and the Hellers originated from Petersheim, near Bingen, along the Rhine River in the province of Pfaltz, Germany. In addition, Christopher Heller's second son, Johan Simon Heller, purchased a two-acre farm along the Saucon Creek, where he built what by 1746 had become Wagner's Grist and Saw Mill. By 1753, a tavern had been added.

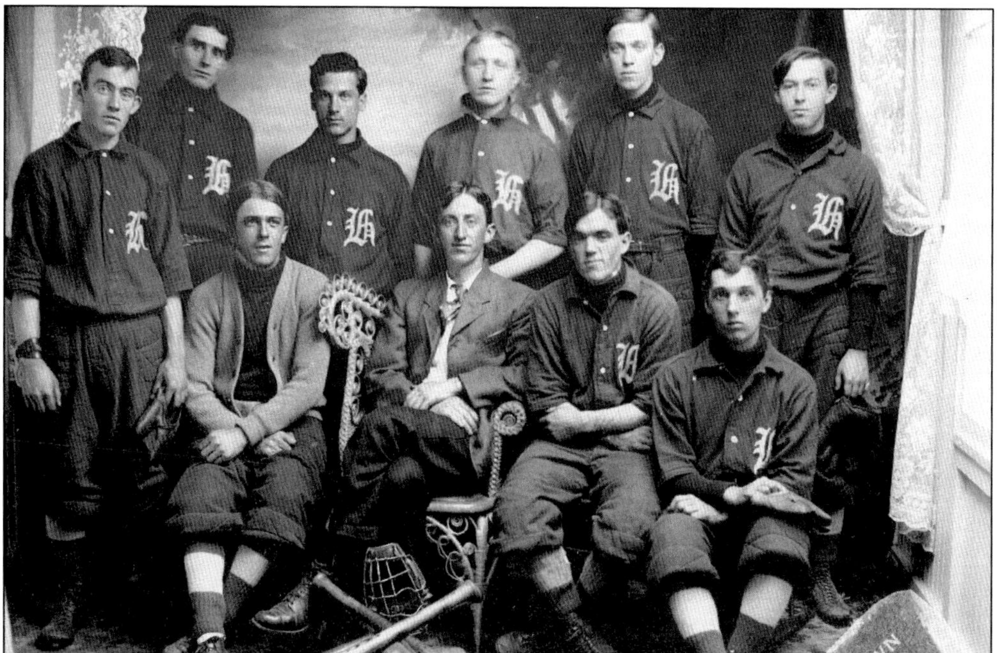

This photograph shows the Hellertown baseball team in 1908. From left to right are the following: (front row) Walter "Dutch" Barnett, manager Luther Eisenhart, William Diehl, and Harry "Stuffy" Barnett; (back row) William Sandt, Harry Harwi, Vincent Ache, Herbert Hoffert, Howard Sutton, and Seymor Heil.

This candid photograph was taken c. 1900. From left to right are Dr. W.F. Detwiller, Henry Eberts, Joley Harris, and the doctor's pet parrot.

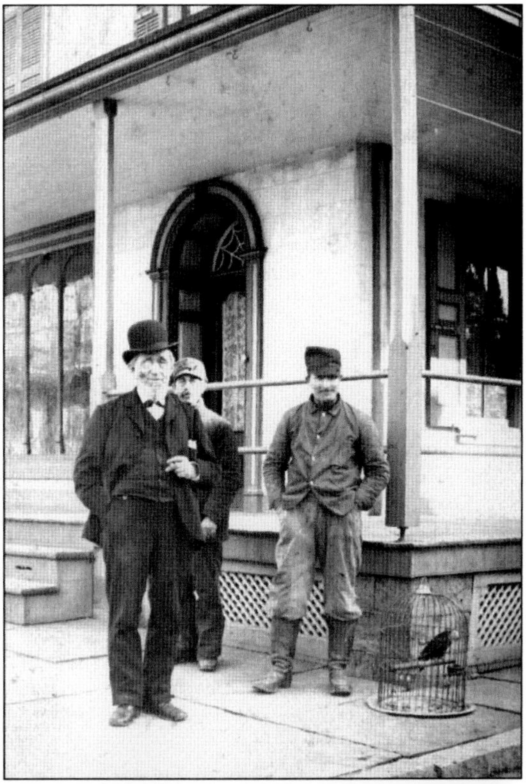

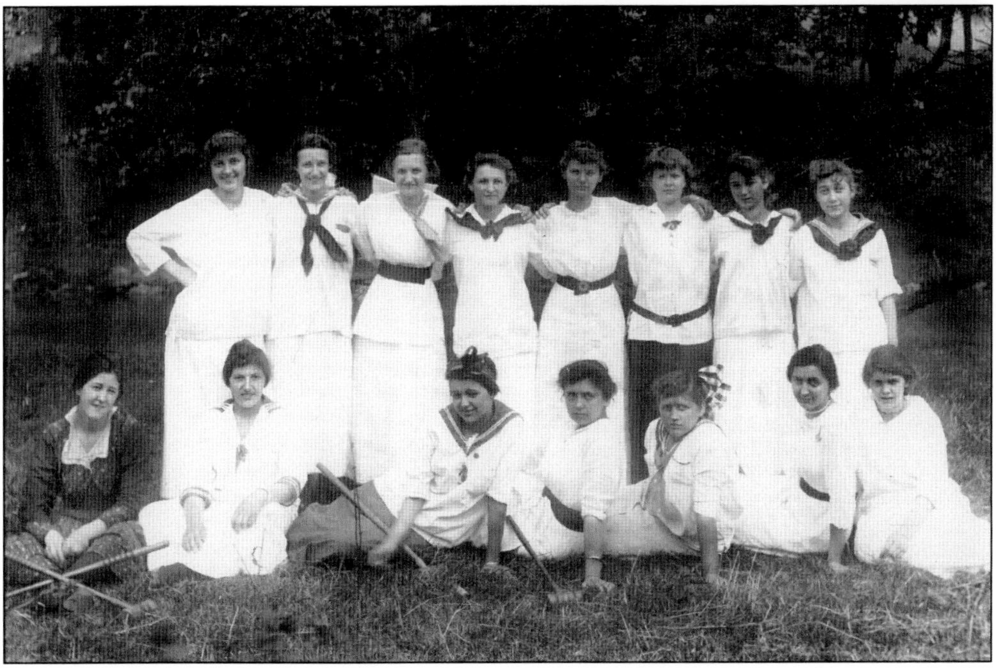

Here we have the early-1900s Hellertown croquet team. Croquet continued to be a popular game on Hellertown lawns until the 1950s. Only two team members are identified: Harriet Hine and Clemmie Bergstresser (front row, fourth and fifth from the left, respectively).

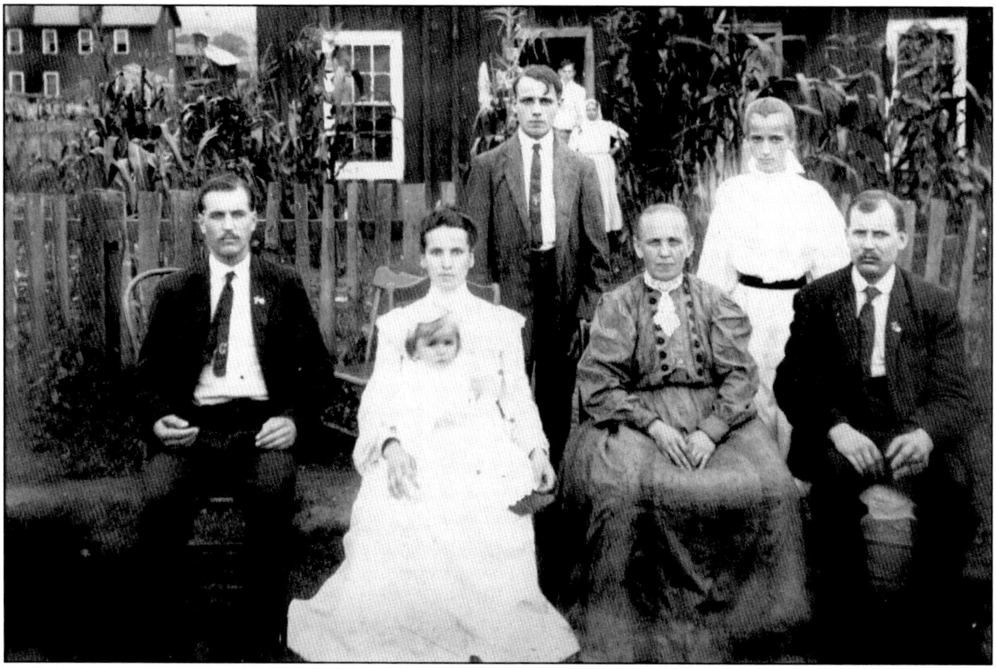

Near the beginning of the 20th century, there were several boardinghouses in Hellertown. Many individuals were provided with lodging and two good meals per day. This photograph features members of the Bacak family. From left to right are the following: (front row) Michael Bacak, Suzann Bacak, baby Anna Bacak, Anna Bacak, and John Bacak; (back row) Mick Petruno and Mary Sluprik.

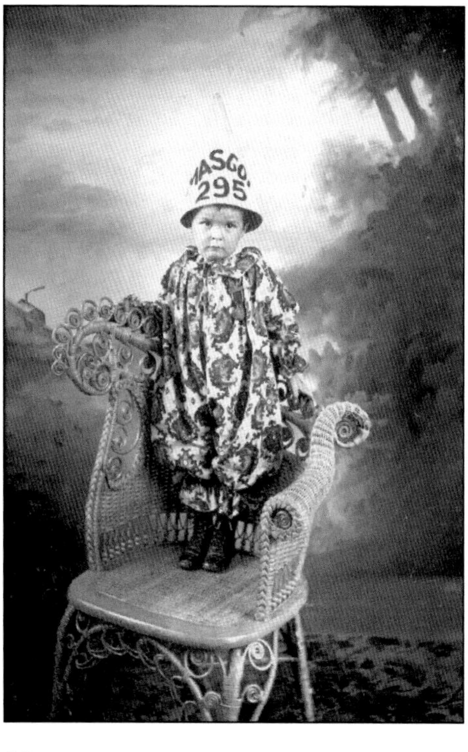

This youngster's image is found on the reverse of a penny postcard dated August 24, 1907. Apparently, it was mailed to Howard Barnet of Wharton, New Jersey, by Titus Ruch of Hellertown. Notice the unforgettable expression on the child's face and his imaginative wardrobe. Also, the cane chair is one of a kind.

This portrait is typical of the time, the late 1800s or early 1900s. The beautiful young woman may be Beatrice Boehm's mother, Mrs. Frank Boehm. Many portraits have no name attached. Perhaps this photograph was taken to mark her graduation or engagement.

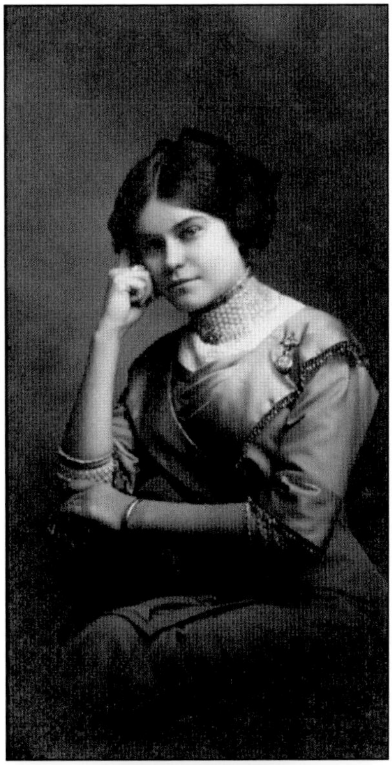

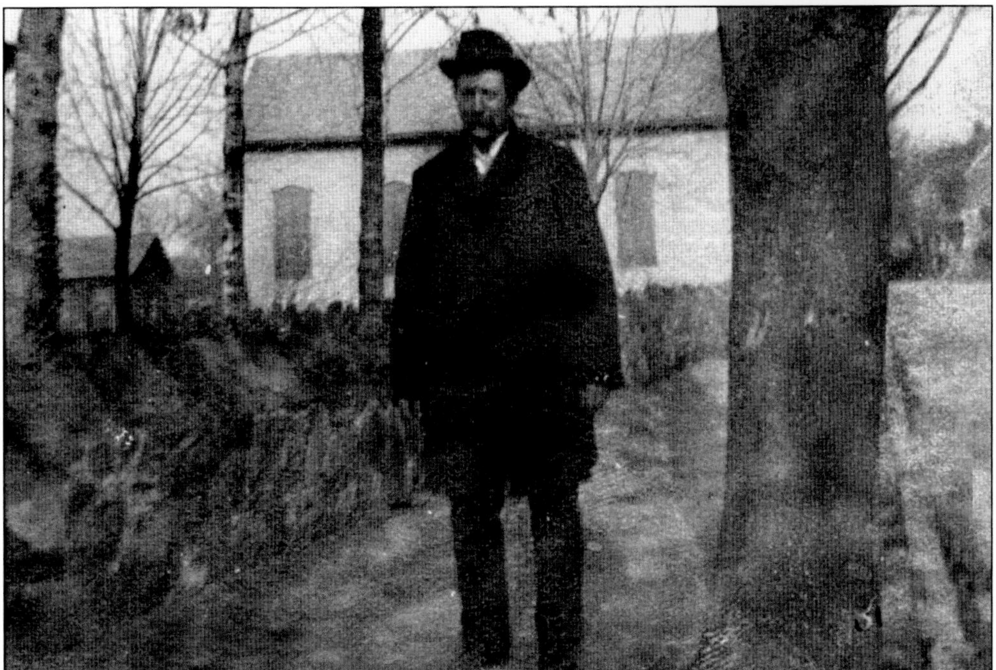

The Hess residence is to the left in this view. In the background is the building that temporarily housed the first high school in town, from 1896 to 1910. This building was mainly the Hess Lumber Company office.

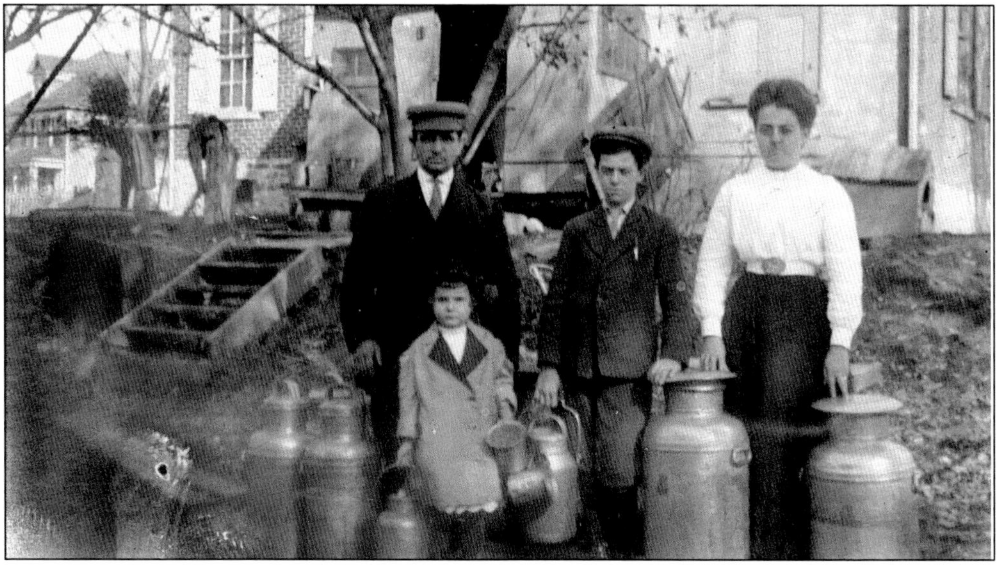

Hellertonians in 1915 walked or drove their horse-drawn wagons or early motorcars to milk-distribution points. Sometimes, a child's errand would be to walk to a dairy with the family's container. Pictured here are Stuart Boehm (left), Charles Seifert, and Sarah Boehm. Evelyn Boehm stands in front.

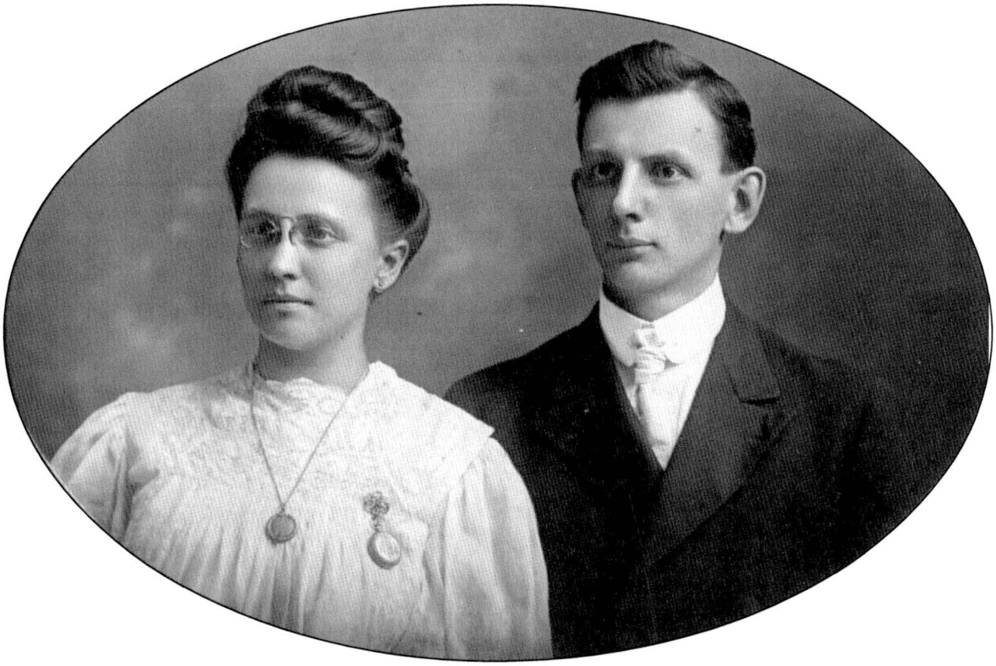

Mr. and Mrs. Joseph Werst were the parents of Estella Werst, longtime U.S. Postal Service worker in Hellertown. They were descendants of the 19th-century Werst family, which included Joseph Werst, who volunteered at an early age to join the Union army against the Confederacy. Werst was killed during the Battle of Gettysburg. He was part of the 153rd Regiment, which was defending Seminary Hill, mistaken for Cemetery Hill due to the Pennsylvania German dialect misunderstood by Gen. Abner Doubleday.

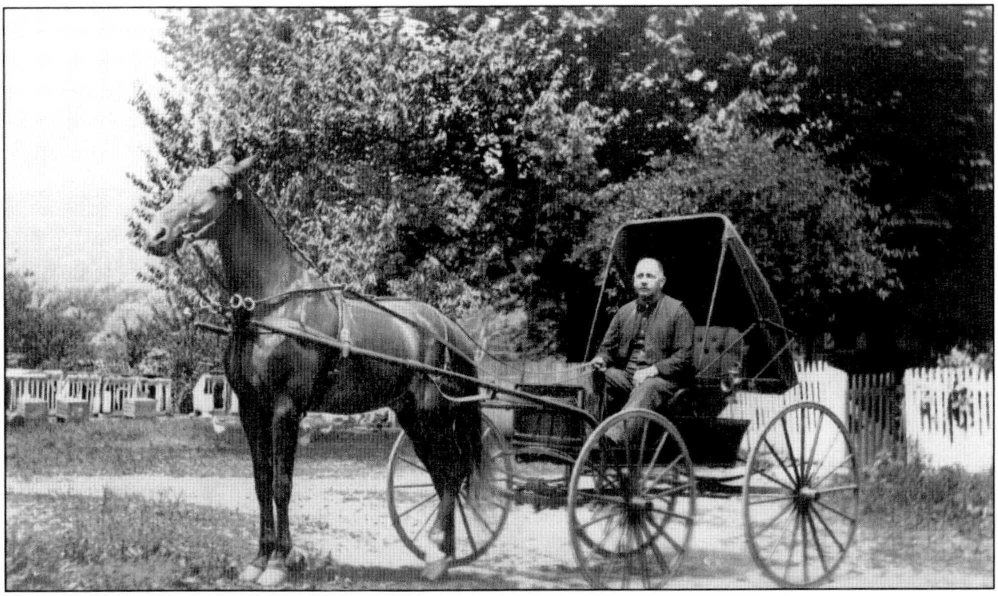

Farmer and owner of a coal company since *c.* 1890, Charles Kichline owned land from Kichline Avenue, named for him, up to High Street. He was active in Hellertown affairs and became president of the Saucon Valley Trust Company.

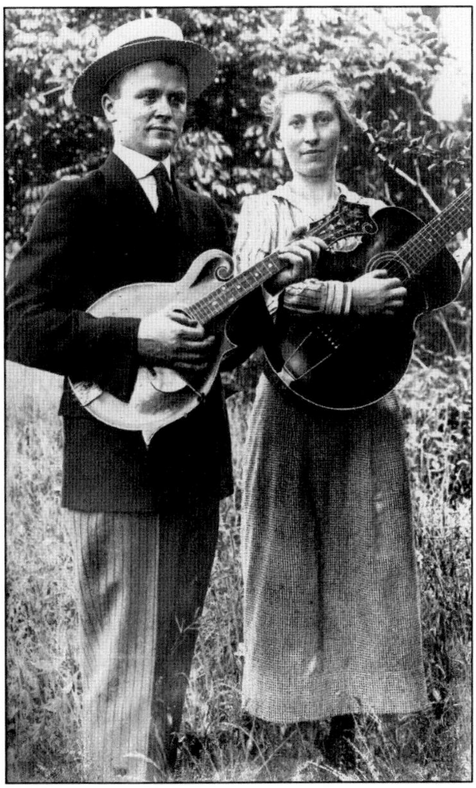

John and Stephanie Nagorski moved to Bethlehem from Erie *c.* 1920, where John learned the shoemaking trade from his father-in-law, John Spadt. The Nagorskis moved to Hellertown, and John began his own shoemaking business in the building that housed the Odd Fellows Hall. After 32 years, they purchased a general store on High Street next to Wolf School.

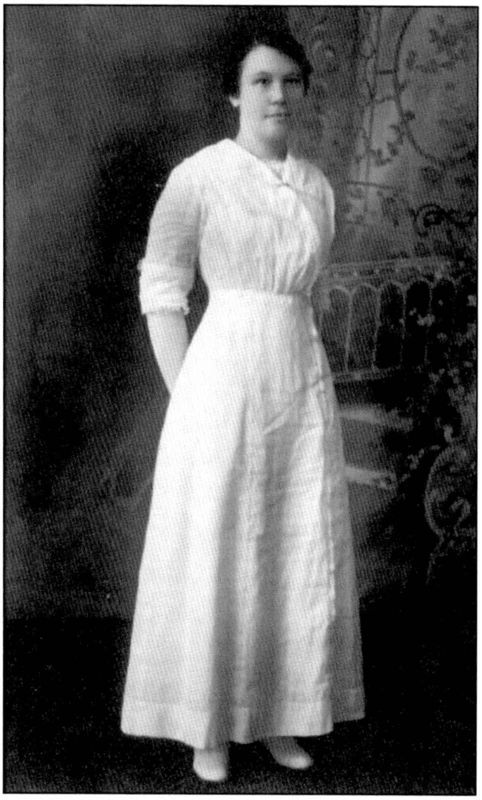

At this point in her youth, Annie Werst (later the wife of Frank Weidner) was about to be confirmed. The author's paternal grandmother, she was noted for her Pennsylvania German style of cooking and baking. Once in a while, she would even serve groundhog to the writer's grandfather. The family still favorably remembers her lattice crust grape pie.

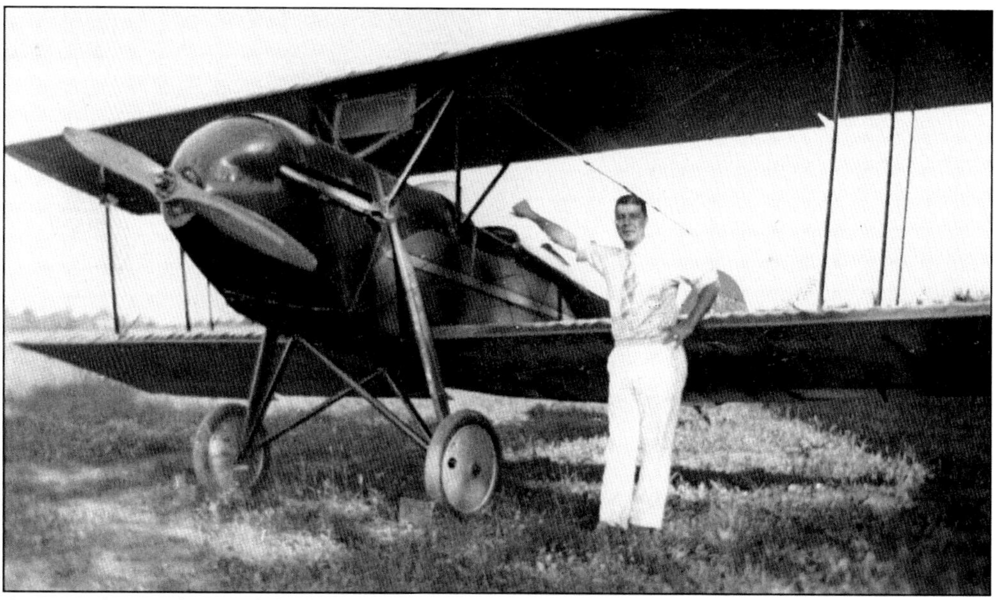

As a youth, Stanley Keck had already earned the nickname "Krazy Keck," but Hellertown had not yet begun to realize how crazy his exploits would become. He became famous for his stunt flying, organizing air shows at the Bethlehem Airport just north of Hellertown, and for assisting with the aerial wedding of Ruth Wagner and J. Harold Stoneback.

Kenneth Dimmick served as bat boy for the Saucon-Crossroads baseball team. He was Marcella Dimmick's brother. Early in their lives, the two had a famed father, Burgess Morris Dimmick.

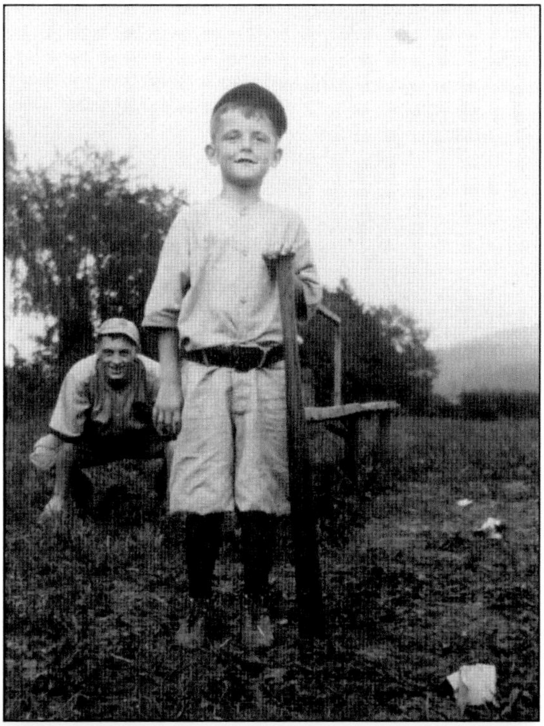

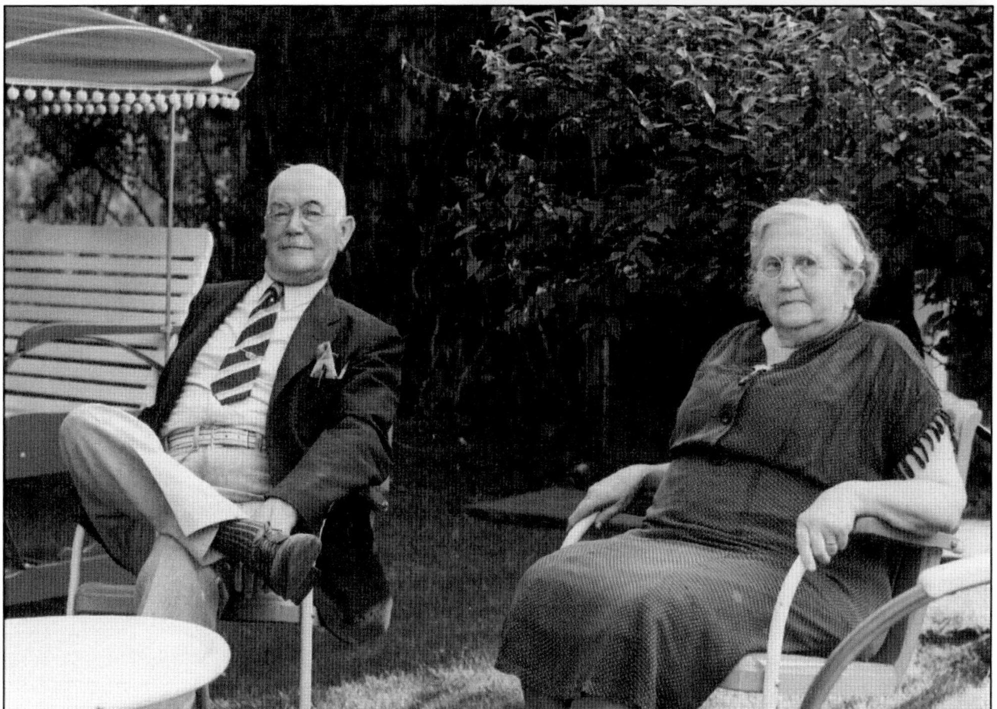

George and Jane Deemer were in the grocery business early in the 20th century on the southwest corner of Main and Water Streets. This would be the site of several other grocery stores, particularly Stern's Market.

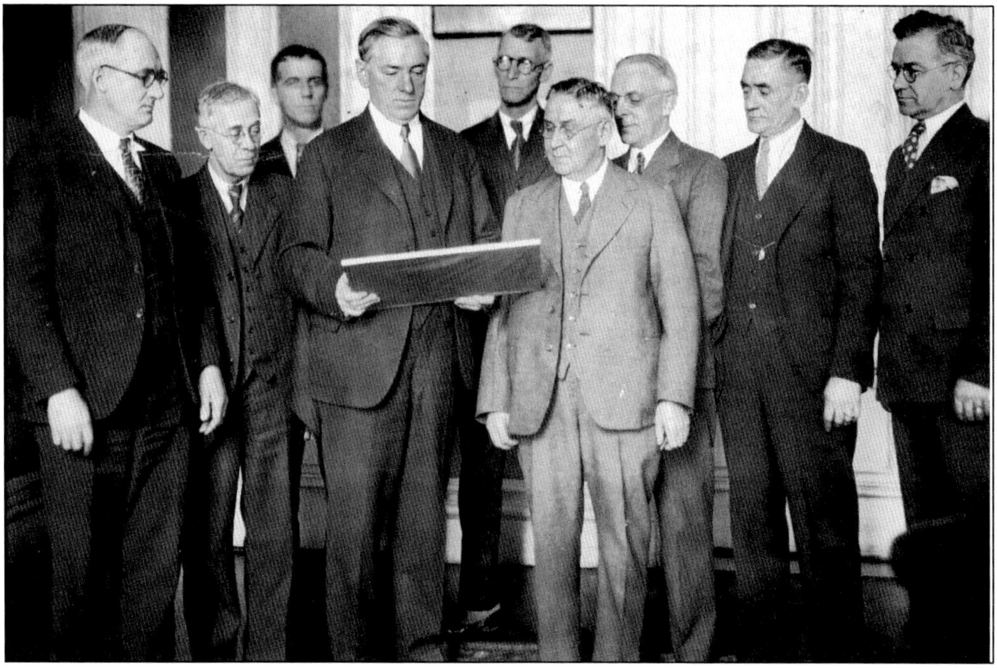

In Boston in 1933, the Sons of Union Veterans of the Civil War were meeting when Titus M. Ruch (up front, in the light suit) was presented with an award. Ruch was the grandfather of Betty McManus, longtime member of the Hellertown Historical Society.

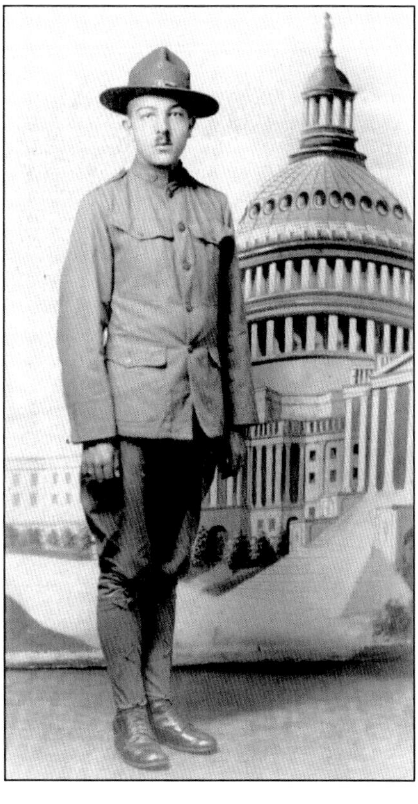

Herbert Weisel is pictured in his World War I army uniform. At this time, he lived at 701 Main Street, his father's harness shop. Weisel would go on to participate actively in community government and church activities. His employer was the Bethlehem Steel Company.

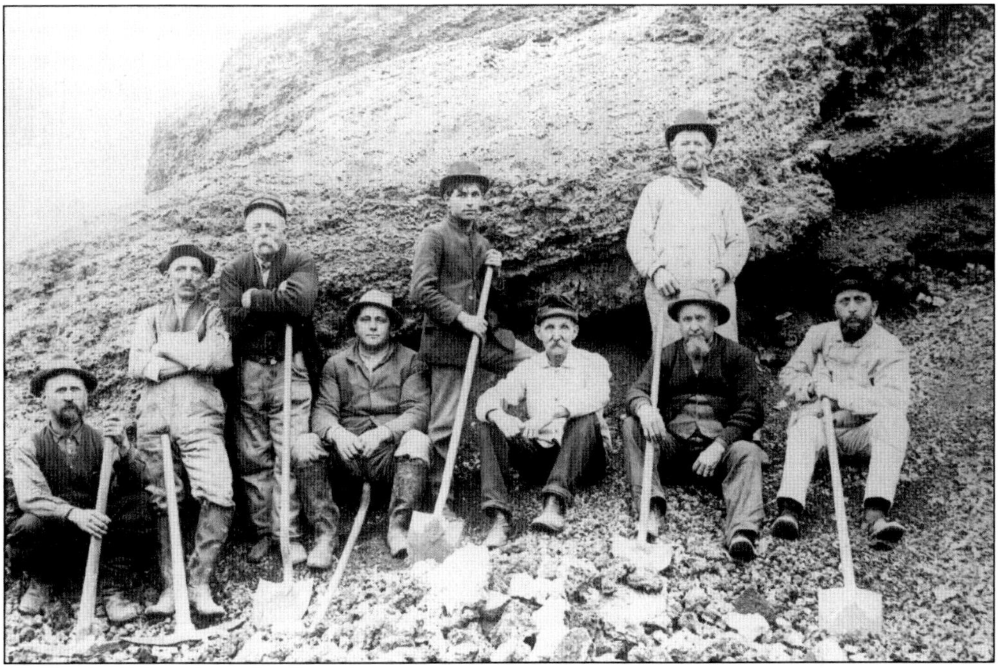

These workers dug in the slag piles, slag being a by-product of iron making. The Thomas Iron Company provided many jobs for Hellertonians. The men assembled here represent various Hellertown families, such as Fehr, Reilly, Leidich, Kichline, Boehm, and Werst.

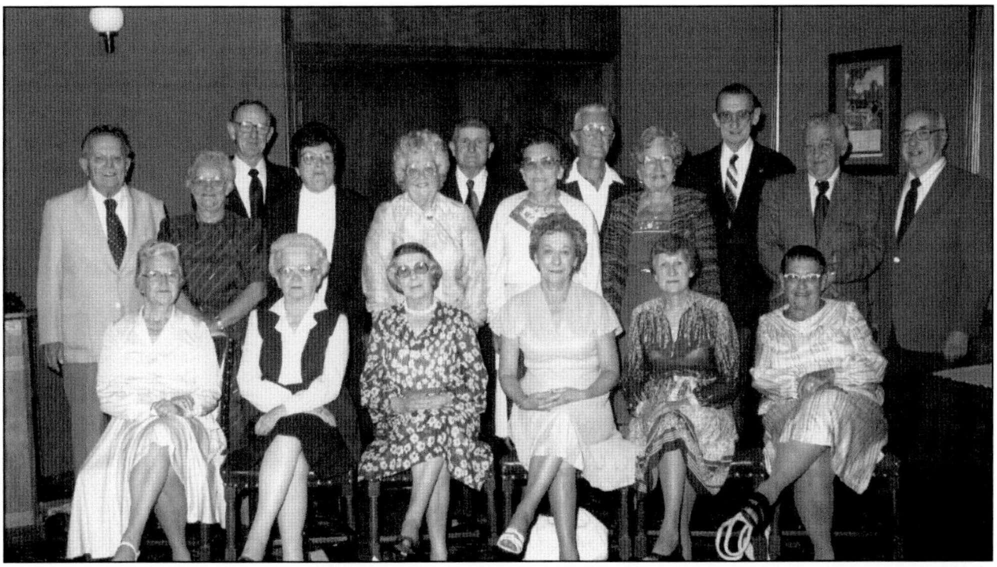

The Class of 1933 held its 50th reunion in 1983. From left to right are the following: (front row) Arlene Nicholas Dieterly, Martha Judd Clark, Mary Barnett Repash, Norma Frederick Lerch, Adelaide Baker Clawson, and Marion Fulmer Cook; (middle row) Henry Buss, Joyce Herman Talaber, Dorothy Johnson La Barge, Vernon Dimmick Muhr, Orpha Diehl Pfeiffer, Adele Moran Brown, Edward Eisenhart, and Howard Clawson; (back row) Stanley Dornblaser, Robert Hoffert, Paul Brown, and Stanley Becker.

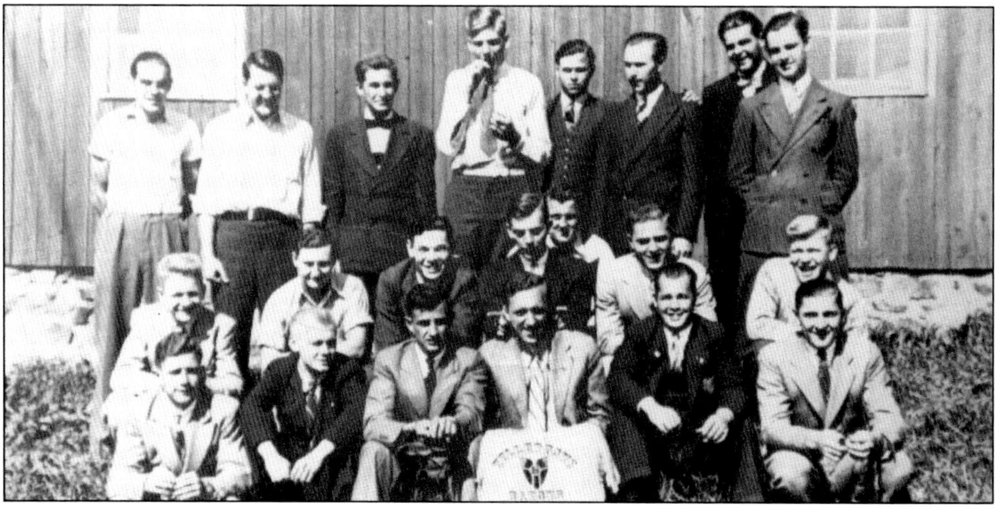

In 1934, a group of young men formed a club in northern Hellertown. They originally called themselves the Bone Crushers and met in the chicken house behind Herbert Riegel's residence. They constructed their own miniature golf course in the Riegels' backyard, and the first president was Kenneth Riegel. As membership increased, the club moved to Herbert Hoffert's barn in the 1300 block of Quintus Alley. They changed their name to the Barons and played ball games against the Hellertown Men's Club, the Bears Club, and the Hines Slicers. Entertainment included playing pool and Ping-Pong, as well as listening to the radio or to J.T. Boatwright play the club's piano. World War II took away many members, and the club disbanded. Pictured, from left to right, are the following: (front row) Bob Hahn, Dave Weidner, Skip Kies, Andy Komar, George Lichtenwalner, and LeRoy Wagner (middle row) Grant Hoffert, Art Shrantz, Junius Boatwright, Kenny Riegel, John Weber, Bill Riegel, and Guy Weidner; (back row) Rodney Johnson, unidentified, Jim Lichtenwalner, Russ Eckert, Bill Trefny, two unidentified, and Cal Boehm.

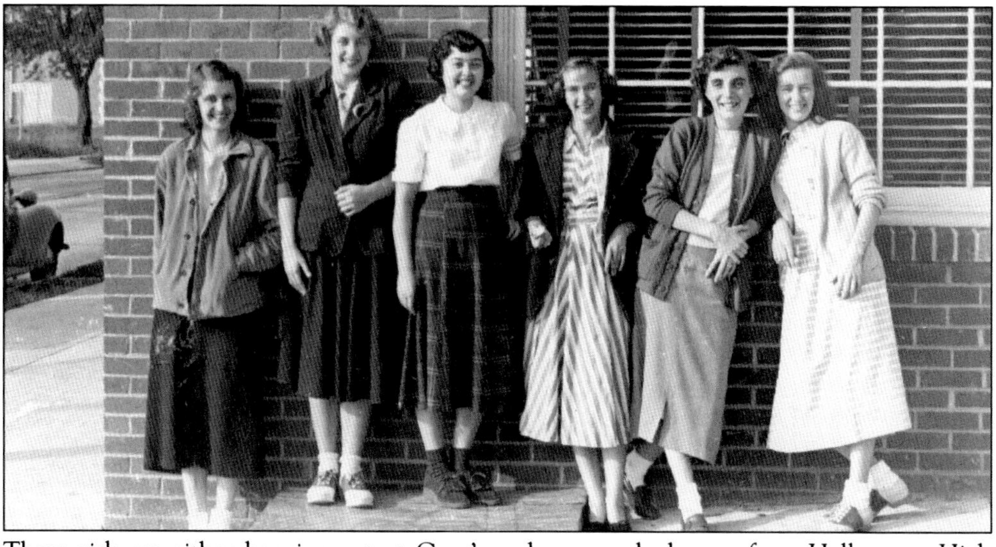

These girls are either hanging out at Guro's or have sneaked away from Hellertown High School. The corner of Main and Thomas Streets was most popular right after school. From left to right are Peggy King Gozzard, Shirley Beil Luybli, Connie Doddy Fluck, Dorothy Spisak, Shirley Durn Stefanik, and Helen Mahaletz Clay.

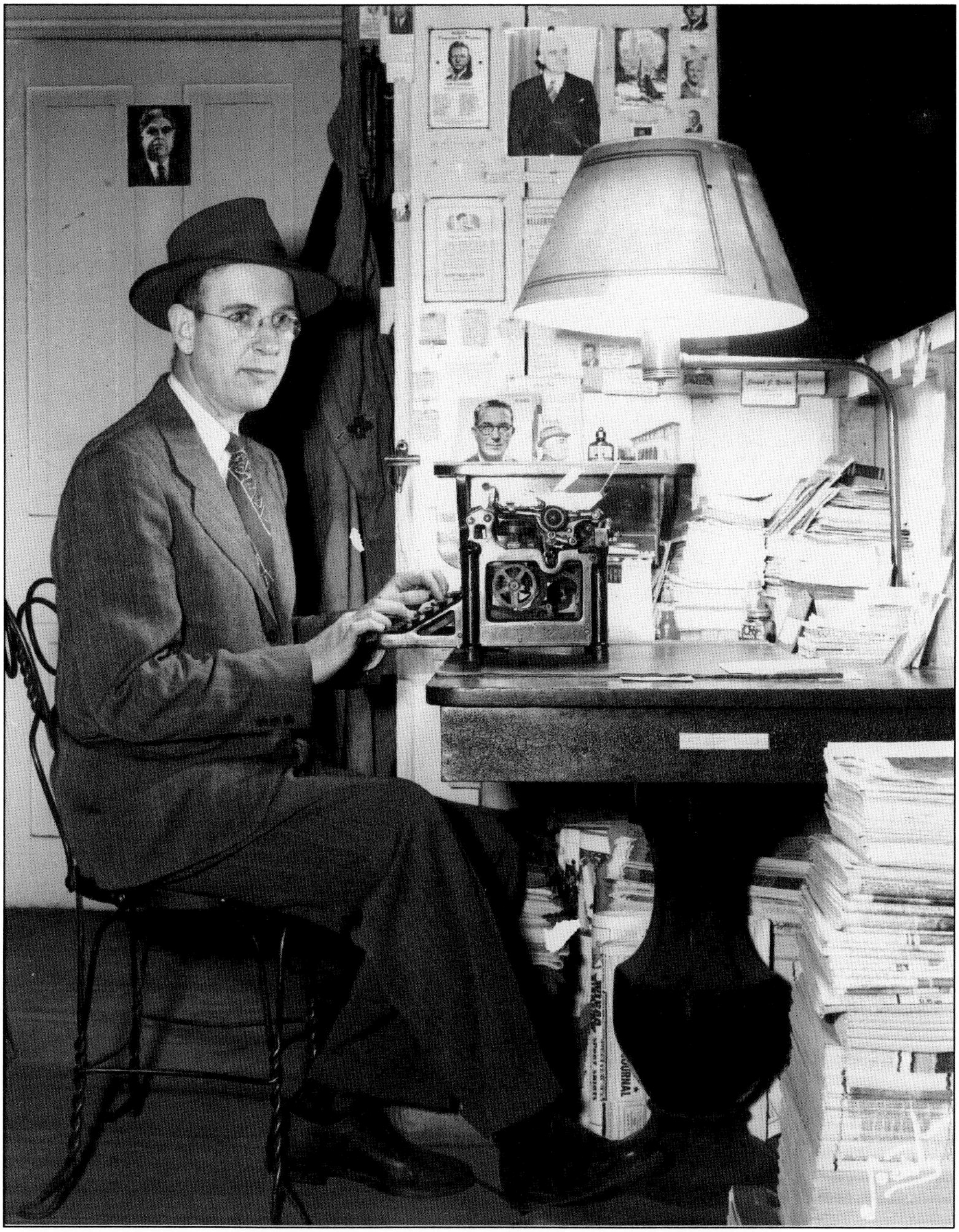

Charles W. Bauder covered Hellertown like a blanket in his weekly *Shopping Journal*. On April 26, 1952, this photograph was taken in his small office, which was located within Ed Brown's Electric Company on Main Street. His office was here between 1950 and 1955, but "Pokey" wore out plenty of shoe leather around town, gathering the big stories.

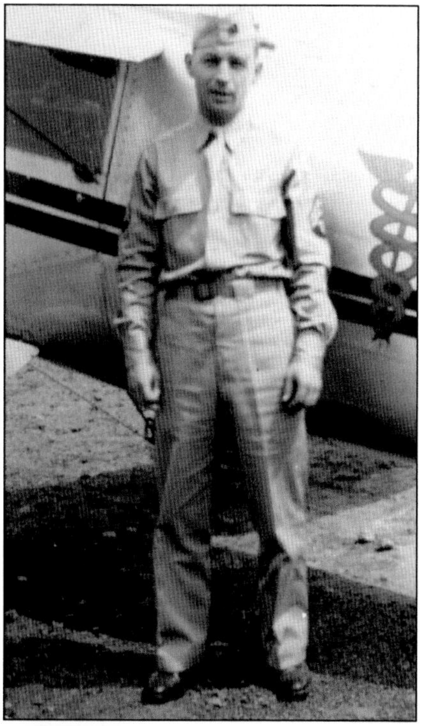

Truman Raudenbush participated in World War II, as did many other Hellertonians whose names appeared on the honor board outside town hall.

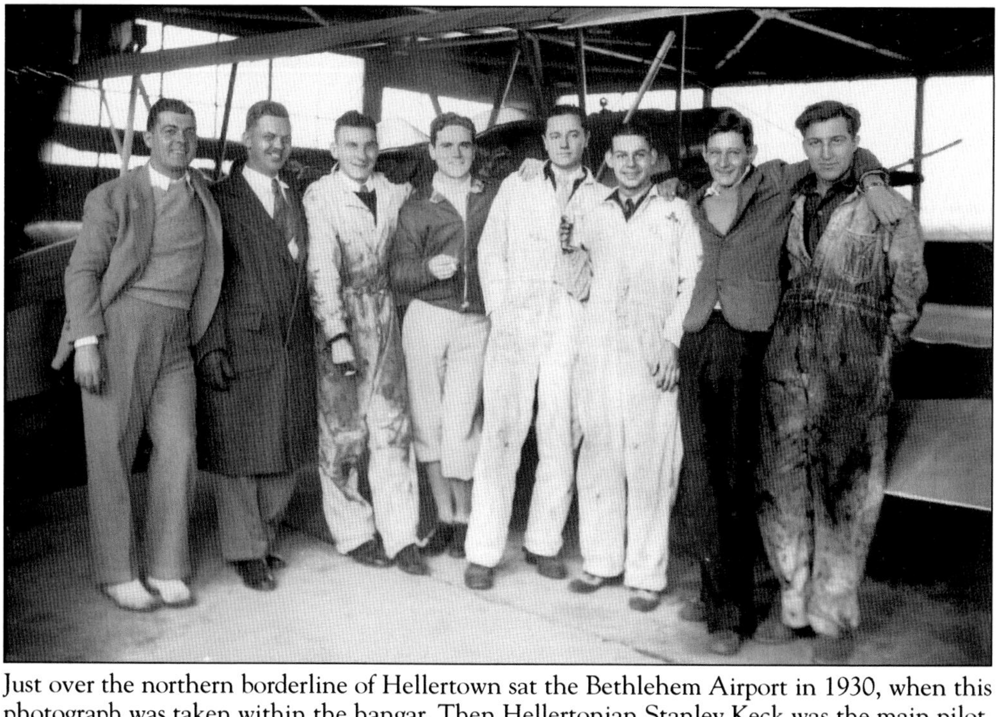

Just over the northern borderline of Hellertown sat the Bethlehem Airport in 1930, when this photograph was taken within the hangar. Then Hellertonian Stanley Keck was the main pilot. From left to right are Stanley Keck; Charles Gerher, engineer; Harold Leamon, mechanic; Nelson Trye, student; Jim Miller, mechanic's helper; ? Traser, mechanic's helper; Slim Wasko, student; and Warren Ohl, student.

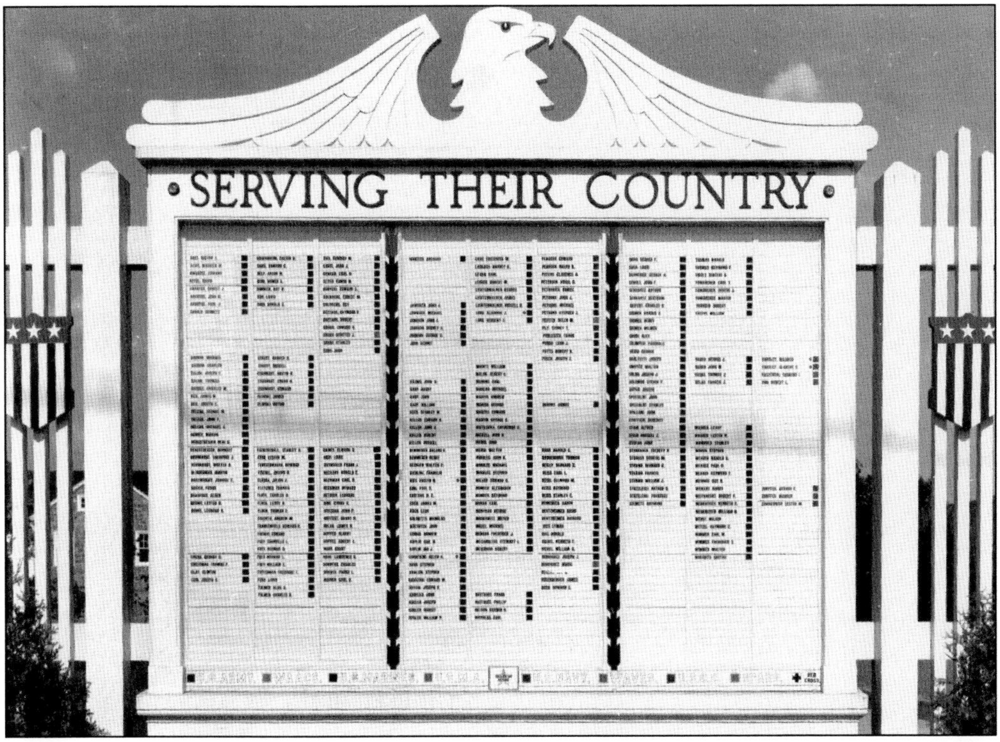

This is one of the few existing photographs showing the memorial board outside town hall. The board listed all Hellertonians who served in the various branches of the military during World War II. No one knows what became of the memorial.

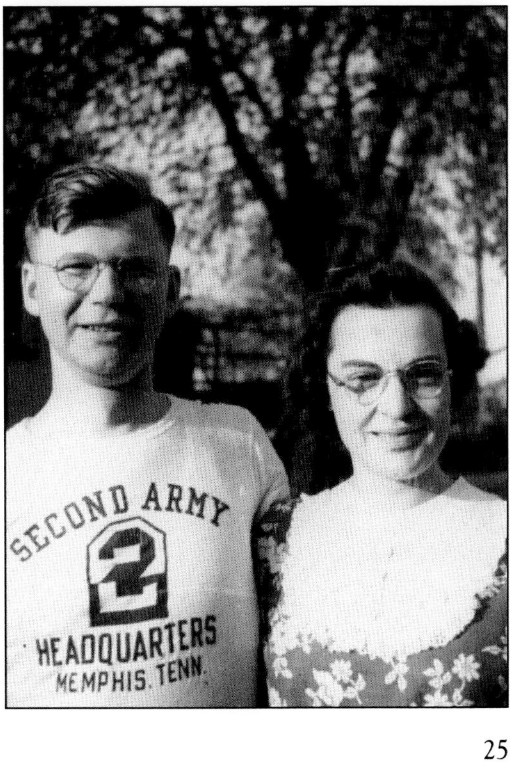

Like so many newly married couples in the early stages of World War II, Guy Weidner was stationed in Memphis, Tennessee, for a time before receiving orders to be transported to the South Pacific. He is pictured with his wife, the former Beatrice Weisel, both natives of Hellertown.

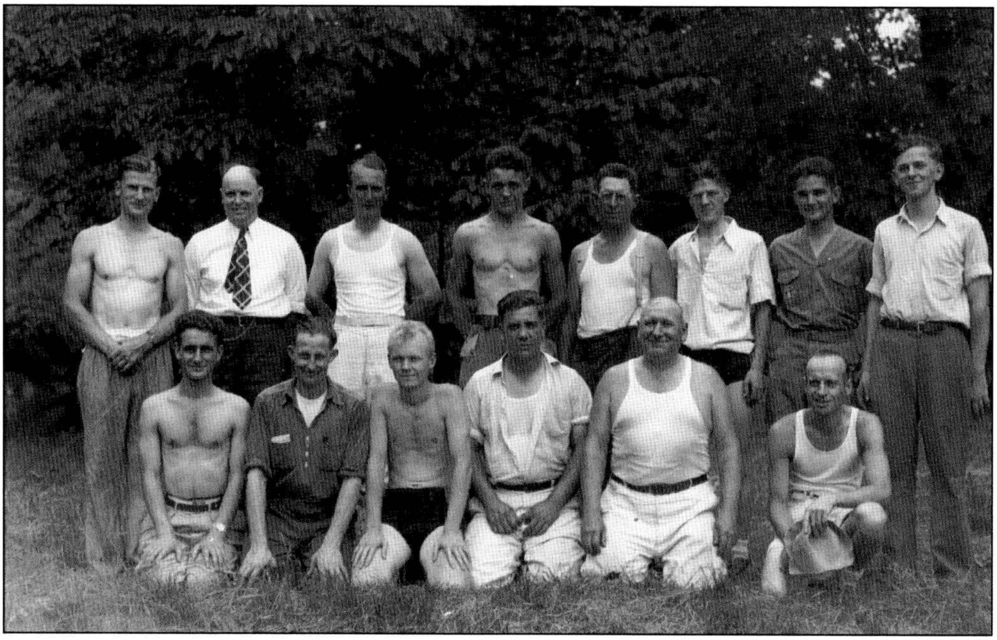

From this 1930s photograph, one can see the many adult and teenage volunteers among various Boy Scout troops in Hellertown. Some among the group are David Eisenhard, John Leith, David and Frank Weidner, John Long, Myron Parsons, Kenneth Nauman, Austin Eisenhard, and Ralph Pearson.

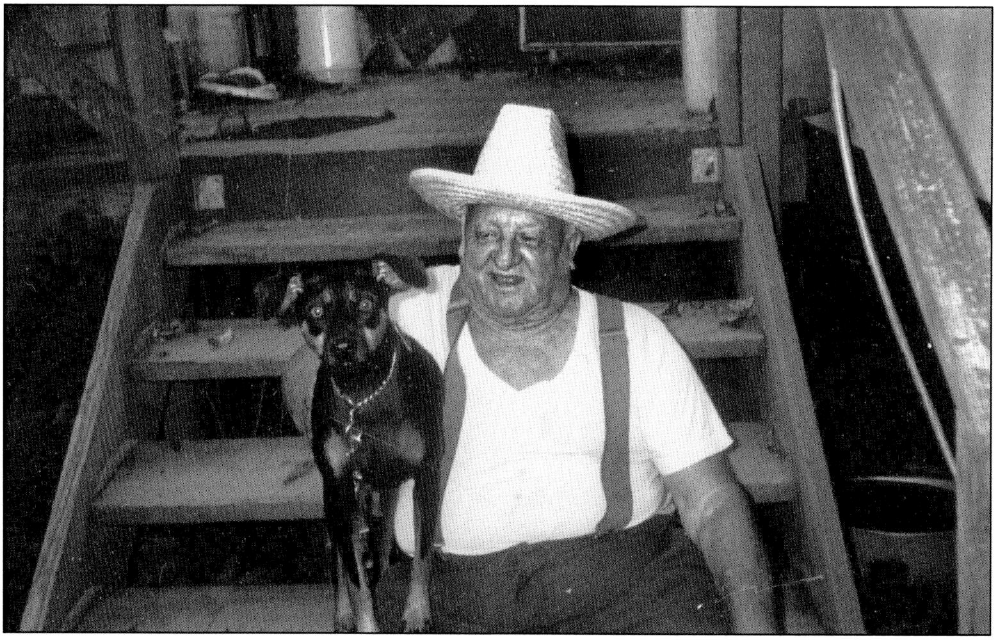

Hunting and fishing since 1927, Al Stair has won three state championships in fly rod casting accuracy. He maintains that the Saucon Creek had been much deeper before the Thomas Iron Company shut down. Over the years, Stair has worked with other sportsmen to maintain the Saucon and continues to volunteer with the Northampton County Conservation School.

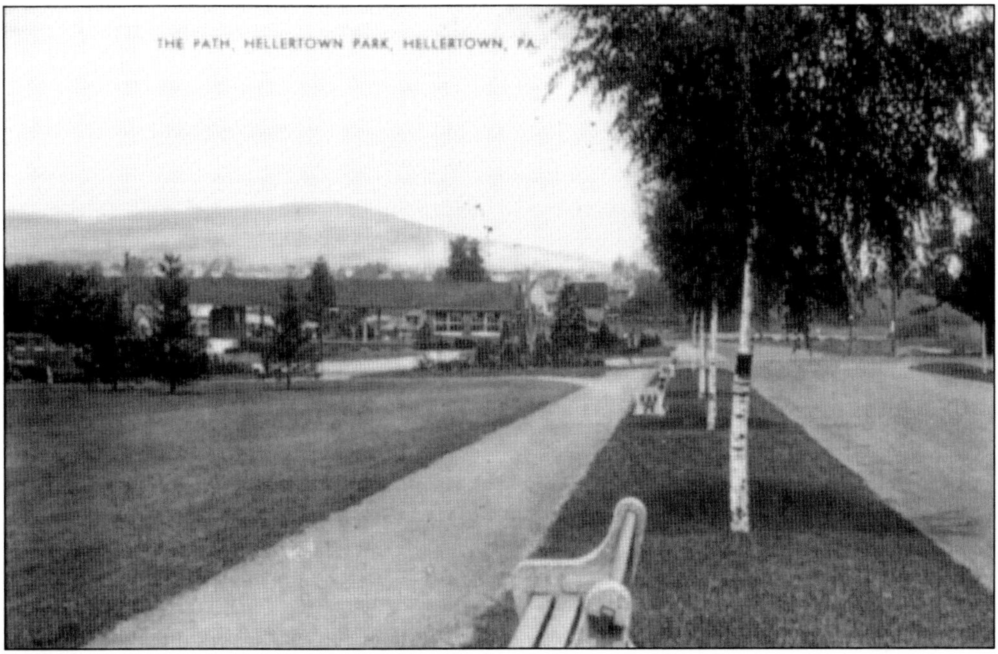

This Dimmick Park path has been traveled often since its construction during the 1930s. The grassy area on the left has been the site of many American Legion and Dewey Fire Company carnivals over the summer. In the background is the Hellertown Municipal Swimming Pool.

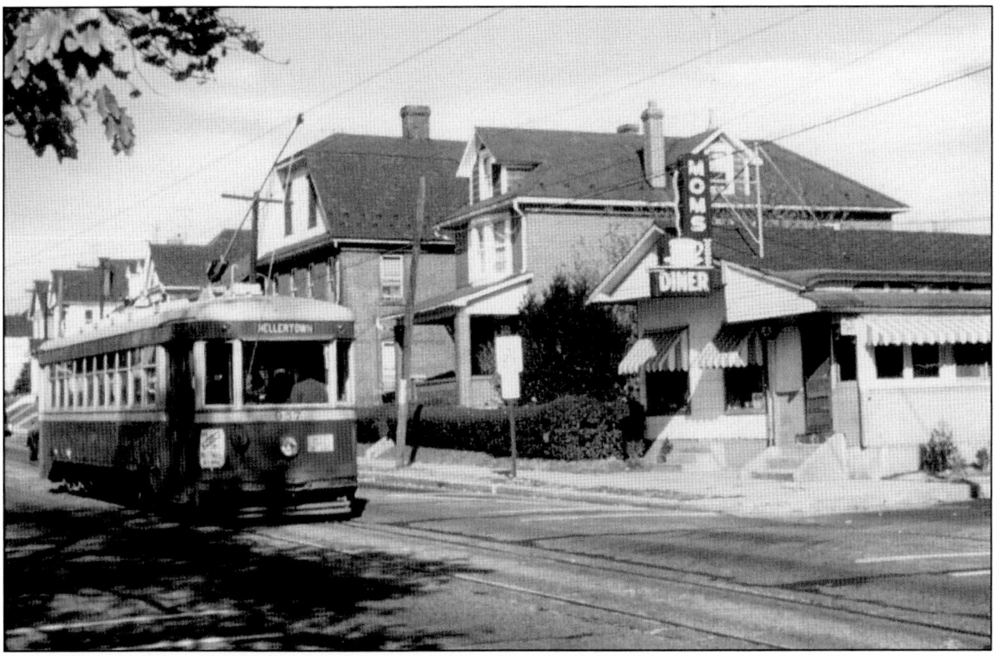

This early-1950s photograph shows Mom's Diner, at 1333 Main Street. Earlier, in the 1940s, it was owned by Andy Komar and John Khula. It was then managed by a Mr. Cope and renamed Cope's Diner. Edna and John Grogg bought the diner from the Copes. In 1950–1951, Doris Weida Magocs owned it. Edith Graham Hoffert bought the diner from Magocs. Hoffert was the last owner, and it was she who named it Mom's.

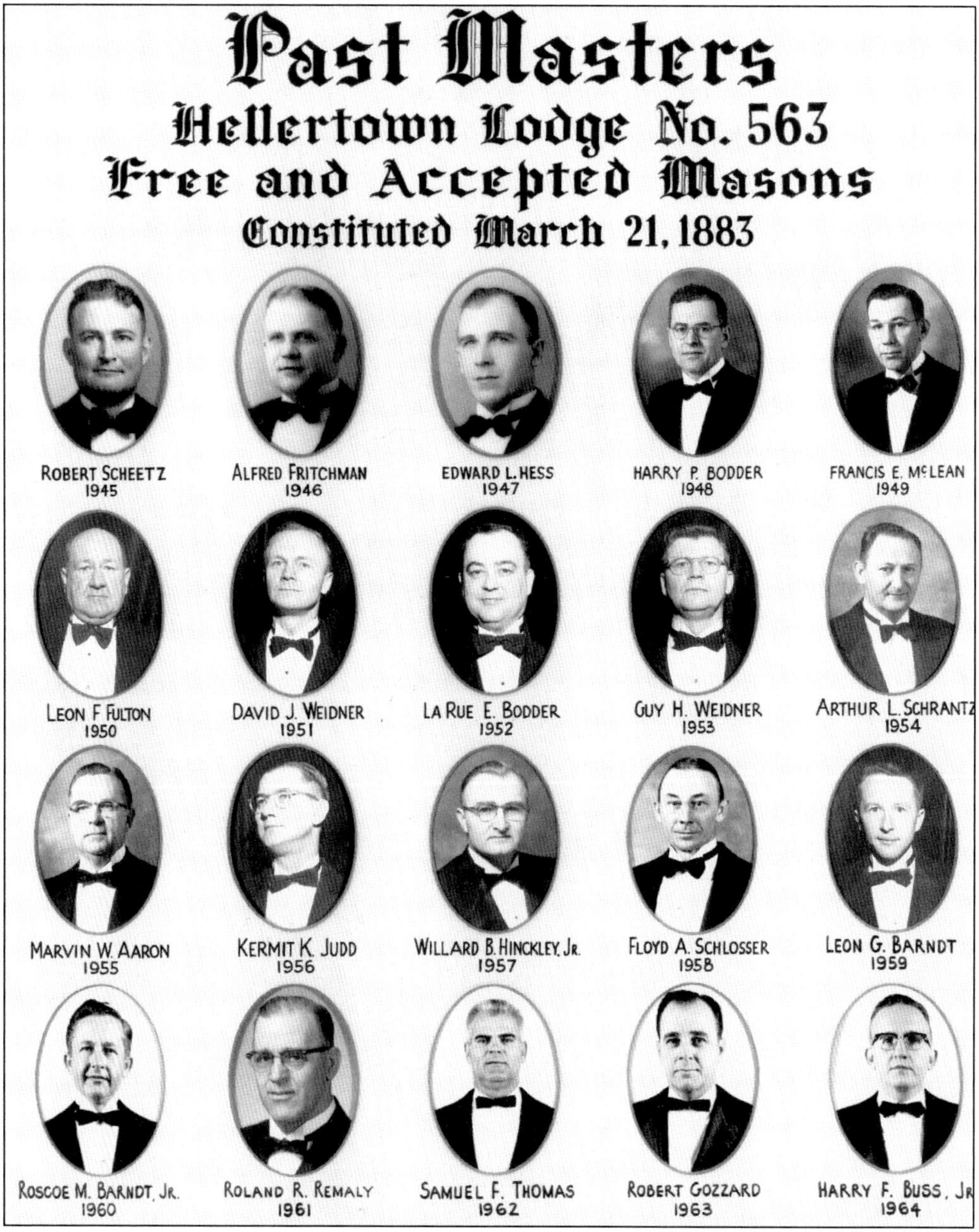

Organized in 1883, Hellertown Lodge No. 563 met weekly upstairs in the Odd Fellows Hall, which housed the original Yeager's Pharmacy on the lower floor. This collection of distinguished gentlemen includes those who served as the leader of the lodge for one year.

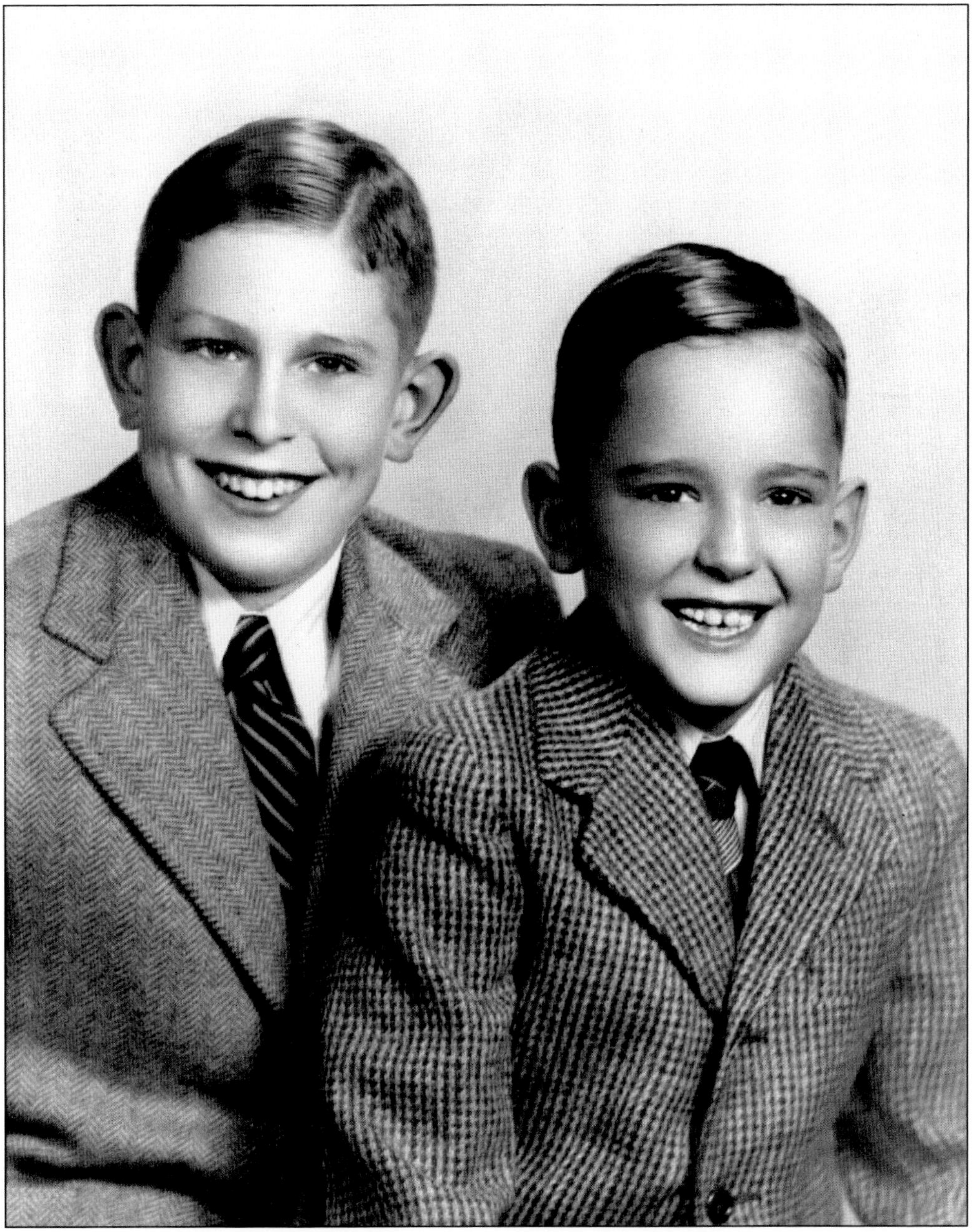

This photograph was taken in December 1944. On the left is Earl "Skip" Prosser, who was 12 at the time, and on the right is Stanley "Bud" Prosser, who was 7 at the time. These boys went on to become pharmacists and instrumental members of their communities.

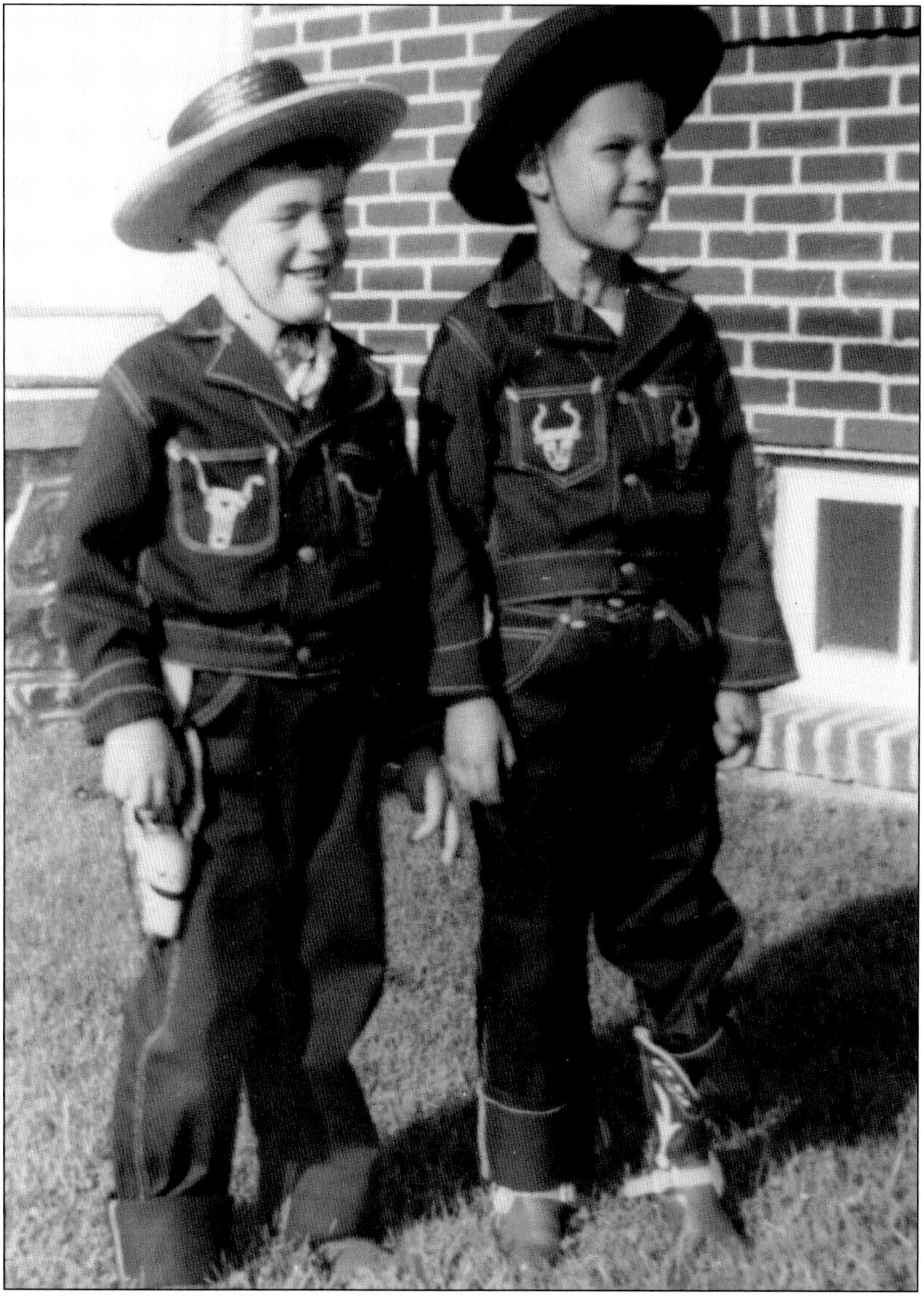

During the 1950s, with the advent of television, cowboy shows, such as those featuring Gene Autry, the Cisco Kid, and Roy Rogers, were most popular along with continuing serials, such as Lash Larue. On Saturday, many Hellertown youths made their way to the Sauconia to see their stars on the big screen. This photograph shows the author on the left and his best pal, David Kantor, keeping watch over their herd.

Two

LANDMARKS

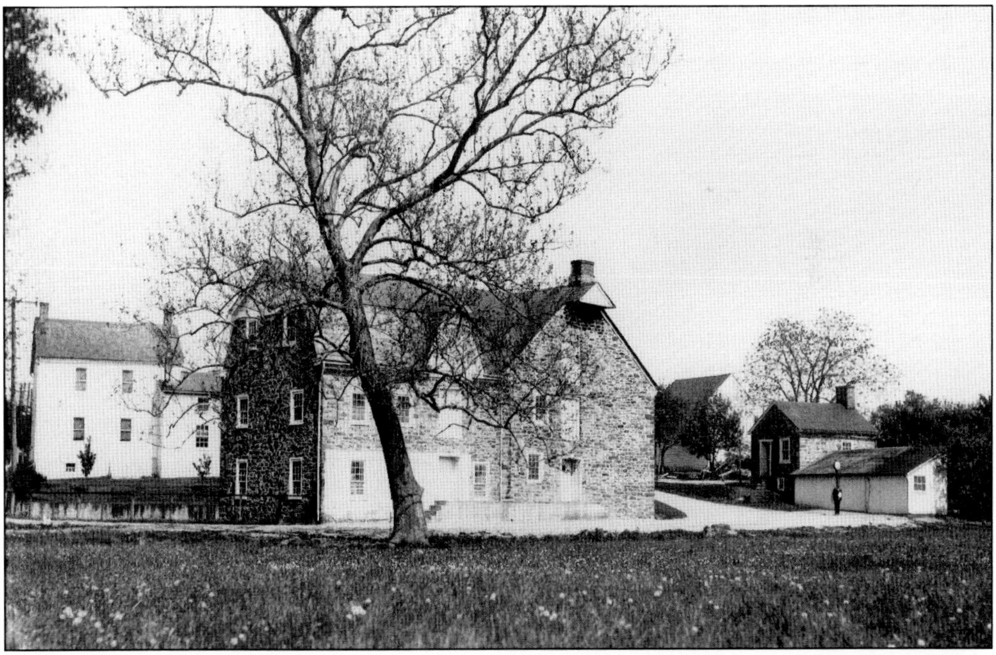

Christopher Heller's second son, Johan Simon, purchased a 200-acre farm along the Saucon Creek in the early 1740s, where he built a grist- and sawmill. By 1746, Christopher Wagner had purchased the mill and, by 1750, had obtained a tavern license for the same site, seven-tenths of a mile from the central part of Hellertown. It is believed that French General Lafayette, a great friend of the colonists during the American Revolution, stopped at the tavern on his journey from Brandywine to Bethlehem.

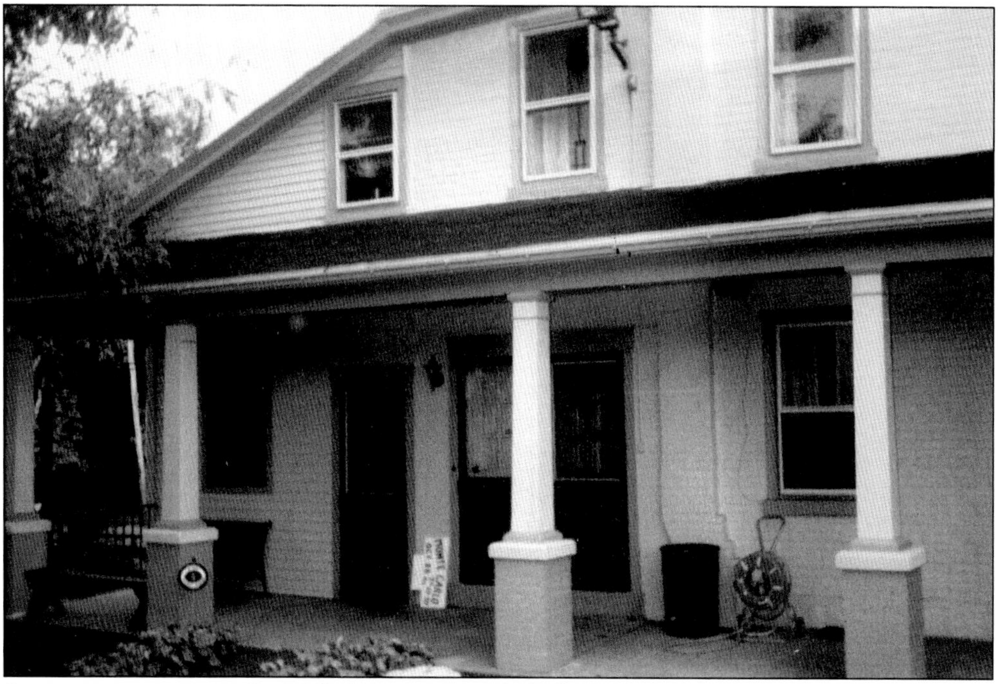

Since its construction, the Miller's House provided a home for the mill operator. Located along West Walnut Street just before the mill, it now provides housing for the Hellertown Historical Society, whose task is to preserve Hellertown's heritage. Now volunteers man their stations between 9:00 a.m. and 11:30 a.m. on Tuesdays and Saturdays.

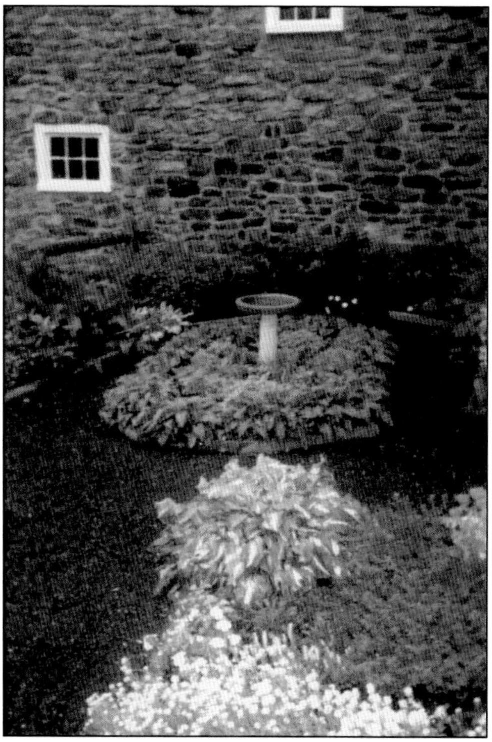

For a place of personal respite and restoration, a visit to the herb garden is satisfying from late spring to late fall. There are nearly 30 varieties of herbs and flowers to observe and to smell. For years, Polly Metzger has led a team of volunteers to care for this place of tranquility, also a necessity in Colonial times.

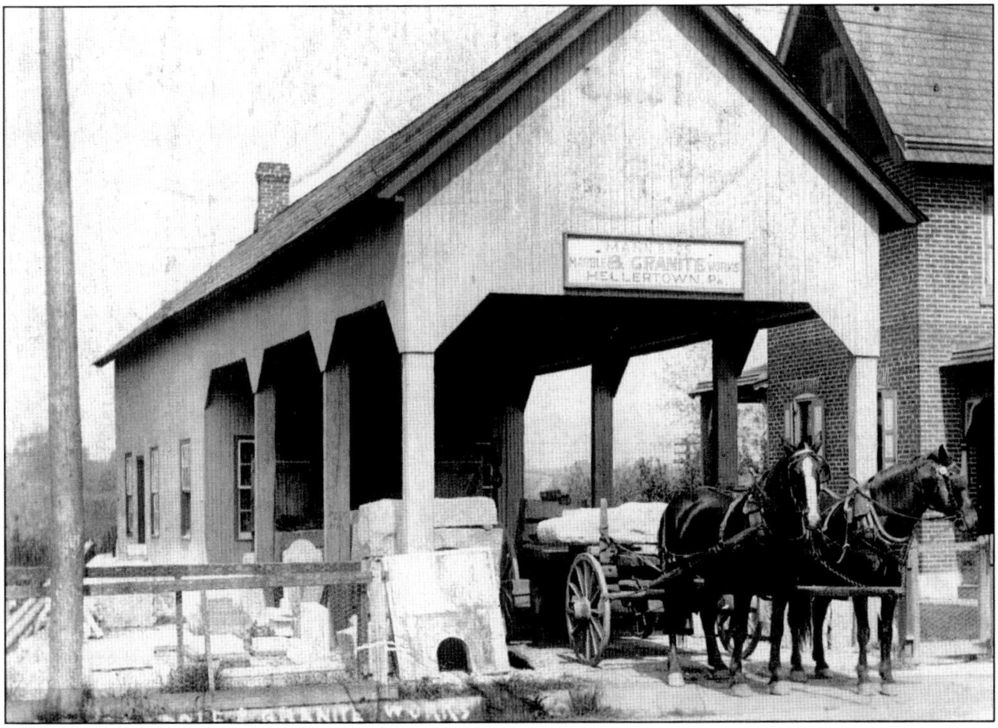

This picture postcard was sent to Ella Trumbauer of Applebachsville from Hellertown on August 1, 1906. It depicts the Mann Brothers Marble and Granite Works. The photograph was taken by Cal Bergstresser.

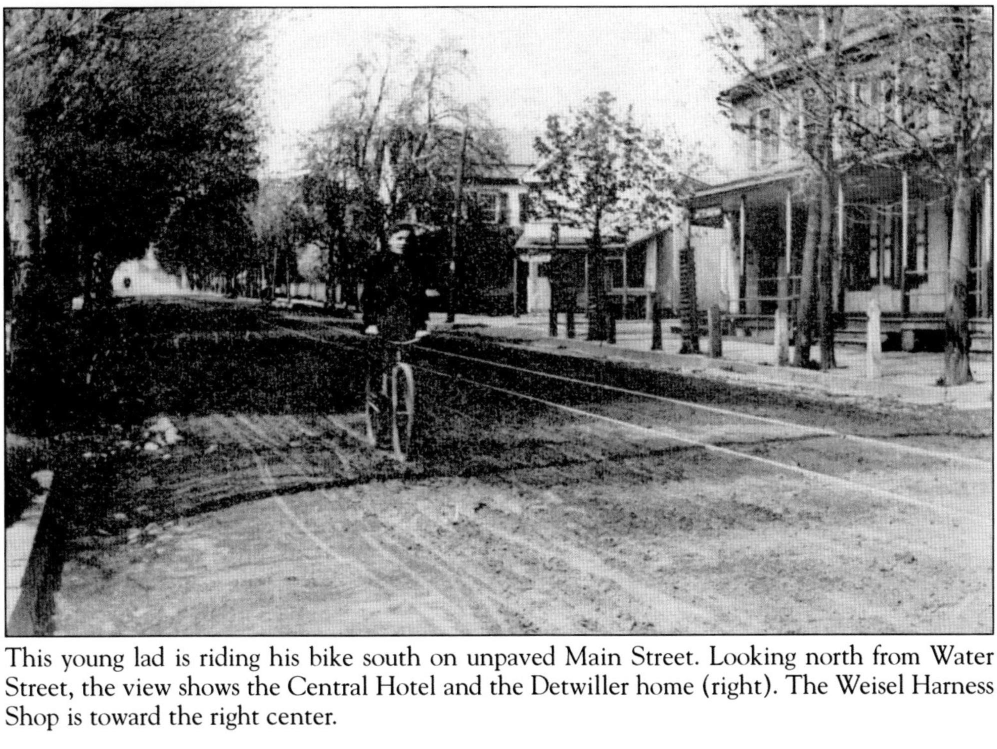

This young lad is riding his bike south on unpaved Main Street. Looking north from Water Street, the view shows the Central Hotel and the Detwiller home (right). The Weisel Harness Shop is toward the right center.

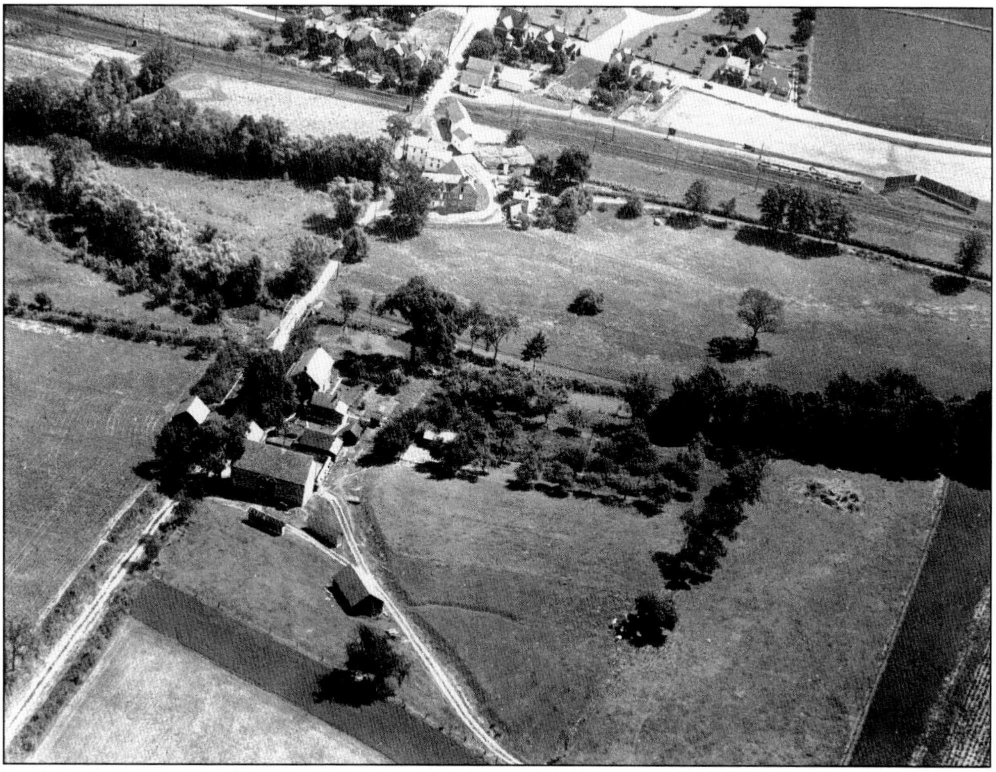

In the center, notice the Saucon Creek running north and south. The Pony Bridge was still in use at the time Stanley Keck took the photograph. The gristmill complex is located near the top of the photograph. Skibo's Farm can be seen in the center.

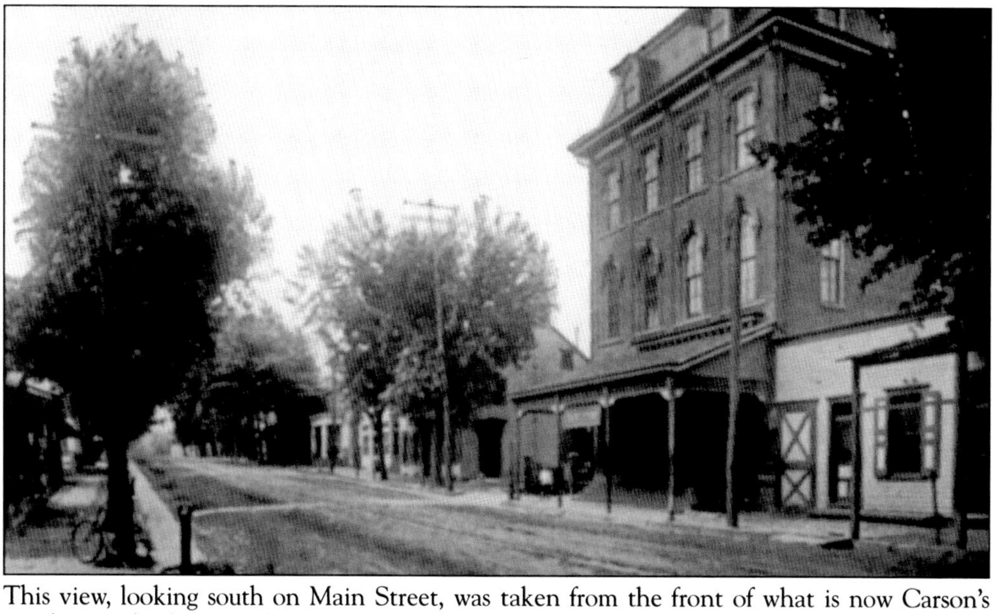

This view, looking south on Main Street, was taken from the front of what is now Carson's Hardware. The former Odd Fellows Hall can be seen on the right. The trolley tracks are shown to be in the center of Main Street, surrounded on both sides by the hardened street surface.

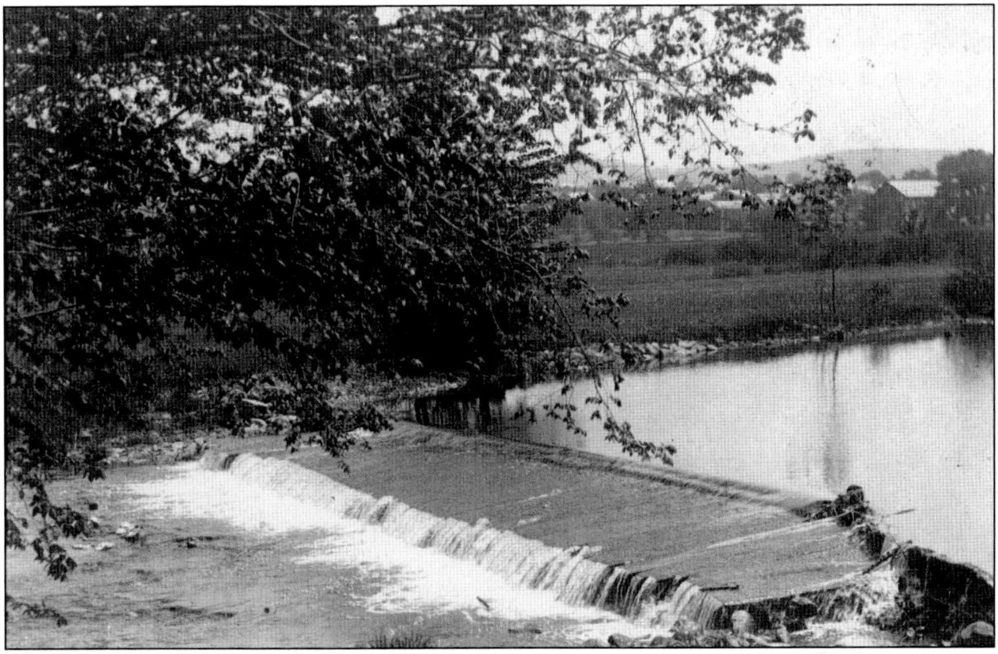

This photograph by Cal Bergstresser shows one of the dams built by conservation-minded citizens. The sportsmen have sought to preserve the Saucon to benefit the native trout.

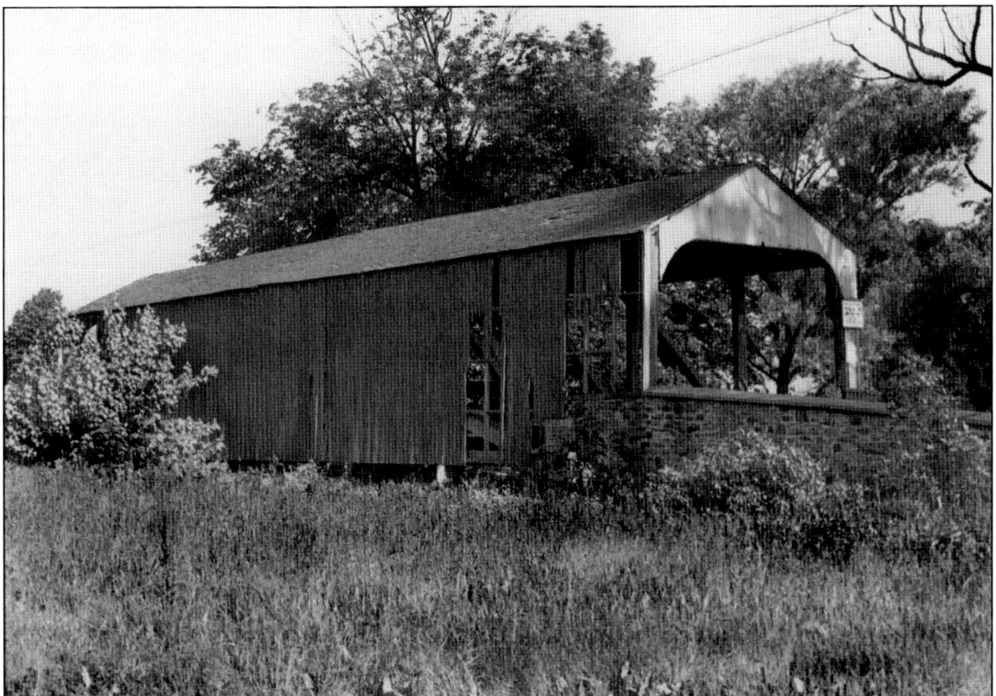

The covered bridge on Water Street spanned the Saucon for many years. The bridge provided protection from the elements and a good fishing spot. It also provided an excellent place for children to hoot and holler or for girlfriend and boyfriend to do some spooning. The bridge was torn down in 1938.

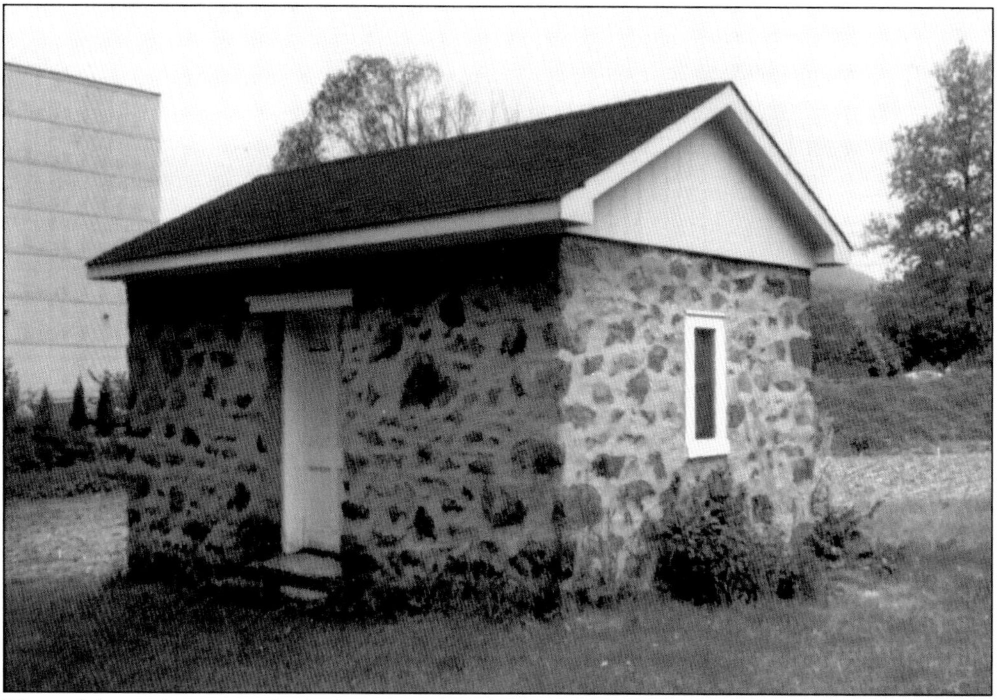

The jail, better known as the lockup, stood in close proximity to the police station. The primary residents consisted of those who had a little too much to drink or those who disturbed the peace. However, Hellertown had its own organized group of men to watch over more serious crimes, such as horse thievery, one of the most heinous crimes in its day.

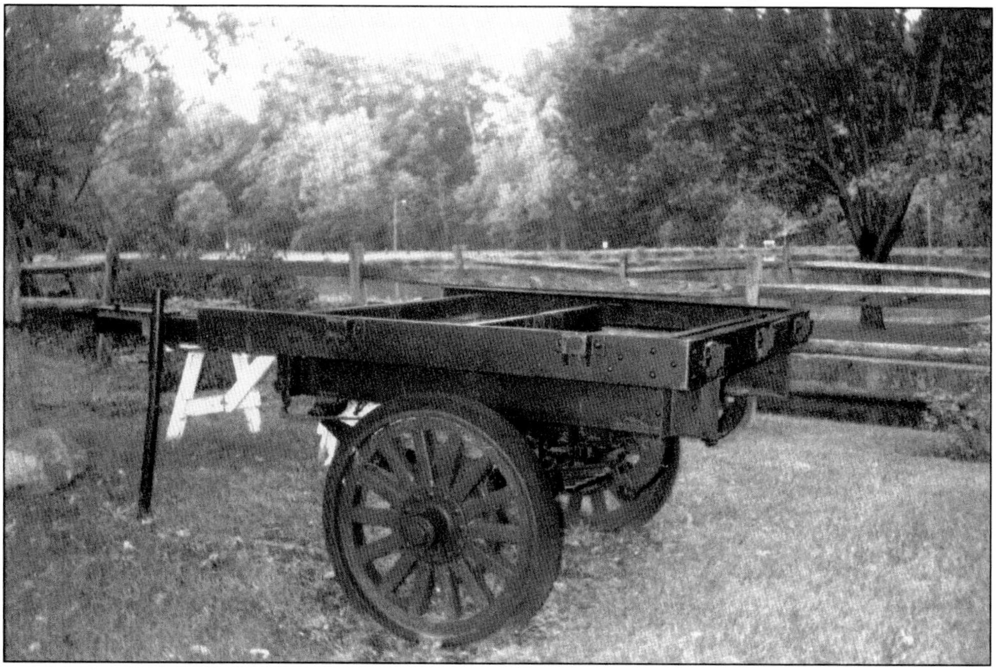

During the late 1930s, this wagon was used by the Hellertown Water Department to haul cast-iron pipes to replace the old wooden pipes from *c.* 1898.

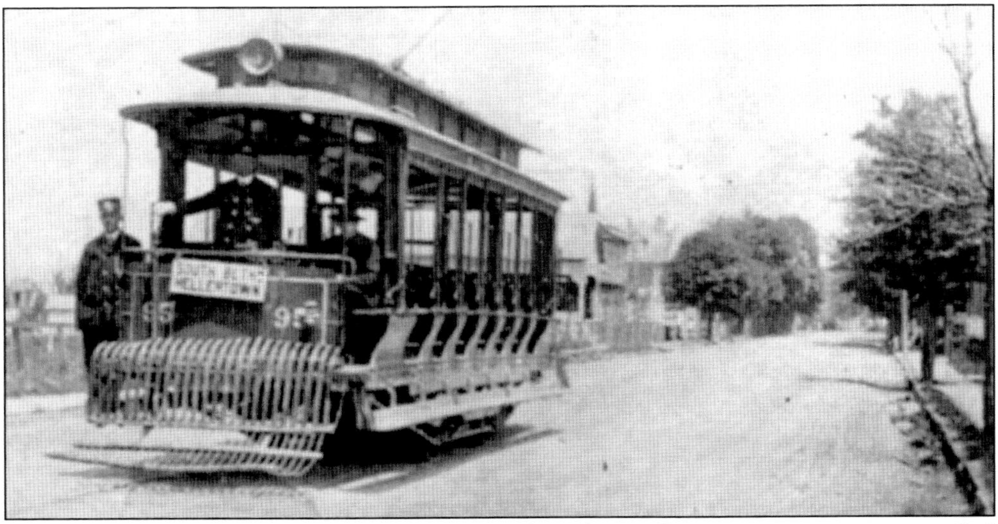

According to Russ Sloyer's article in the 1982 *Look Back*, a trolley transportation system called the South Bethlehem and Saucon Street Railway Company was in business until 1929. These trolleys were equipped with hand brakes and held a motorman and a conductor, along with 40 passengers. A trolley system that connected Hellertown, Bethlehem, and Allentown operated until the early 1950s, when they were replaced by buses.

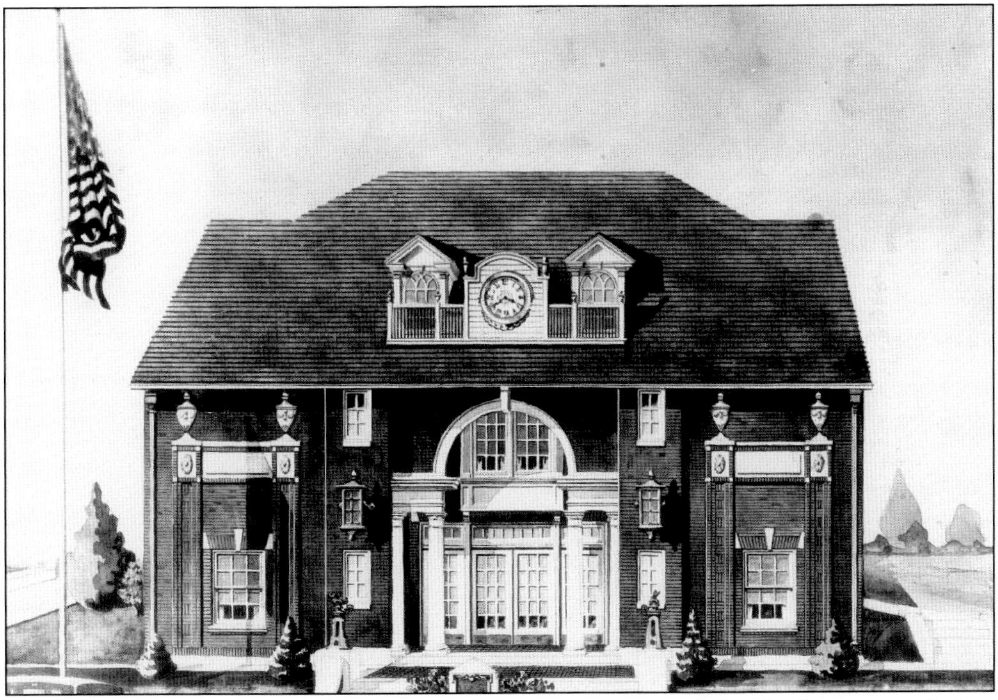

In one issue of the *Ackerman Post News* in 1923, it was announced that final actions and plans to finance and build the proposed home of the post were taking place. The estimated cost would be $150,000, and the construction would be done by Comrade Yeager. A new source of revenue would result from the construction of an auditorium, which would satisfy a long-felt need in the community. Post commander Herbert S. Weisel urged all comrades to be present at the next meeting to discuss this important issue.

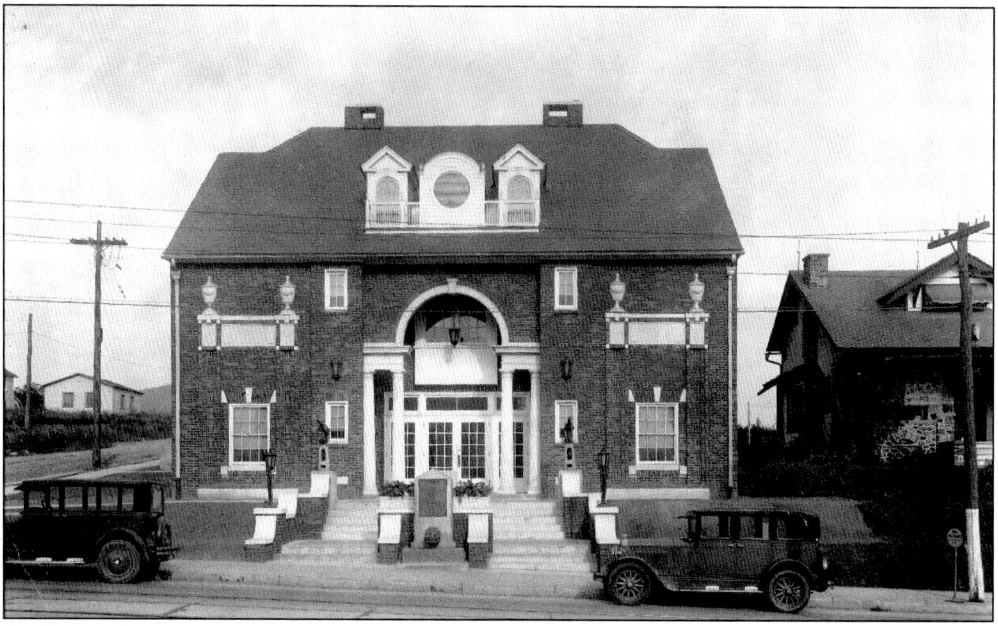

At the southeast corner of Main and Chestnut Streets sat the finished product, the brand-new American Legion building. The World War I memorial plaque had been moved to the center of the front stairs.

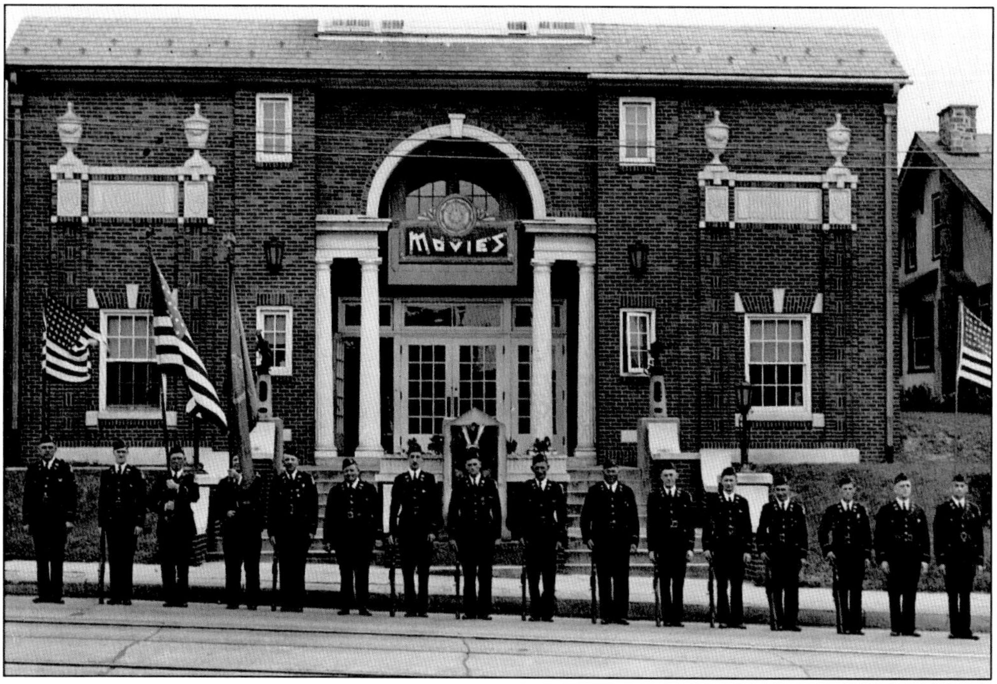

In 1935, the front of the American Legion held a sign front and center—"Movies," which would be shown until the opening of the Sauconia. From left to right are Clarence Clark, Charles Seifert, Charlie Durn, Frank Weidner, Herb Weisel, Stanley Yeager, Bill Potts, unidentified, Charlie Hagel, George Koder, Charlie Heft, two unidentified, Olie Frey, John Waidner, and Clem Halteman.

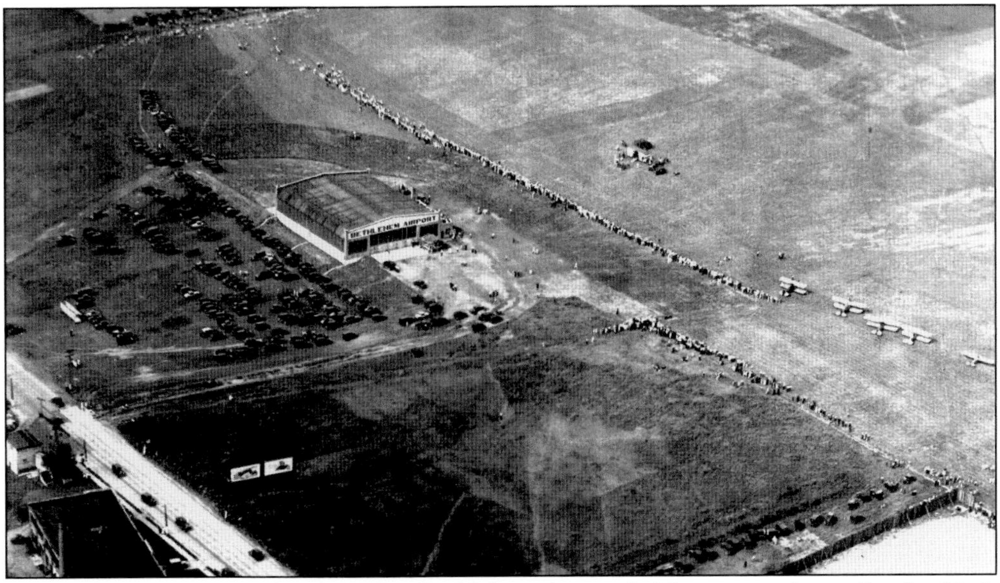

During the late 1920s and early 1930s, Bethlehem Airport held many air shows. Stanley Keck refueled Amelia Earhart's plane here. At one event, more than 1,000 spectators attended and witnessed Eddie Emmerman of Easton perform his parachute stunt. Keck later arranged for a giant 14-passenger Ford Tri-Motor to pay a visit. Many Hellertonians were able to walk to the airport just north of Hellertown, and children would climb trees for a view of the planes landing or taking off.

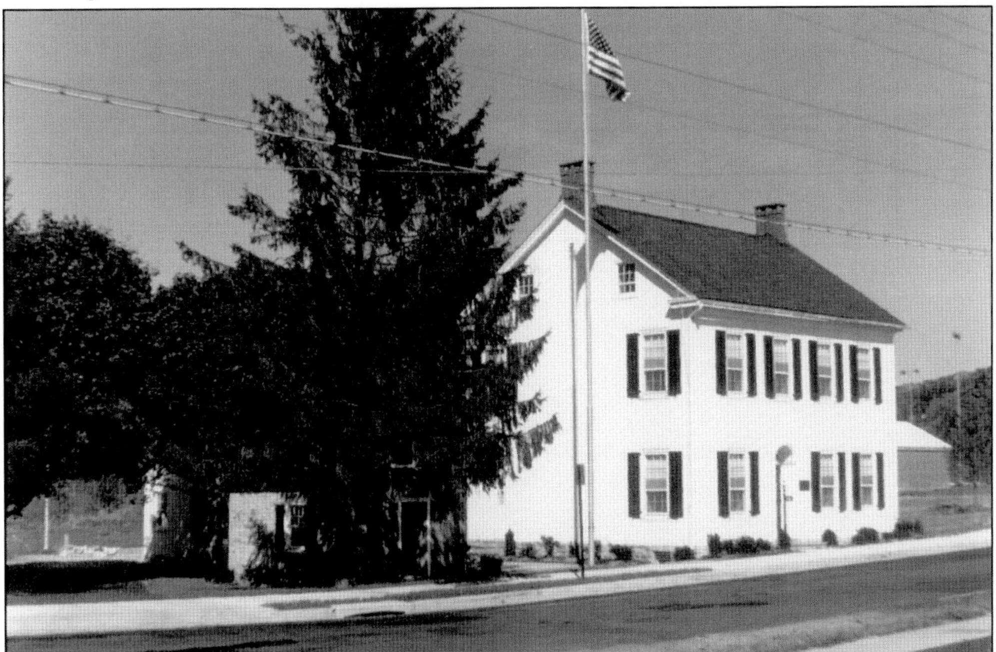

Now housing the Borough of Hellertown Water Authority, this building was originally a farmhouse in the possession of Dr. William Rentzheimer and then Charles Judd. Also, the Youngkins were tenant farmers here. There was quite an apple orchard and black cherry trees, which youngsters would concentrate on "procuring by art," as Mark Twain phrased it.

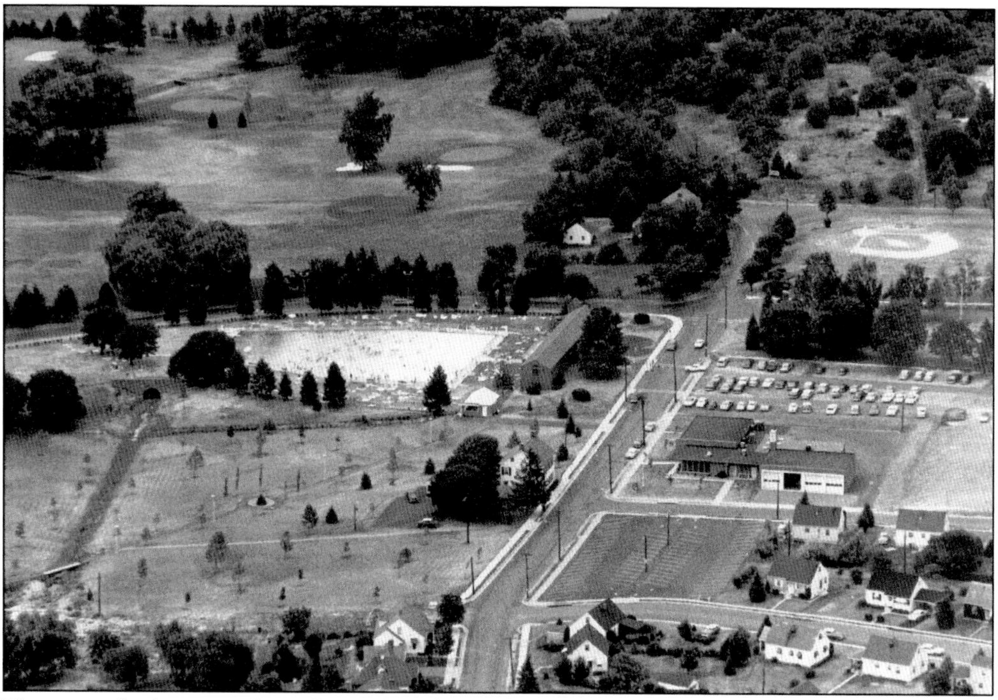

This view, looking north in the 1950s, shows the municipal pool, with the Bethlehem Steel Club Golf Course in the background. To the right, part of Dimmick Park and Dewey Fire Company are visible. The photograph was taken by local pilot Stanley Keck.

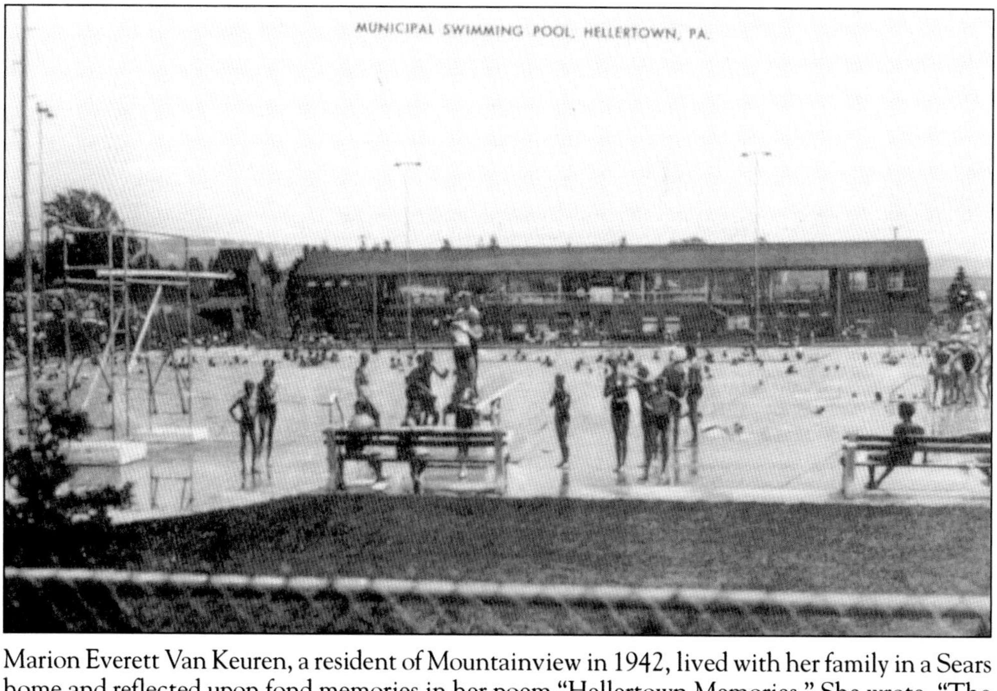

Marion Everett Van Keuren, a resident of Mountainview in 1942, lived with her family in a Sears home and reflected upon fond memories in her poem "Hellertown Memories." She wrote, "The park, the pool, those lazy summer days, the laughter of children in many ways still remain."

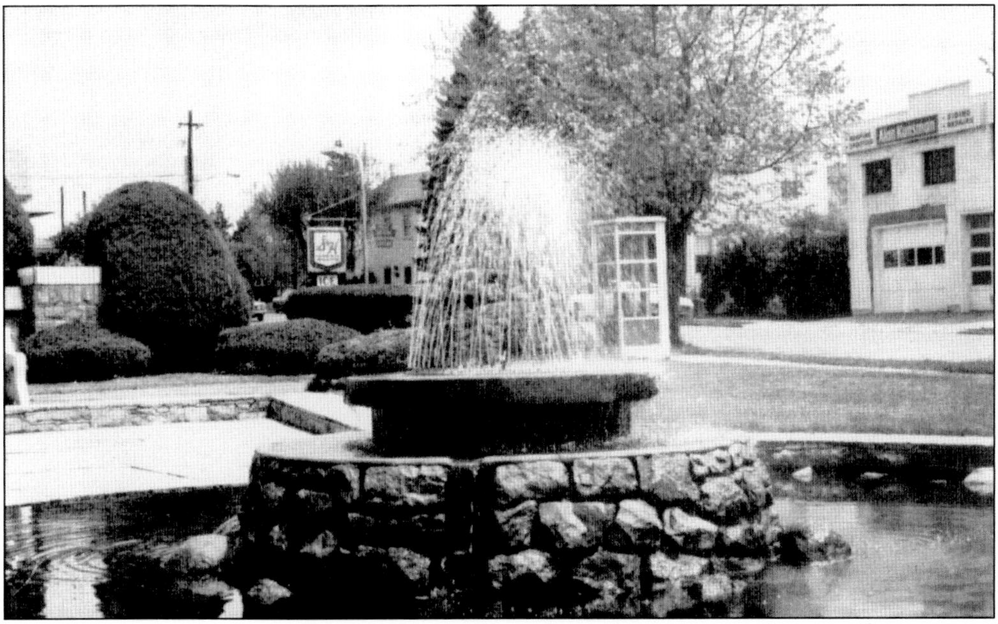

On the former site of the Weisel Harness Shop, Detwiller Plaza stands across Easton Road from town hall. Noted for its fountain, floral beauty, and recently the clock tower, the plaza was named in honor of Dr. Henry Detwiller, who began his homeopathic medicine practice in Hellertown in 1818. He not only practiced medicine in town for 34 years but also assumed the responsibility of an active citizen, serving as school director, cataloger of botanical species in the area, and one of the founders of the Thomas Iron Company.

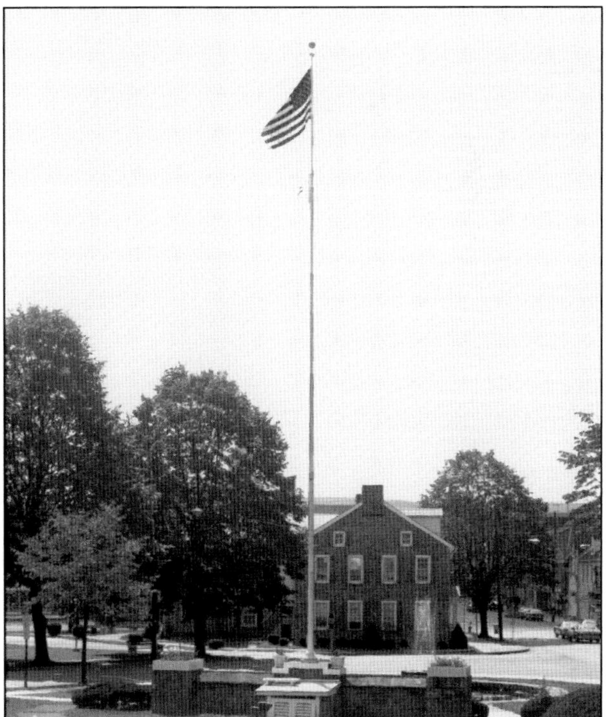

Dedicated on July 4, 1942, Detwiller Plaza is seen in the foreground, while the background shows town hall during the 1960s. Stern's Market can be seen on the southwest corner of Main and Water Streets.

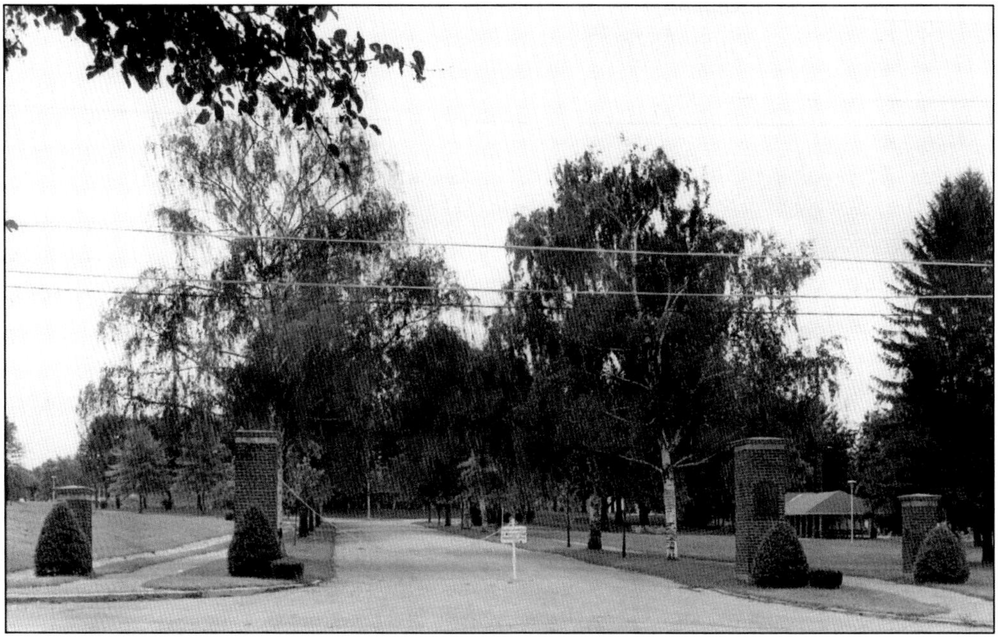

In this view looking south is the main entrance to Morris J. Dimmick Park, dedicated in 1939. Burgess Dimmick was able to acquire federal assistance to have the park built during the Great Depression after negotiating with Bethlehem Steel, which had owned the land.

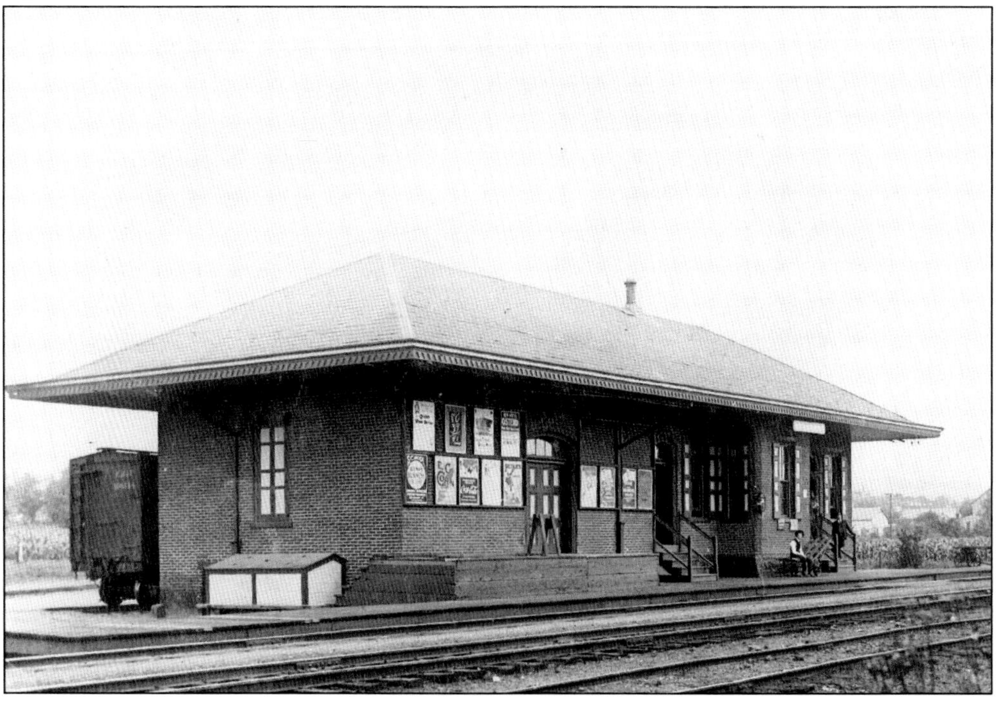

The Hellertown train station was a main hub of activity for many decades. Judging by the advertisements and the men's clothes, the photograph seems to have been taken during the 1920s. Unfortunately, it could not be preserved as a historical site.

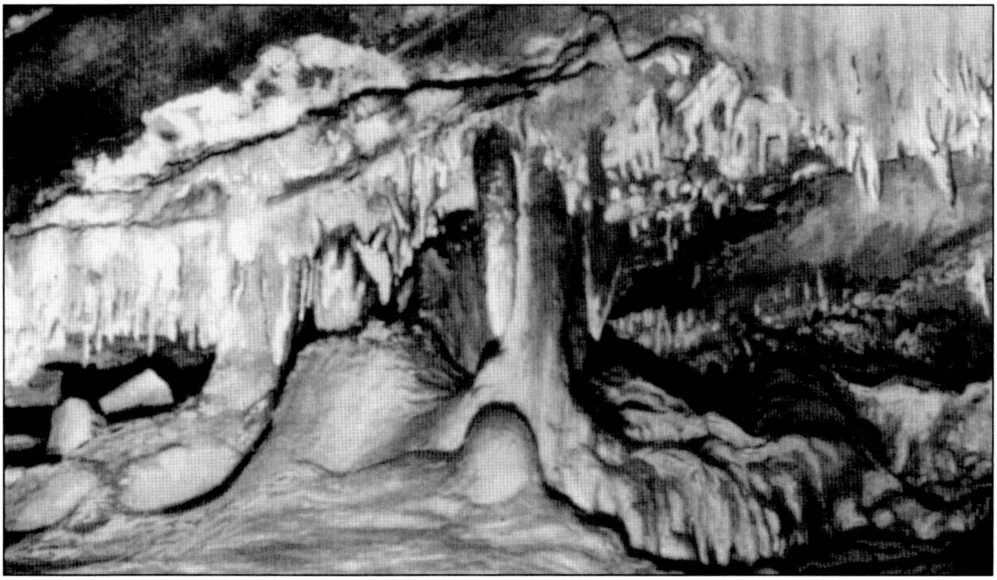

Lost River Caverns, otherwise known as Lost Cave, contains five crystal chambers. The lost river flows two million gallons of water daily through the length of the caverns. The Crystal Chapel is open for weddings, baptisms, or other services.

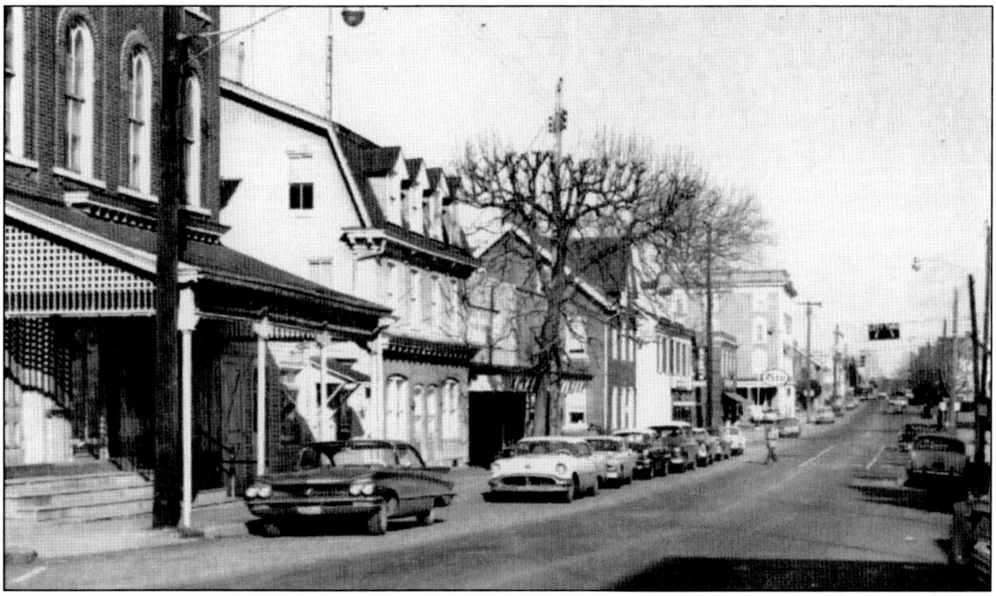

This view of the Hellertown downtown business section shows the 1950s in detail. The site of the original Yeager's Pharmacy is to the left. The new Yeager's is three cars down on the left of this view looking north. Still seen in the background are Geyer's Esso station and the Park Hotel.

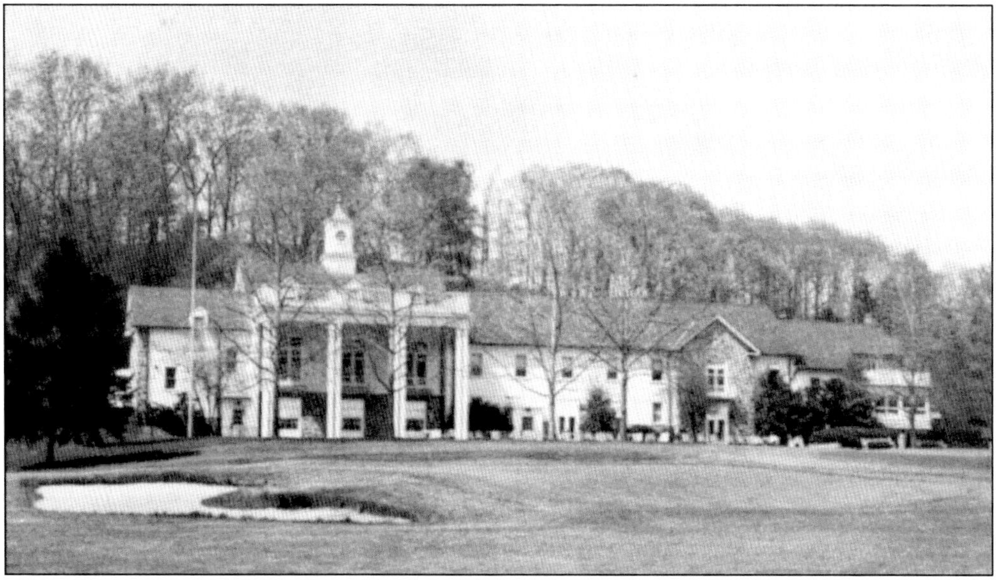

For many years, the Bethlehem Steel Club, at the east end of Linden Street, provided the upper echelon of Bethlehem Steel Company staff with one of the most beautiful golf courses in the Lehigh Valley. The excellent cuisine in the dining area was well known.

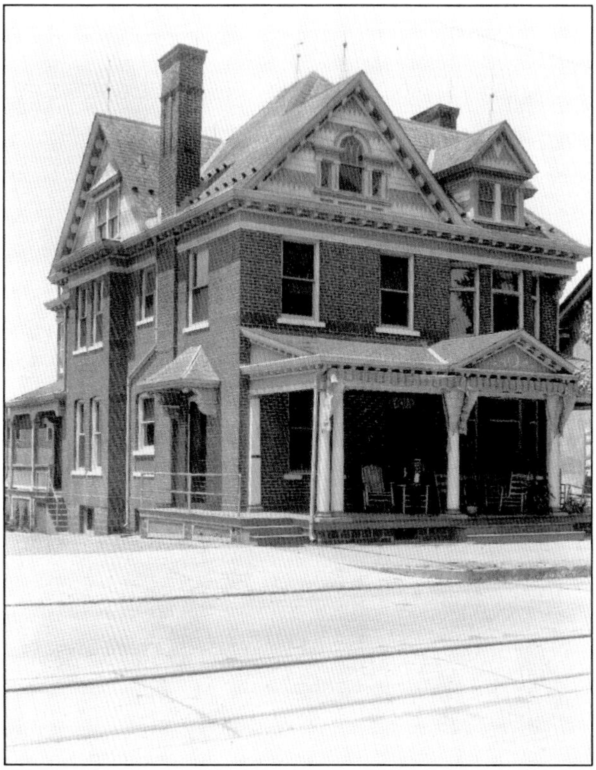

Dr. William H. Rentzheimer set up his professional practice on Main Street in town in 1883. In addition to supplying Hellertown with expert medical care, he also served as secretary on the Hellertown School Board and five years as treasurer of the borough.

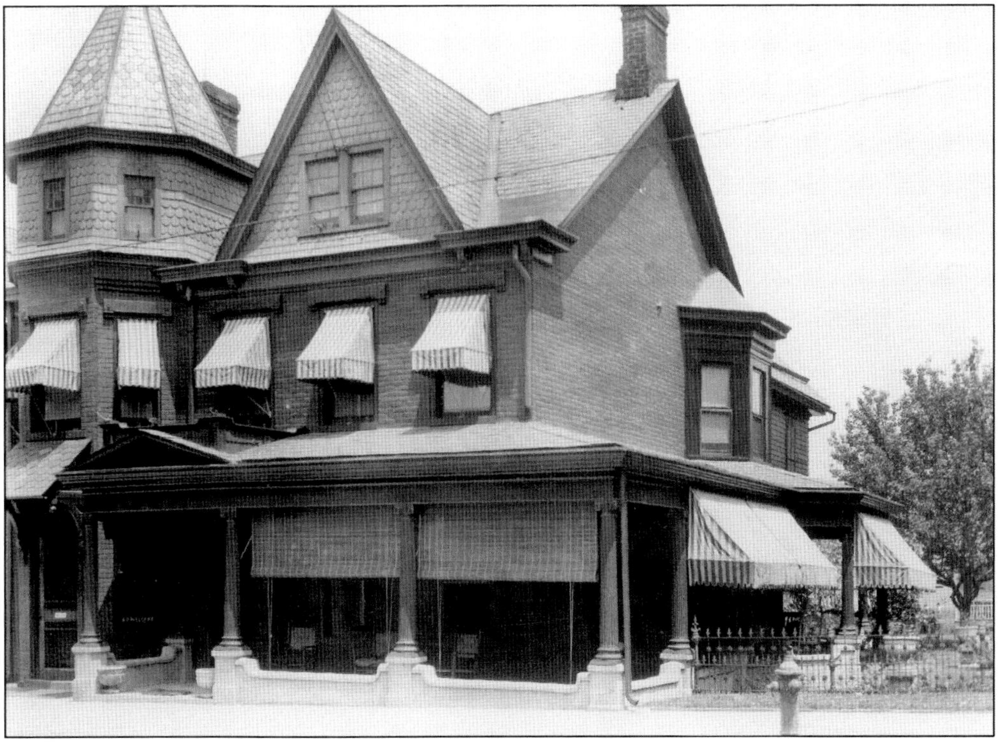

Dr. Henry D. Heller's home, in the 600 block of Main Street, exemplifies the stately Victorian architecture that was popular in the late 1800s and early 1900s.

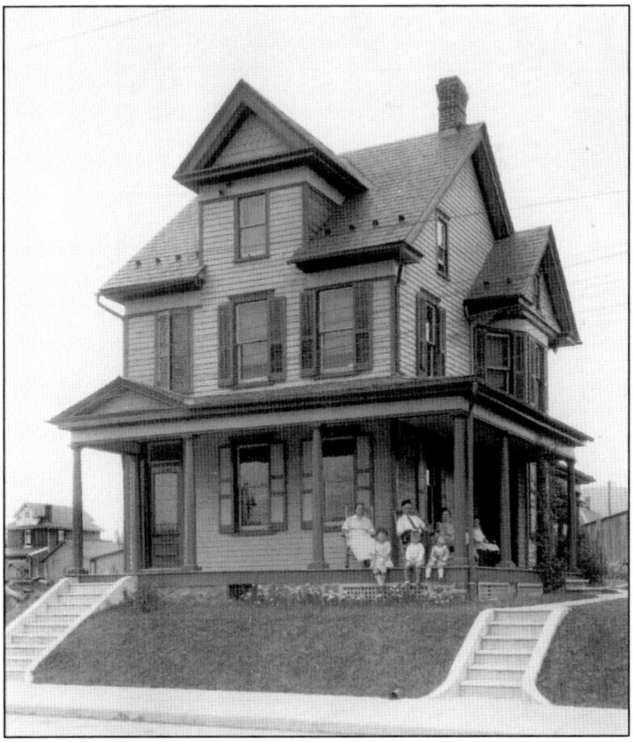

The home of the William Scholl family was built in the 1000 block of Main Street. The design of the two-story structure still shows signs of the 19th-century Victorian influence. Wraparound porches were typical, and a major form of entertainment was to sit outside while listening to favorite radio programs and viewing passersby.

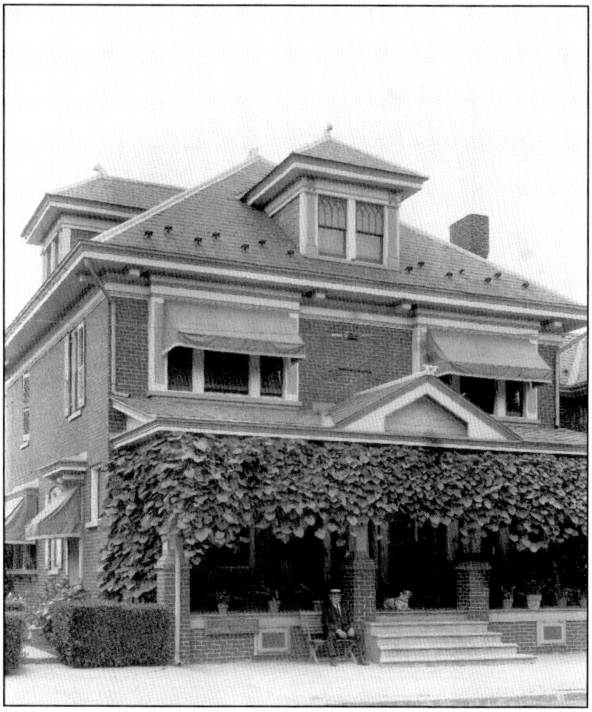

The Bergstresser Funeral Home was built at 326 Main Street and served Hellertown for many years. In this photograph are funeral director Pliny Bergstresser and his dog Rex.

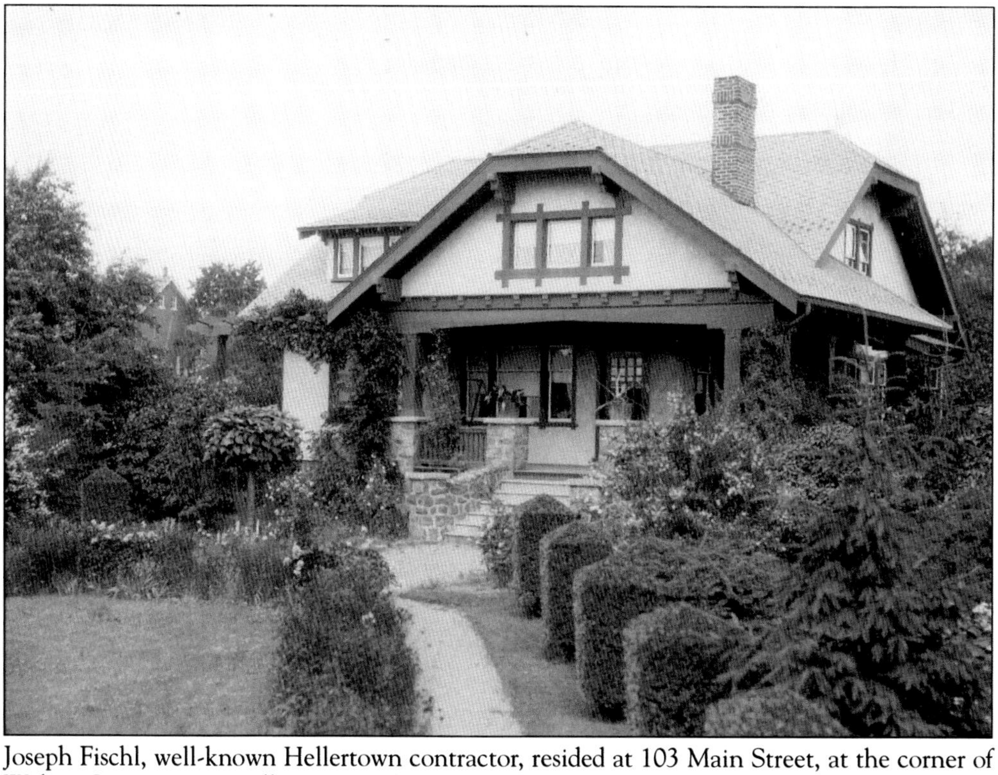

Joseph Fischl, well-known Hellertown contractor, resided at 103 Main Street, at the corner of Walnut Street. Many Hellertonians planted magnificent combinations of trees and hedges and featured colorful flower gardens in season.

Three

Civics

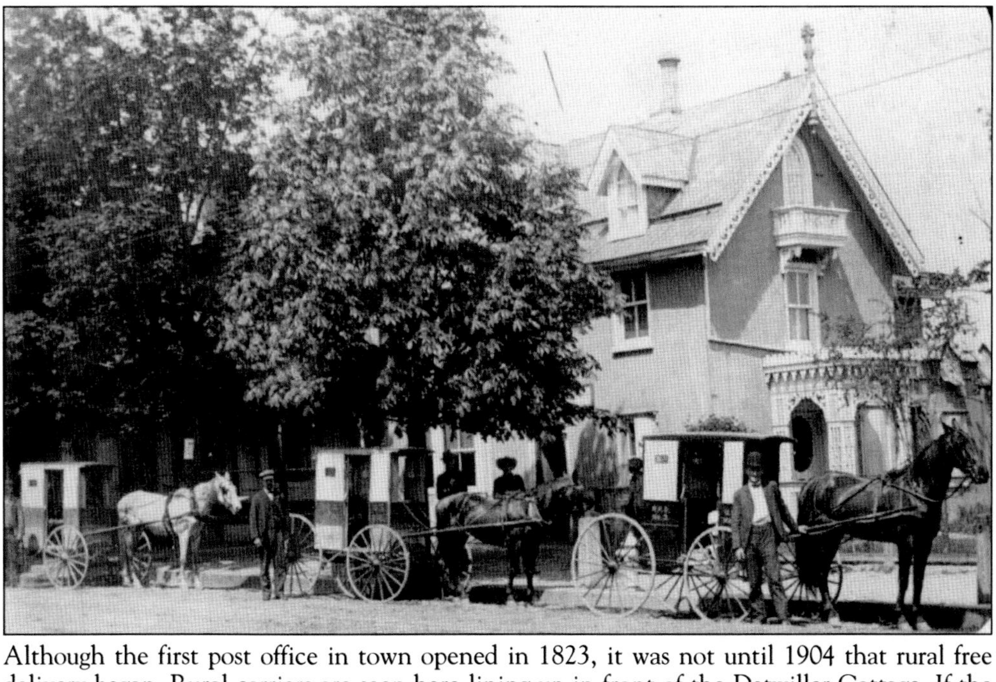

Although the first post office in town opened in 1823, it was not until 1904 that rural free delivery began. Rural carriers are seen here lining up in front of the Detwiller Cottage. If the building stood today, it would be located on the southeast corner of Main and Water Streets.

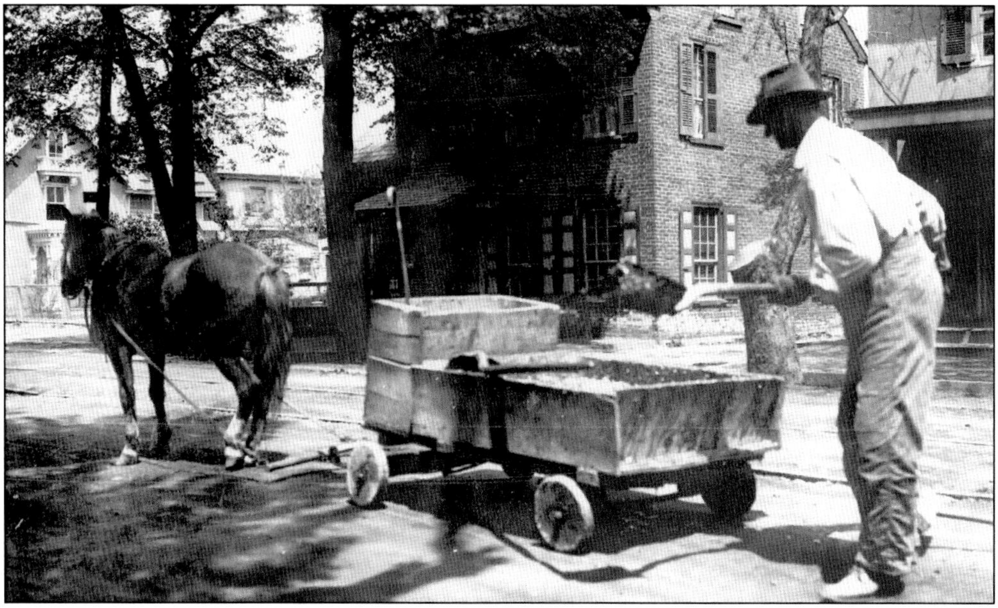

An unidentified man works with the Hellertown Street Department repair wagon in May 1920. Notice that the front end of the cart is out of alignment.

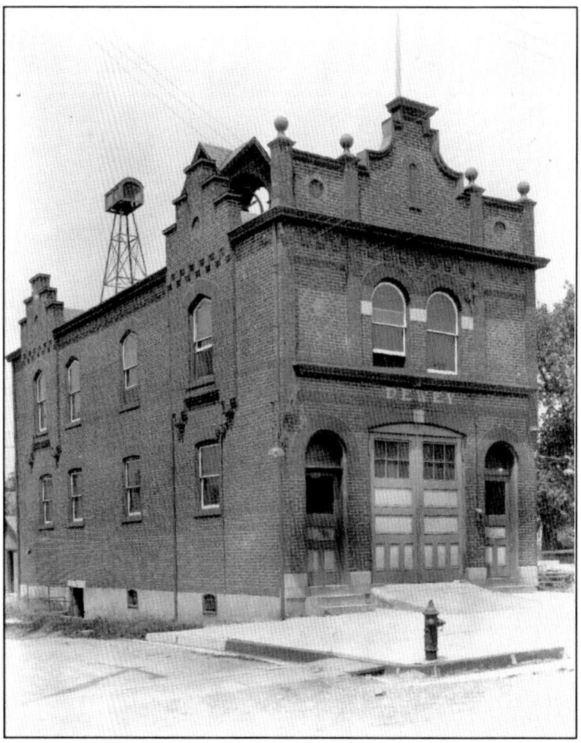

On January 18, 1898, the Dewey Fire Company was organized after Christ Union Church and several other structures had burned down. The company was named for Adm. George Dewey's victories during the Spanish-American War. The equipment had to be manually pulled and operated. In 1925, the first motorized truck was purchased.

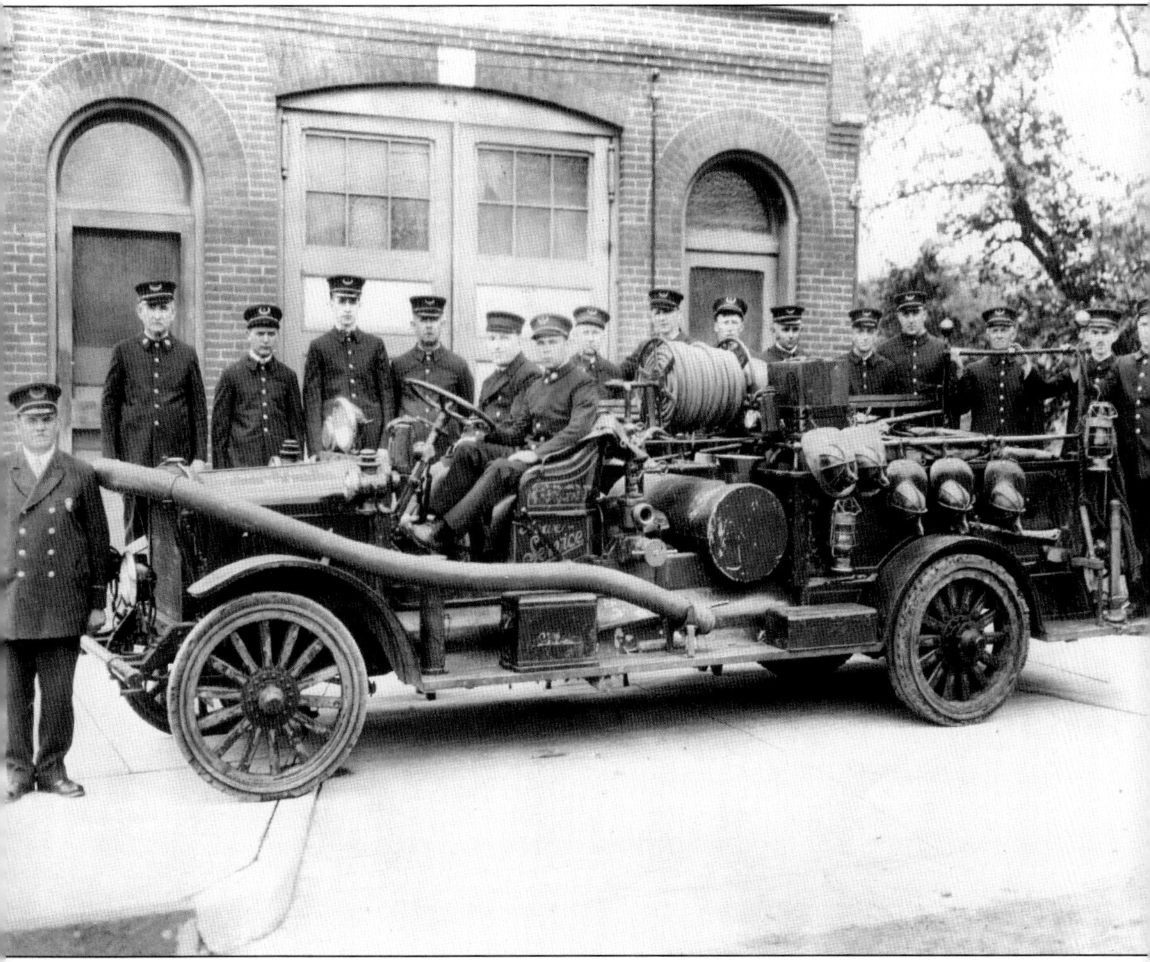

The first firehouse in Hellertown was built in 1900 for $4,000. The Saucon Street building would serve the community as headquarters for nearly half a century.

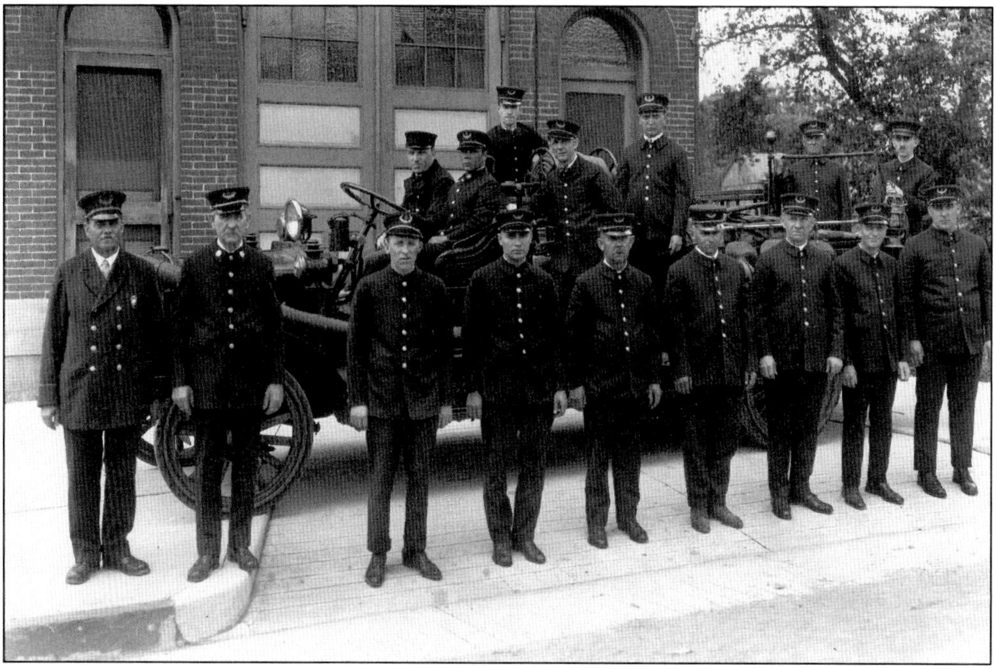

Shown in front of the original Dewey Fire Station are, from left to right, the following: (front row) Chief Charles Zimpfer, Jerry Angstadt, Ed Zimpfer, four unidentified, Ed Frey, and Ed Gross; (back row) driver Wally Zimpfer, Herb Cless, Bill Potts, Shad Frey, Charlie Ackerman, Dewey Fritchman, and Elmer Zimpfer.

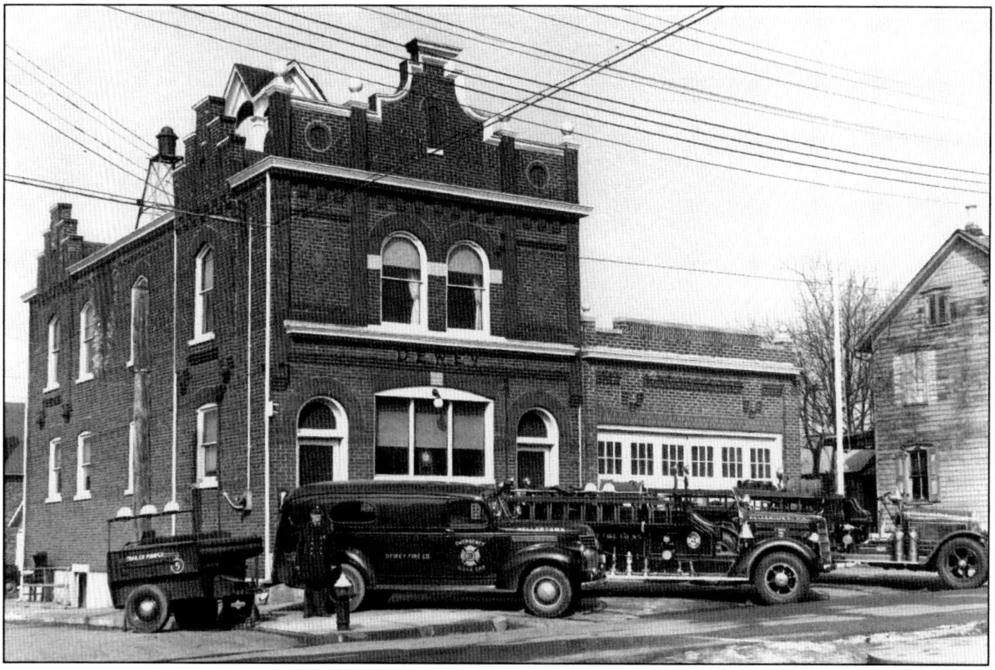

Here is a display of Dewey Fire Company No. 1 equipment in front of the original facility (with its garage addition) on Saucon Street. Notice the first "Agony Wagon" on the left. This building also housed the police and other borough departments. The upstairs was used for civic affairs.

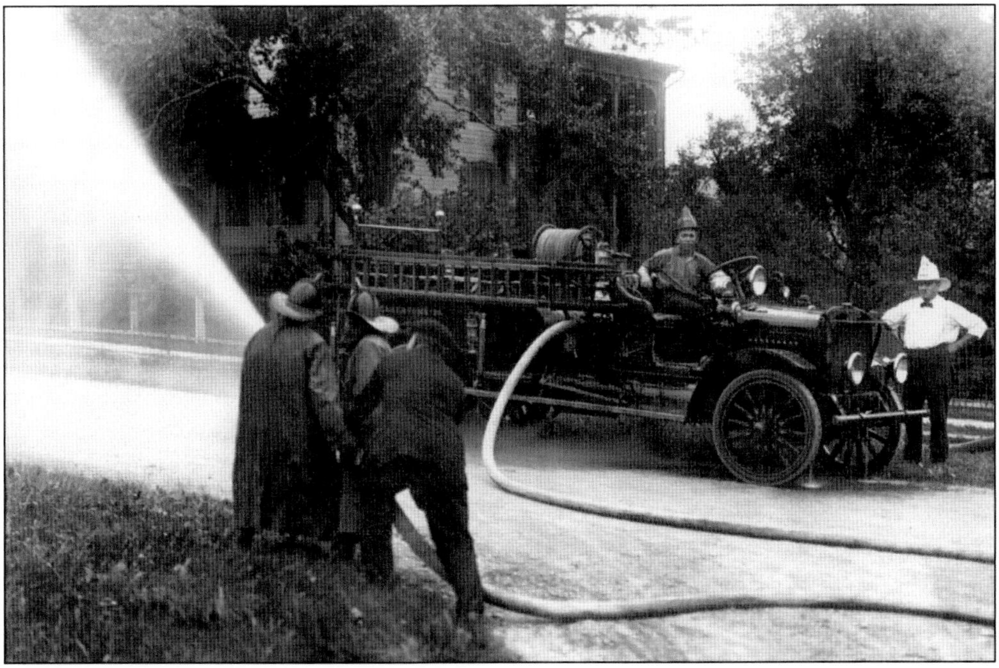

Members of Dewey Fire Company No. 1 are shown in action. Bill Snyder is in the driver's seat, and Chief Charles Zimpfer is standing in front of the truck.

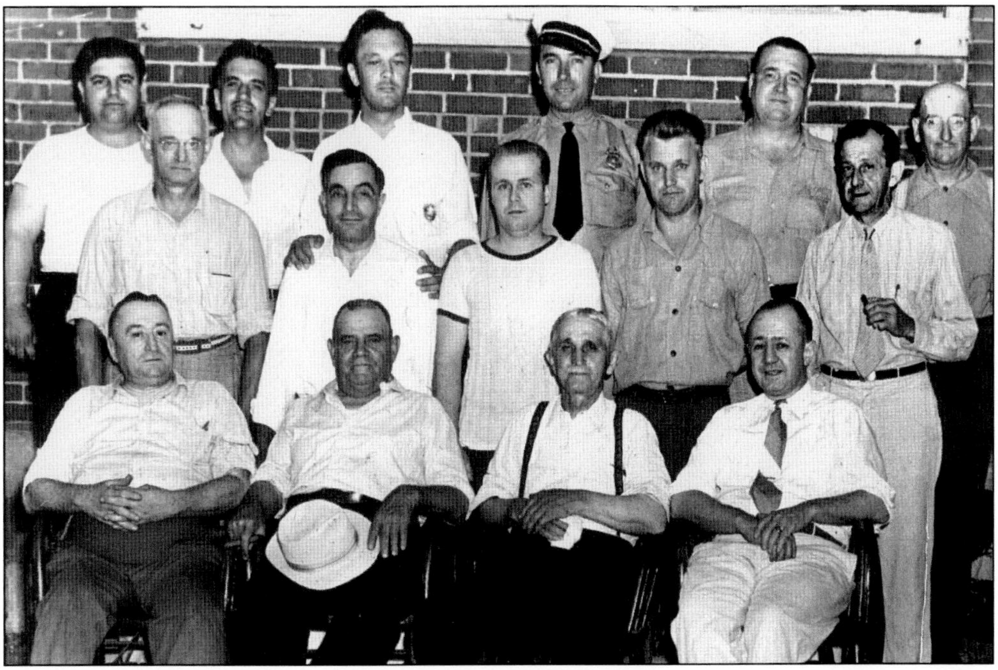

These men organized the Dewey Fire Company Fourth of July celebration in 1941. They are, from left to right, as follows: (front row) Al Muschlitz, Chief Charles Zimpfer, Pete Boehm, and Art Anders; (middle row) Ben Kreidler, John Horvath, Paul Ruch, Darwin Rohrbach, and Shad Frey; (back row) Harry Leidich, Orville Grube, unidentified, Vince Coughlin, Earl Judd, and Charles Bauder Sr.

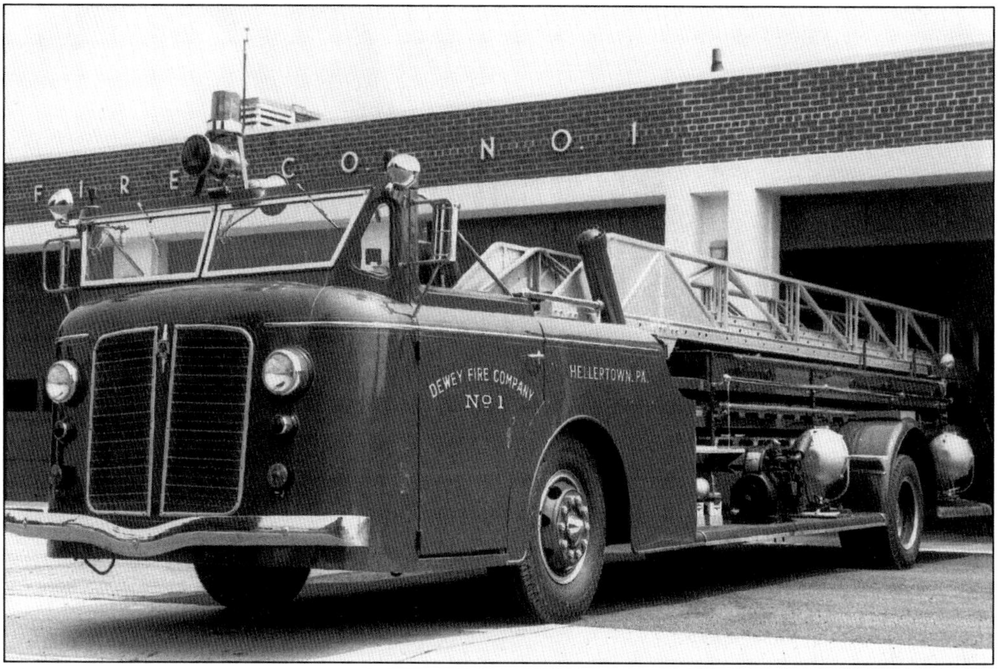

The fire truck known as "Big Bertha" was built in Hamburg by the Hahn Company. This truck was very difficult to handle by its two drivers, Bill Sontak and Joe Poluka. It was soon determined that the vehicle could not negotiate many streets in town, particularly in Mountain View and Durham Terrace. Big Bertha was finally diagnosed as a "lemon" and sold at public auction.

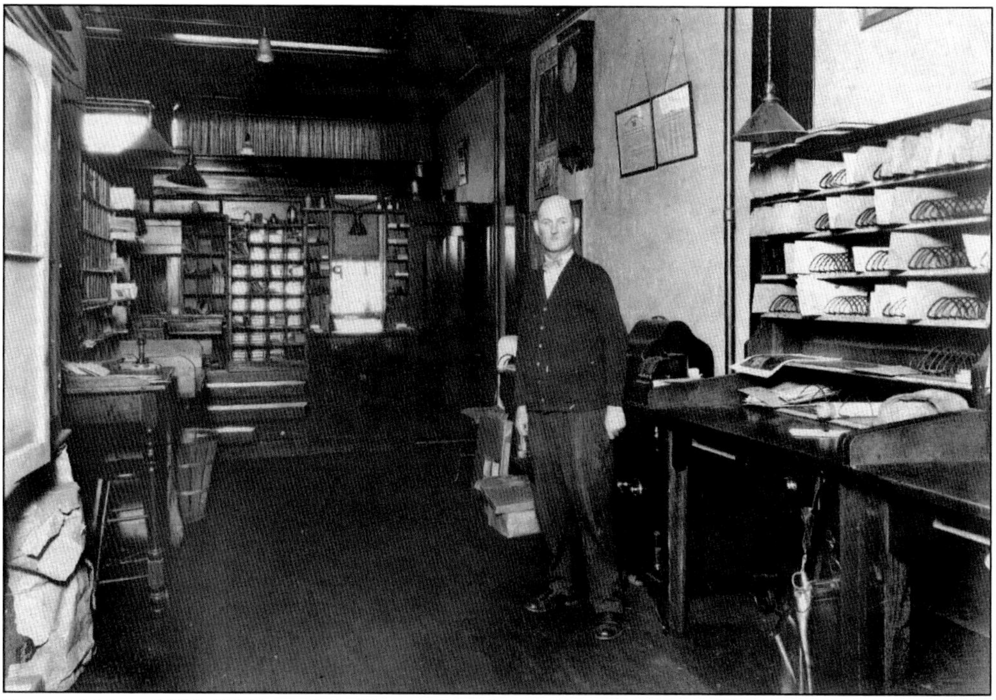

From 1925 to 1932, William Scholl served in the Hellertown post office, which was then part of Prosser's Drugstore, at 834 Main Street.

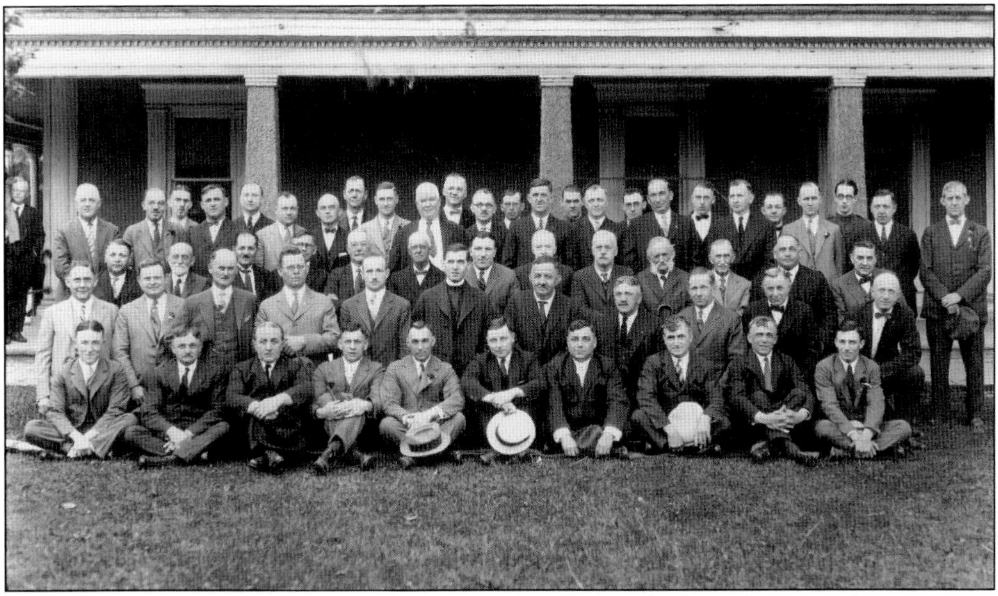

Before 1924, Main Street had been a dirt road with trolley tracks along the east curbing. In 1925, the Hellertown Businessmen's Association, borough council, and the state highway department combined their efforts to pave the street. The trolley tracks were moved to the center. The all-day celebration, made possible by those pictured here, was held on July 4, 1925.

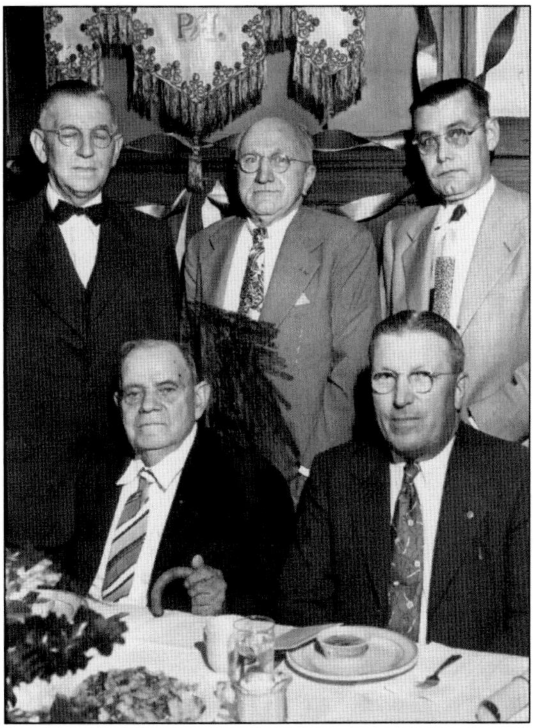

Shown here are five pillars of the community during the first half of the 20th century. They are attending Charles Zimpfer's retirement dinner. From left to right are the following: (front row) Charles Zimpfer and Herb Cless; (back row) Rev. Robert Krause, Herb Hoffert, and Lloyd Hand.

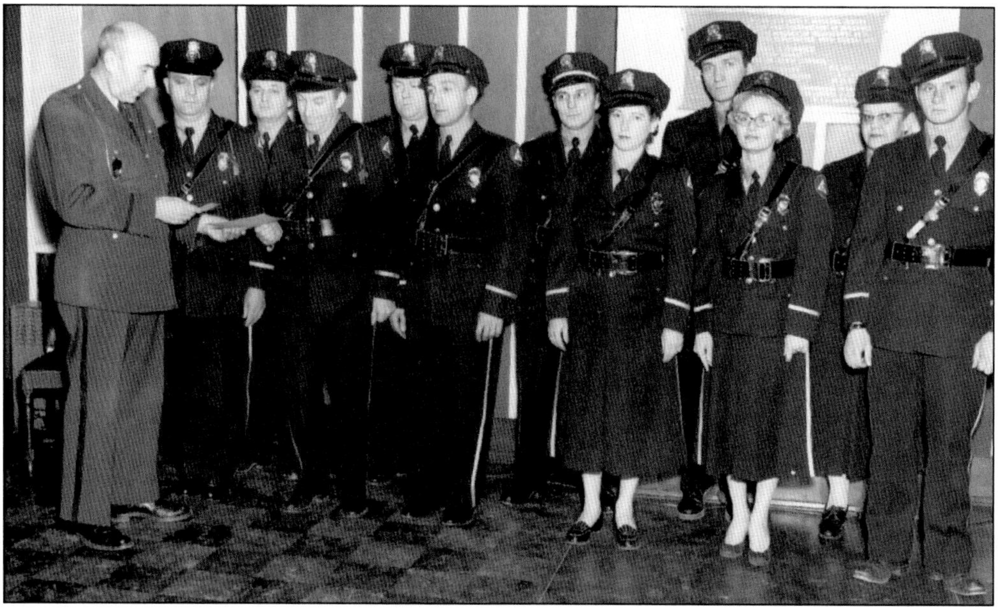

At special events, such as carnivals and parades, the Hellertown Auxiliary Police Force would assist the regular force. They would direct traffic and assist in keeping peace. Pictured, from left to right, are Vince Coughlin (chief of police), Elias Grube, M. Fritzinger, Stephen Bartakovitz, John Spillane, Albert Tarquin, James Ortwein, Grace Ackerman, Bert Stehly, Mrs. Harold Keck, Estella Werst, and Harold Keck.

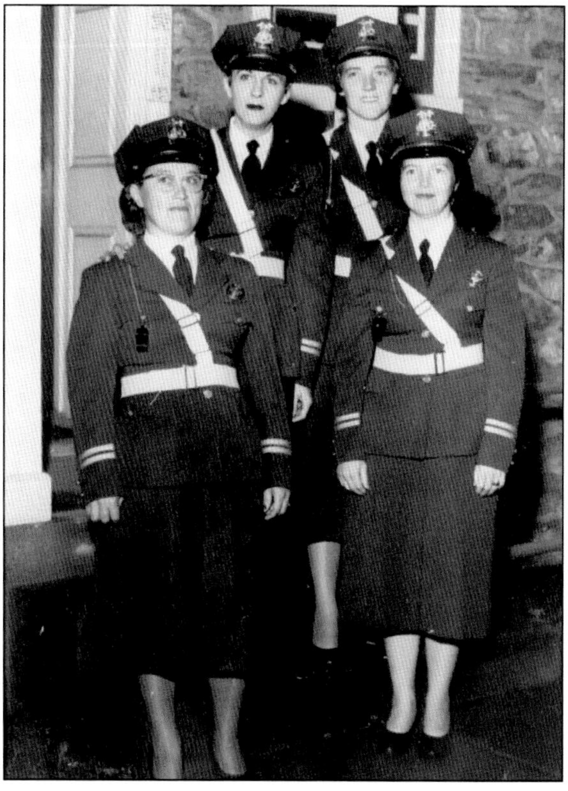

In November 1957, the first uniformed school crossing guards were hired to protect the students attending various schools. Shown, from left to right, are Marion Schneider, Carol Germick, Dorothy Spangenberg, and Margaret Hayes.

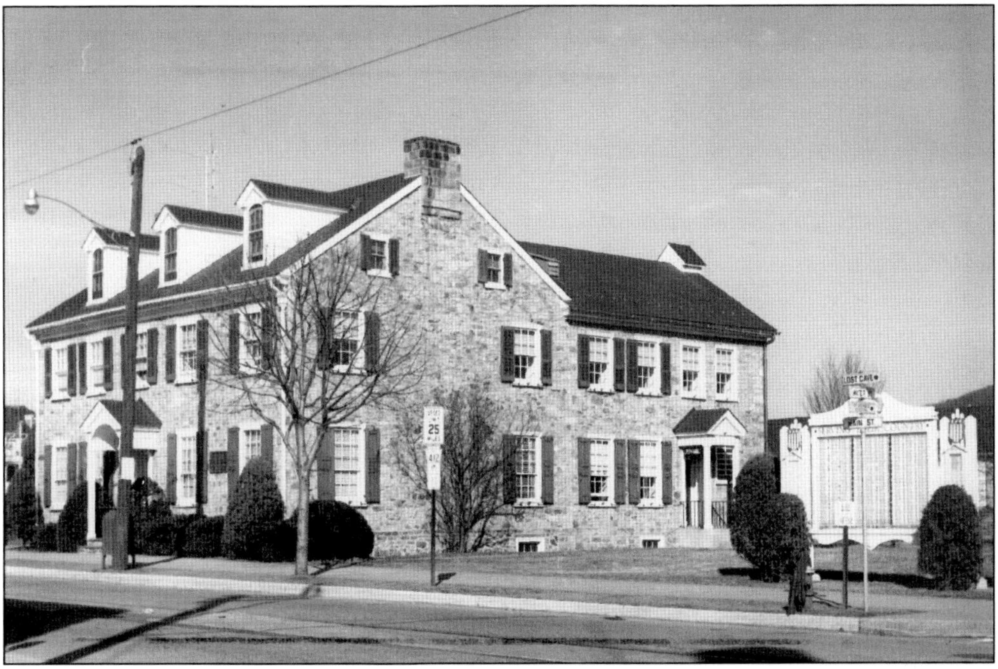

This view of town hall shows the World War II memorial dedicated to those Hellertown men and women who served their country. It must be the late 1940s or early 1950s, after which time the memorial disappeared, never to appear again.

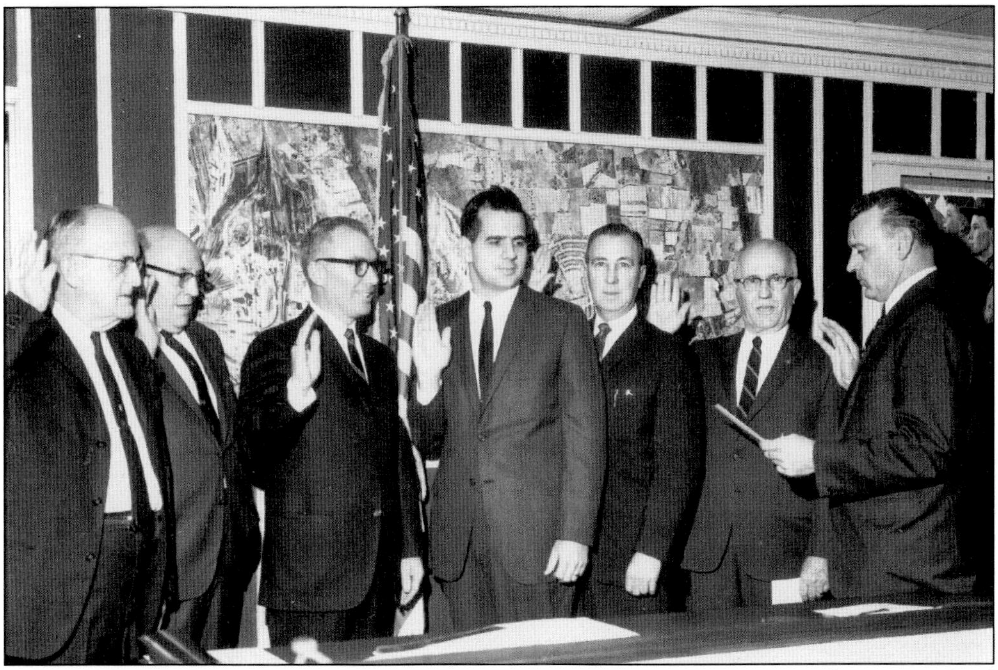

Notice that this council swearing-in ceremony includes Montford Illick, Hellertown School District superintendent, one of the greatest minds of the 20th century in Hellertown. From left to right are Poppy Hahn, Al Beneck, Murphy Ruch, Jerry Long, Owen McCall, Montford Illick, and Edward Johnson.

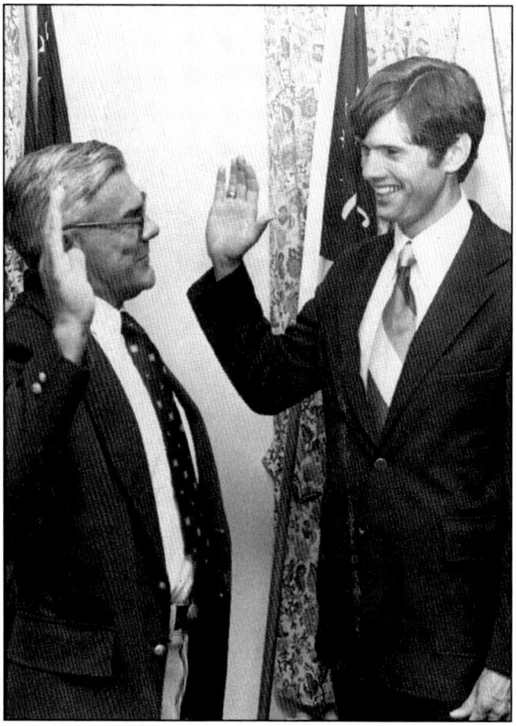

Mayor Emerson Mills swears in the new chief of police, Alfred Shaw, the first new chief in 33 years. Vincent Coughlin was previously the chief.

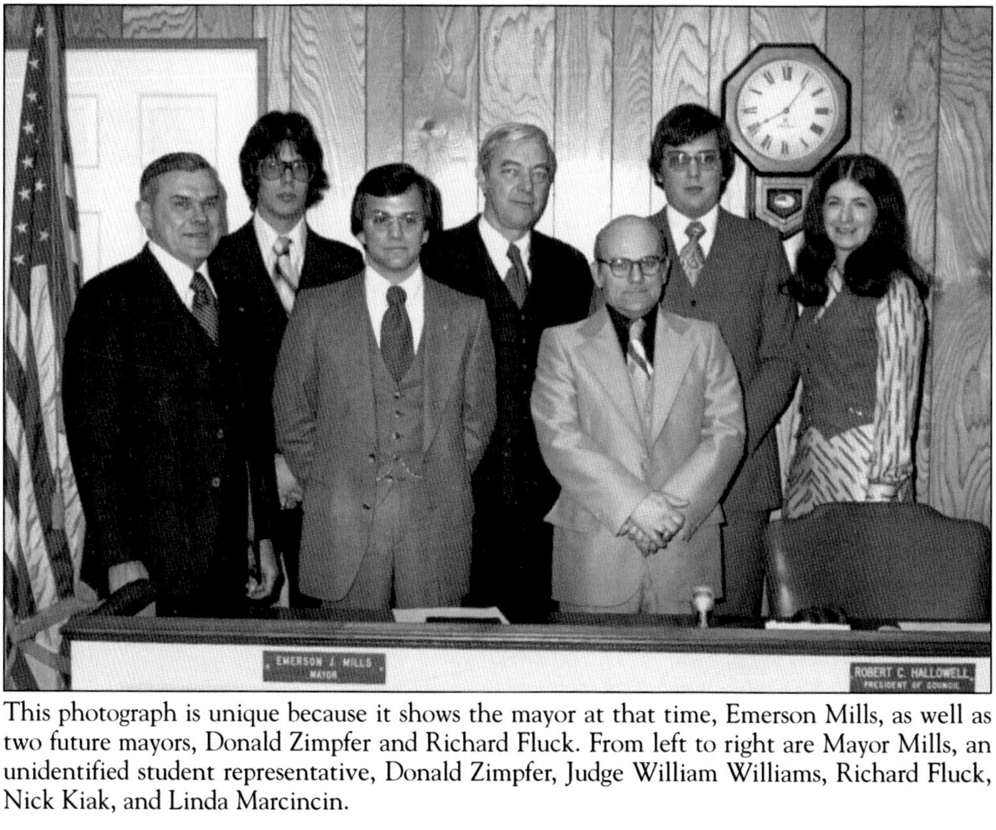

This photograph is unique because it shows the mayor at that time, Emerson Mills, as well as two future mayors, Donald Zimpfer and Richard Fluck. From left to right are Mayor Mills, an unidentified student representative, Donald Zimpfer, Judge William Williams, Richard Fluck, Nick Kiak, and Linda Marcincin.

Four

BUSINESS

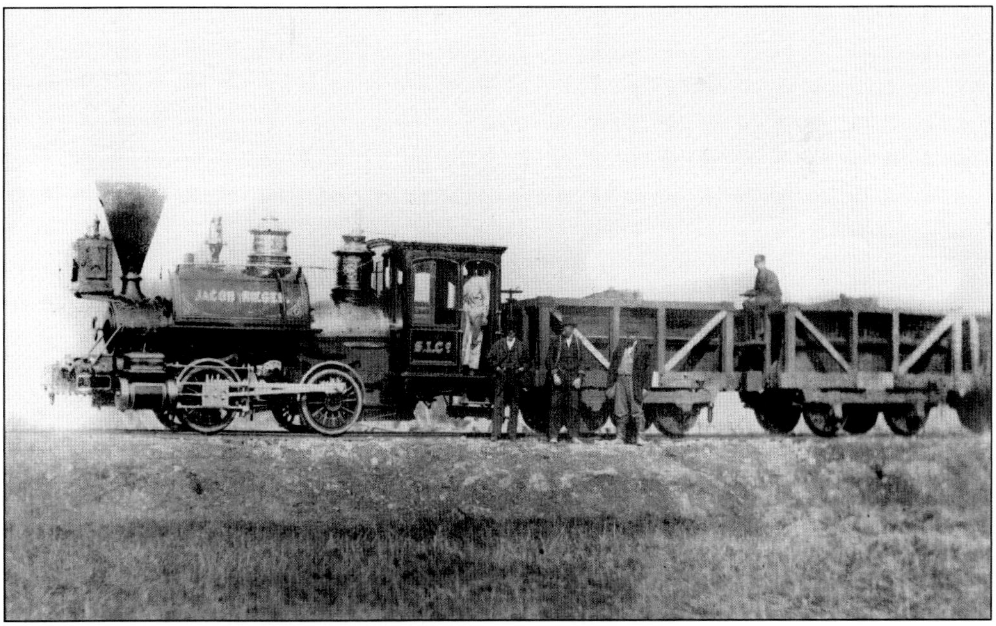

This locomotive is estimated to have been in operation *c.* 1888. The Saucon Valley had rich deposits of iron ore and limestone. Also, the close proximity of anthracite coal made it possible to have a steady source of fuel.

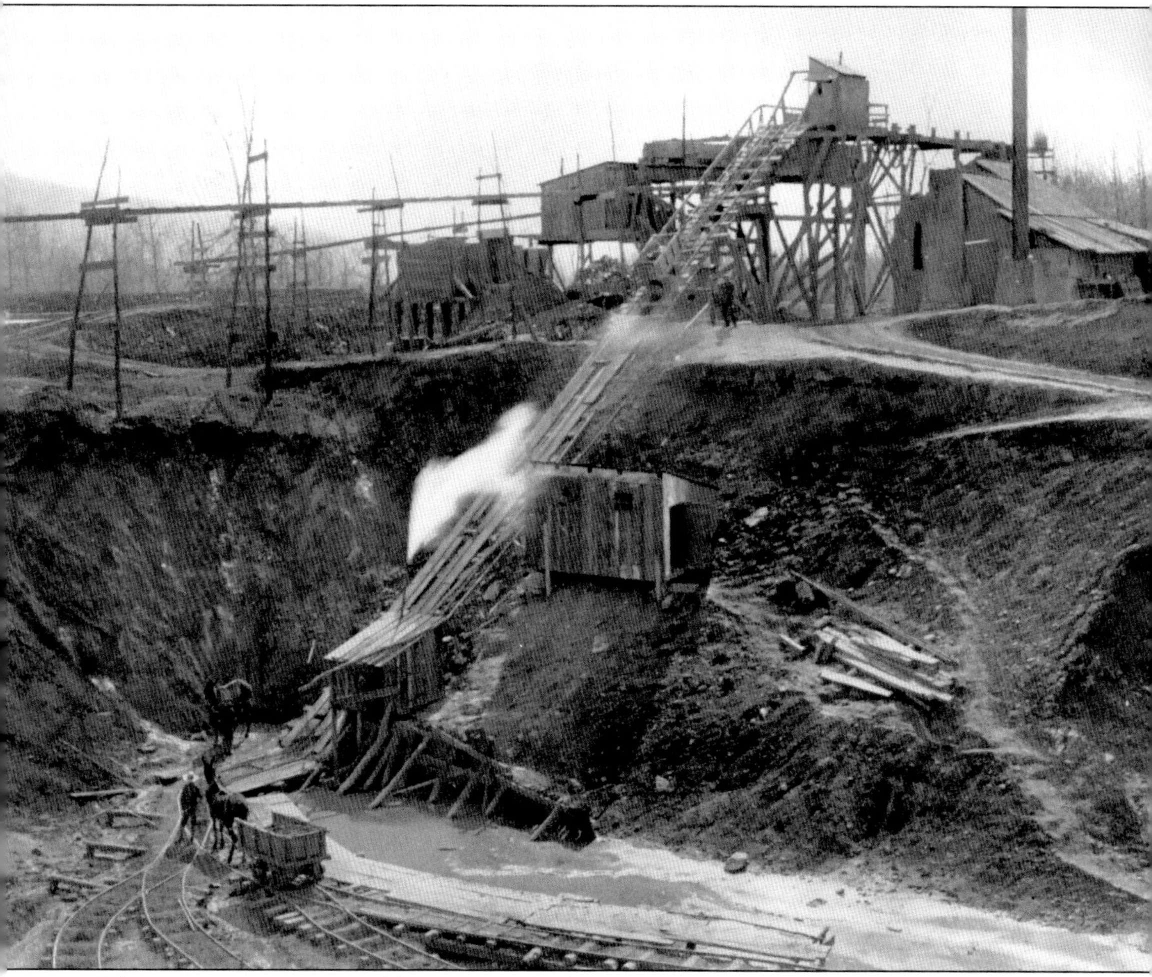

The iron ore mine pictured here was worked by the Saucon Iron Company to be followed by Thomas Iron. This mine was worked between 1903 and 1907. The ore buggies had to be hand-loaded and pulled up by an incline cable. Today, it is part of the water authority's storage dam.

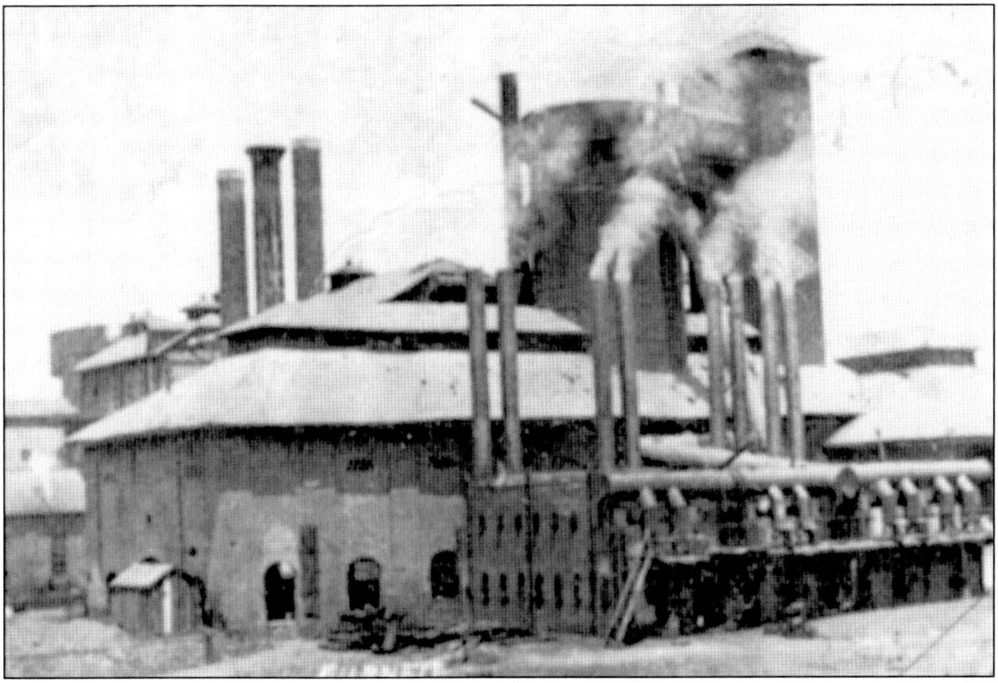

David Thomas is known as the "Father of the American Anthracite Iron Industry." In 1866, the Hellertown branch of the Thomas Iron Company was chartered. The company also owned the Saucon Valley Iron and Railroad Company, which connected to the Philadelphia and Reading Railway near Bingen and ran to the zinc mines in Freidensville. In 1866, Thomas Iron laid claim to being the oldest pig iron–manufacturing company in America.

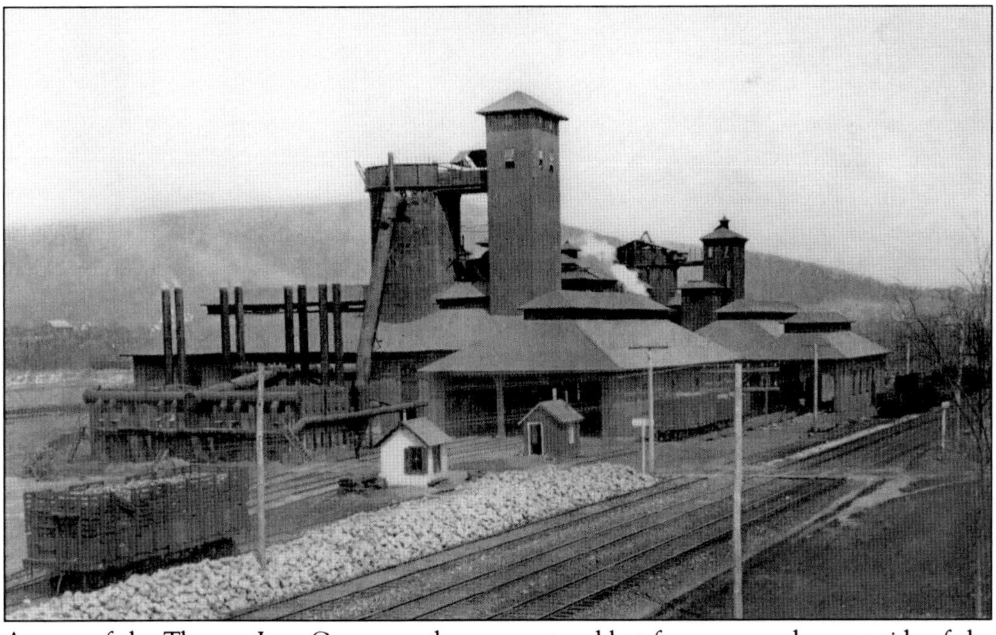

As part of the Thomas Iron Company, there were two blast furnaces on the west side of the railroad tracks behind what is now Saucon Valley Manor. Thomas Iron continued producing until c. 1920.

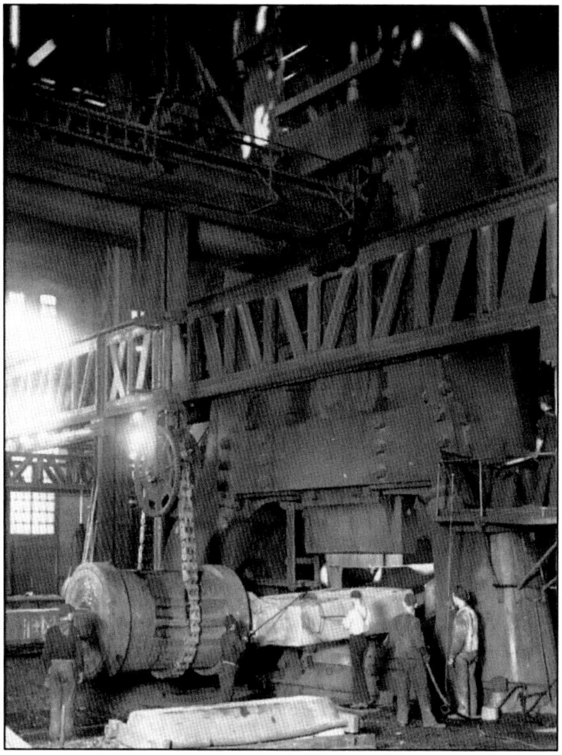

This photograph is one of the few interior views that are available to take us back to the turn-of-the-century iron operations.

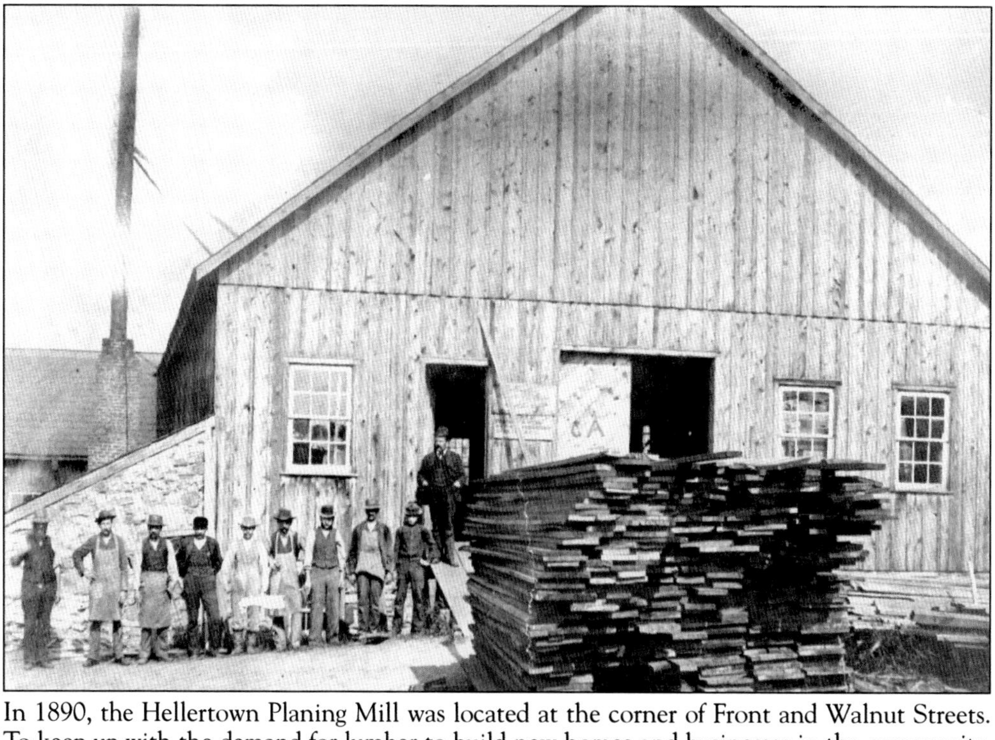

In 1890, the Hellertown Planing Mill was located at the corner of Front and Walnut Streets. To keep up with the demand for lumber to build new homes and businesses in the community, these men transformed a natural resource into a necessary commodity.

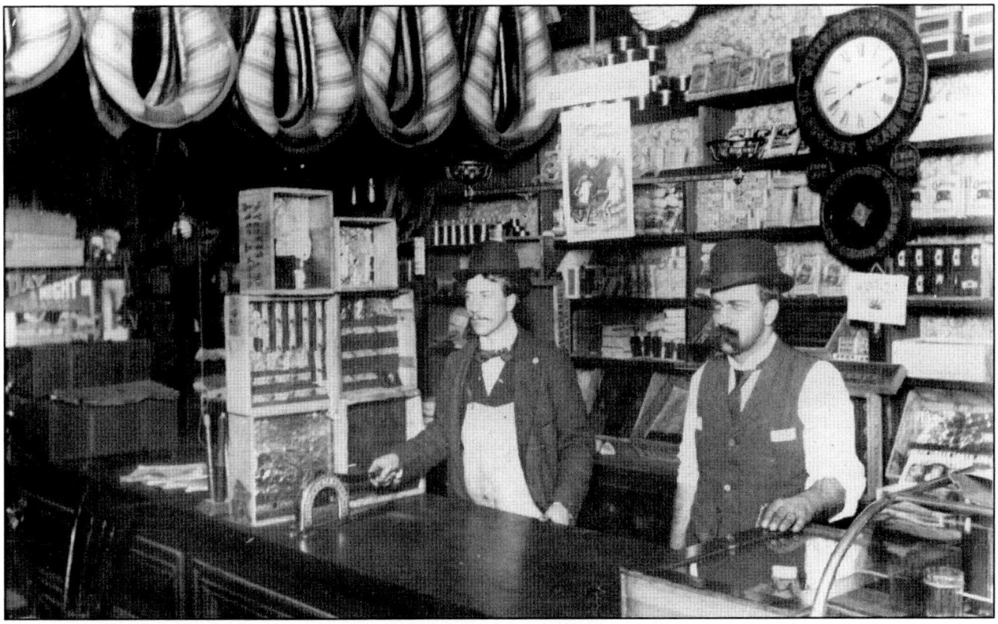

In 1897, Edward Weisel and family moved into a building at Main Street and Easton Road. This building had been erected in the early 1800s by W.K. Witte, who operated a general store. Edward Weisel began a harness shop business that lasted until 1940, when the building was razed. Tobacco products were also sold there, and the store provided a popular meeting place for men where they swapped stories or discussed politics. The sandy surface of the exterior shop walls was constructed similarly to those in certain parts of Germany and reflected the vast influence of Hellertown's Pennsylvania German population.

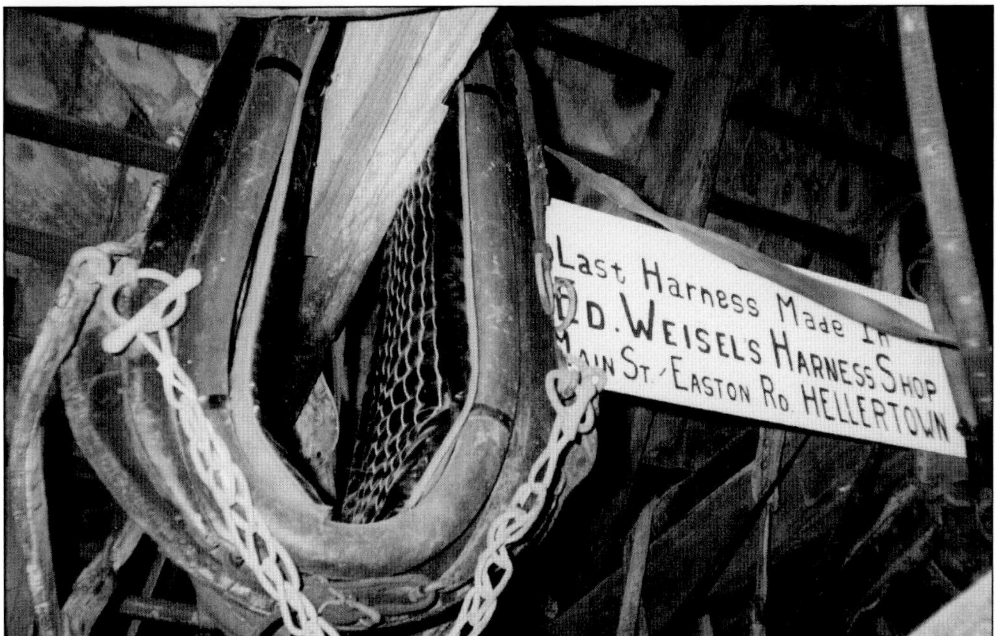

Hanging in the Hellertown Historical Society Museum, this was the last harness created by Edward Weisel on Main Street and Easton Road.

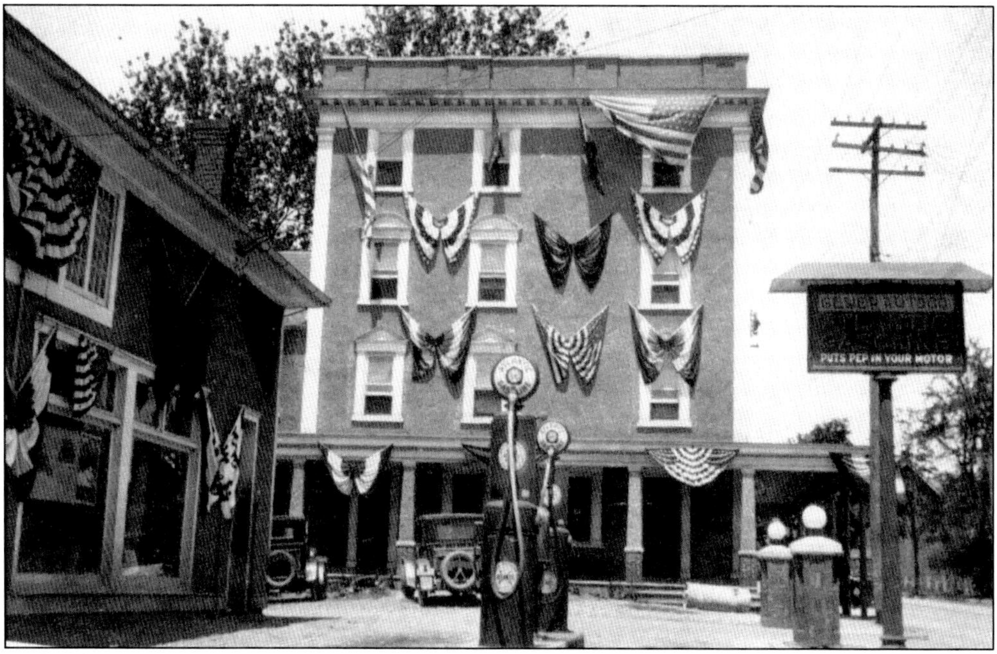

In the foreground can be seen the Geyer Auto Company during the late 1920s or early 1930s. The Park Hotel is in the background. Early touring cars are parked there, and the hotel's livery stable later became obsolete. Near the hotel were large cement pools where trout were raised. Children would stop by the hotel in the evening to watch the quoit competition.

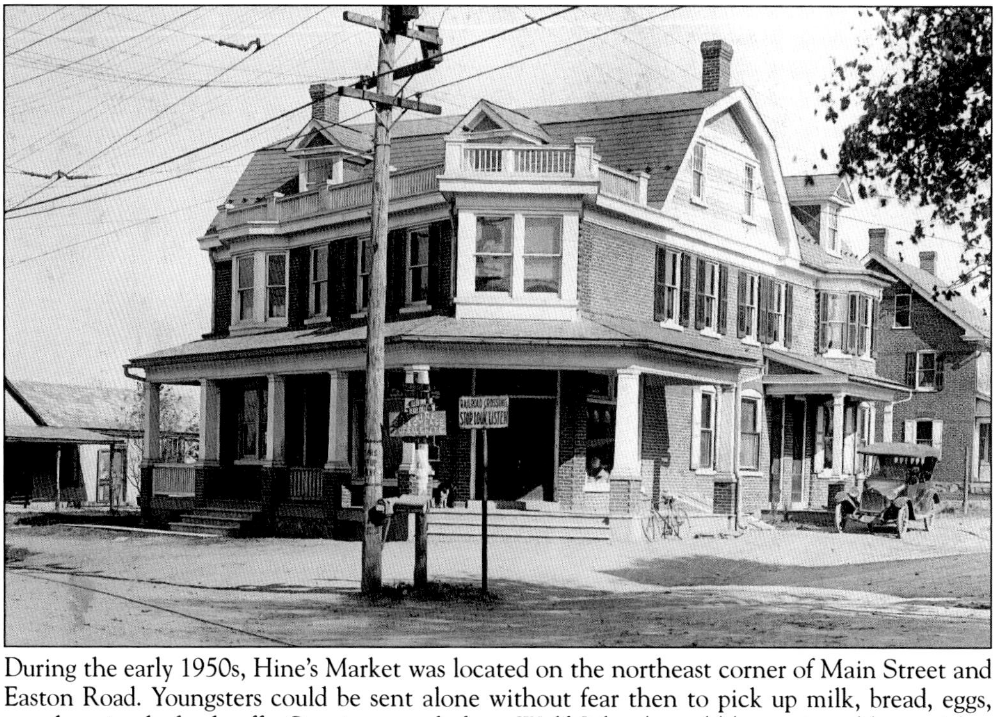

During the early 1950s, Hine's Market was located on the northeast corner of Main Street and Easton Road. Youngsters could be sent alone without fear then to pick up milk, bread, eggs, or other simple foodstuffs. Crossing guards from Wolf School would be stationed here with a policeman before and after school and before and after lunch.

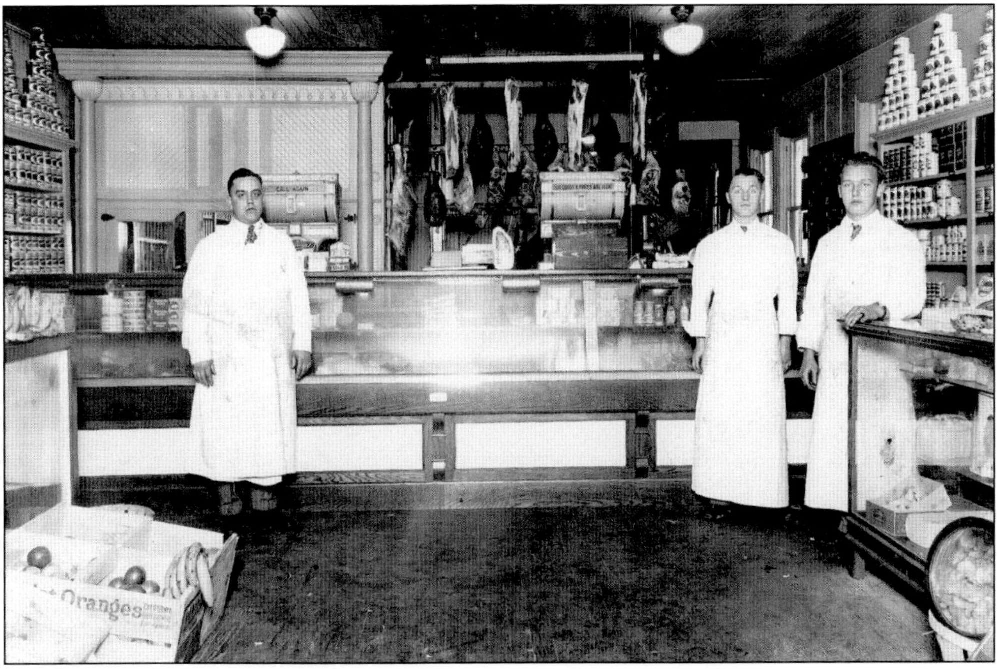

During the first half of the 20th century, many family-owned businesses came and went from Main Street. Ed Hine's meat market was located at 620 Main Street. Posing in the shop in October 1930 are, from left to right, Ed Hine and employees Joe Brown and Bill Barnett.

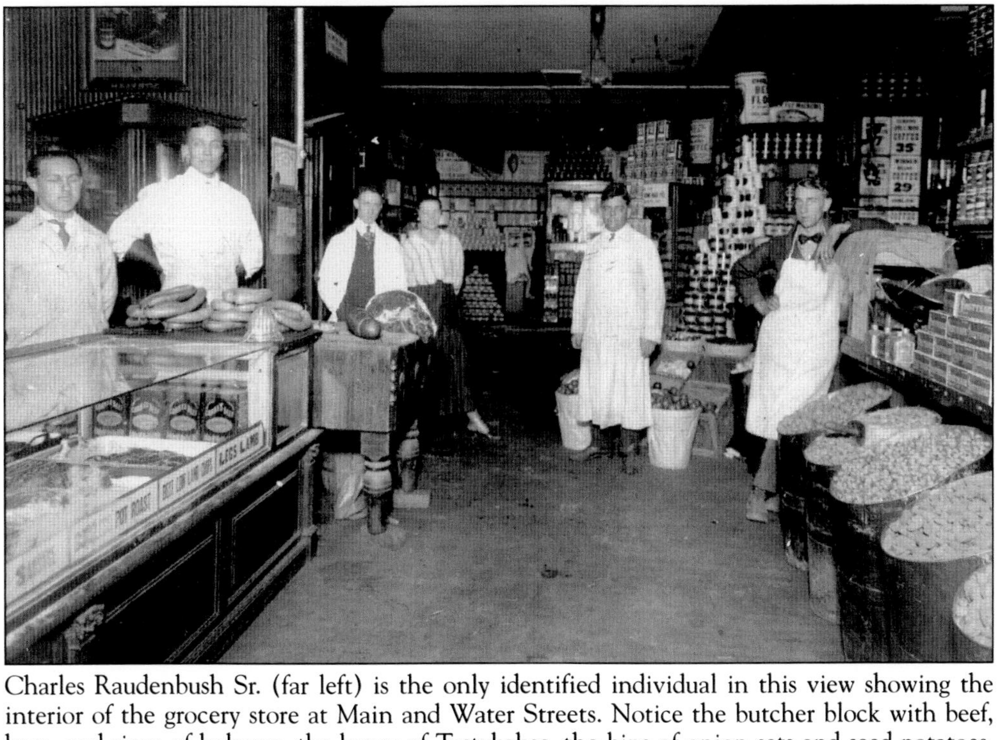

Charles Raudenbush Sr. (far left) is the only identified individual in this view showing the interior of the grocery store at Main and Water Streets. Notice the butcher block with beef, ham, and rings of bologna, the boxes of Tastykakes, the bins of onion sets and seed potatoes, and the pyramids of canned goods.

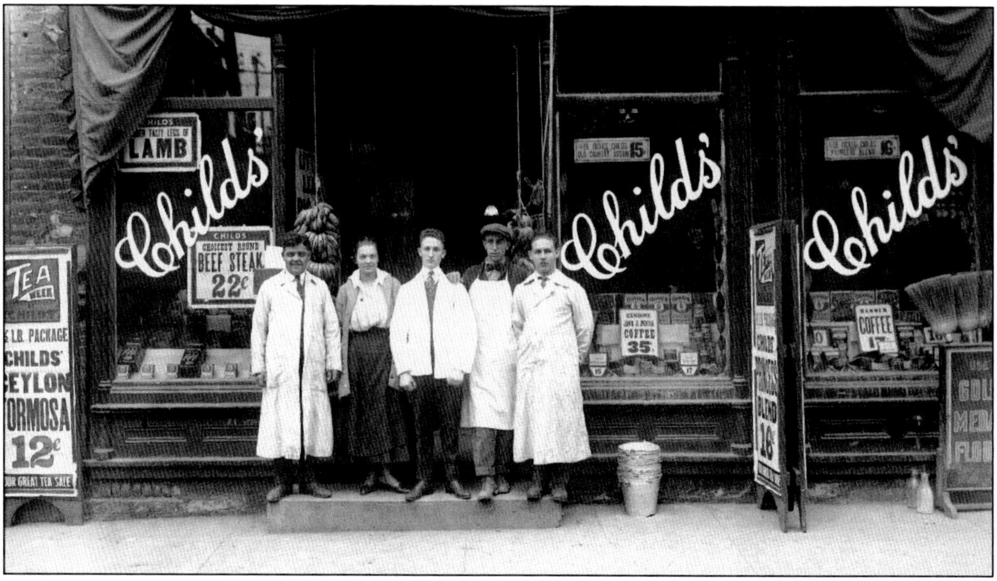

Childs' seemed to have good advertising and a well-organized staff. This Main Street store may have been an early example of a chain store. The only individual identified is Charles Raudenbush (far right). Notice the large supply of bananas hanging by the entrance. The store is advertising its big tea sale, such as a half pound of Ceylon Formosa tea at 12¢. Also, clearly seen are signs for leg of lamb and choice beefsteak.

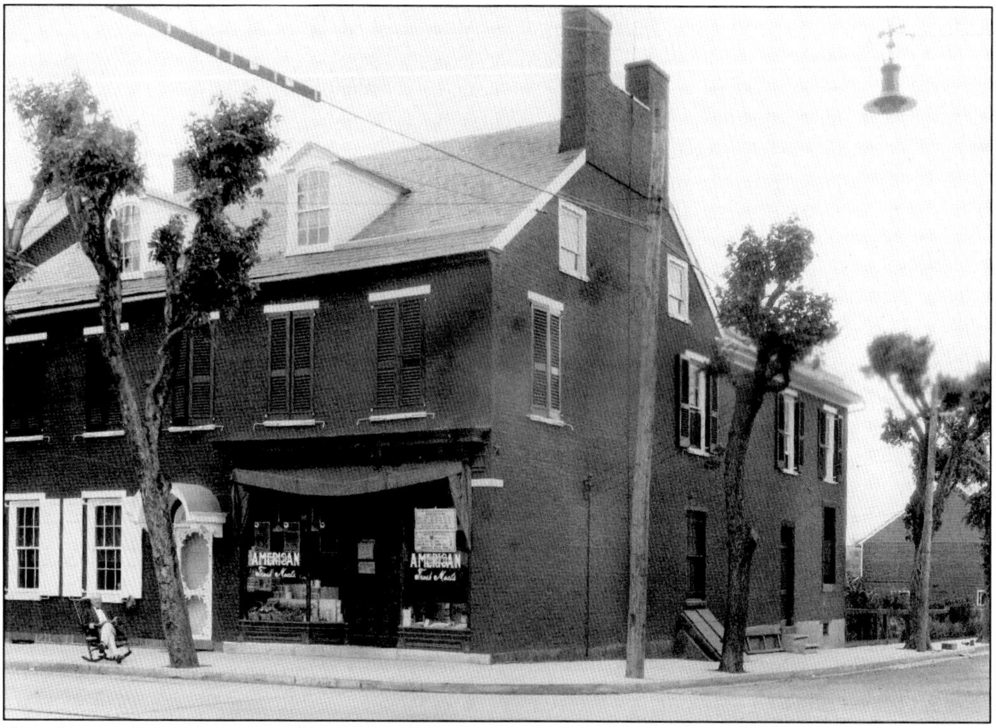

On the southwest corner of Main and Water Streets, George Deemer's American store was one of the true mom-and-pop corner markets from the early 1900s. This photograph shows the owner relaxing in his rocker. The store later became Stern's Market.

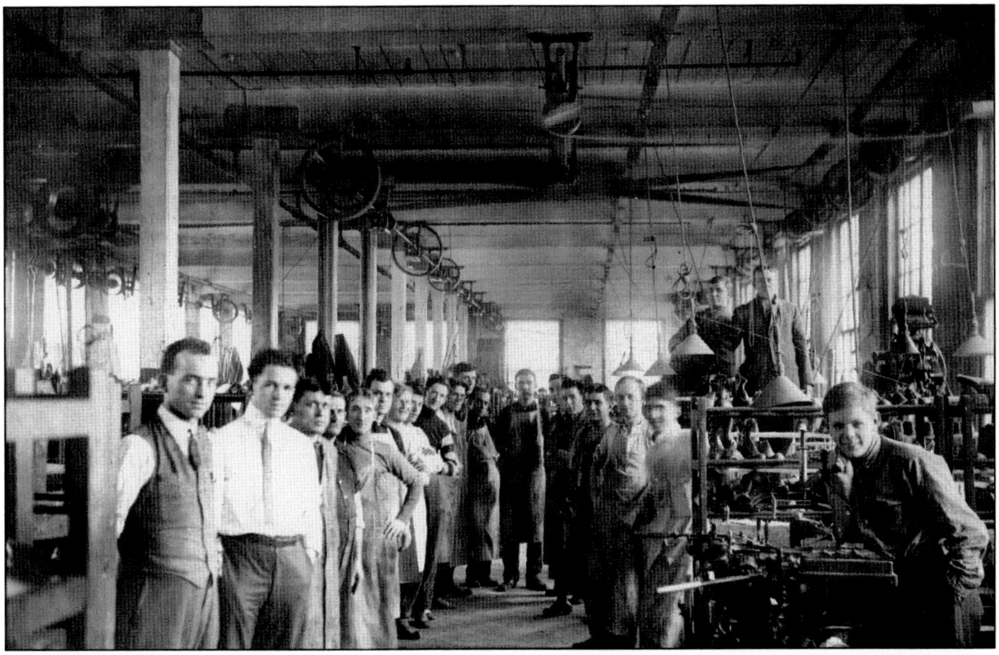

Not much has been documented about the Ronca Shoe Factory, but it was located behind Jefferson Street. Many employees appear to be teenagers.

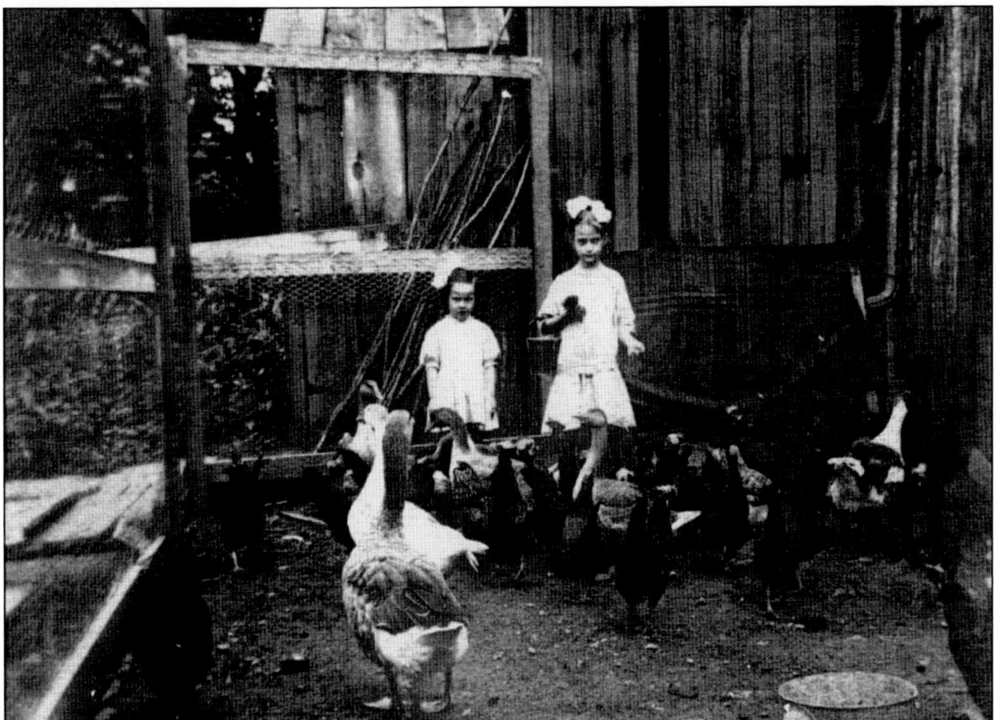

Very early on, there was a butcher shop at the northeast corner of Main and Durham Streets. Pictured is a pair of little girls apparently poised to feed the ducks and geese, which were destined to be served for dinner eventually.

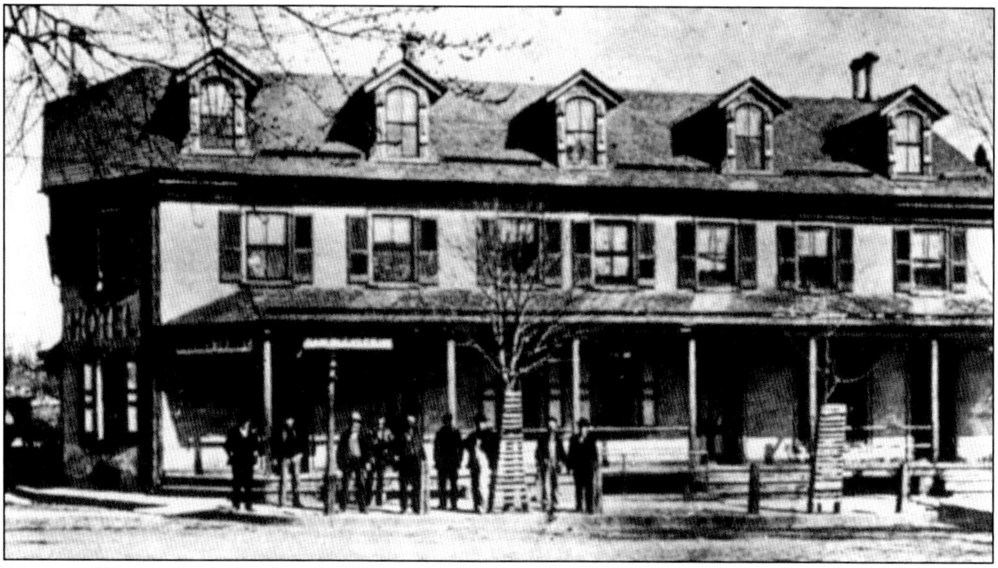

From 1818 until 1853, this building's importance rested with its residents, the family of Dr. Henry Detwiller. Detwiller practiced homeopathic medicine in Hellertown for 34 years. Also, he was school director of Lower Saucon for 14 years and was president during the introduction of free public schools. The doctor also became one of the founders of Thomas Iron. In 1939, the property was purchased by the borough. After extensive alterations, the building was dedicated as Hellertown Borough Hall on July 4, 1942.

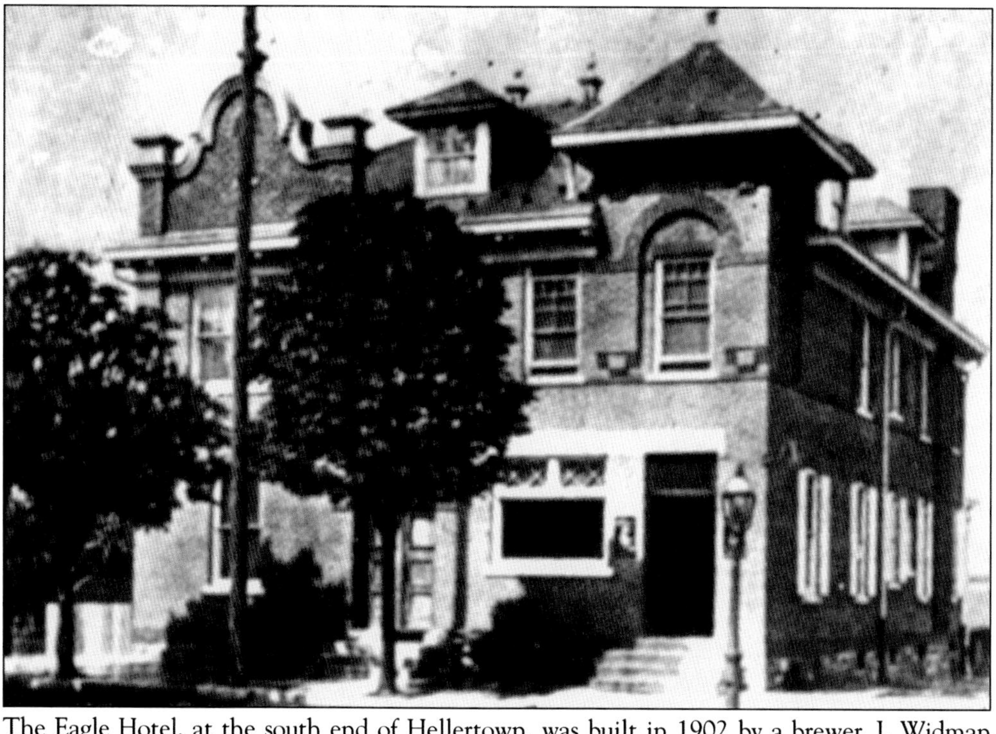

The Eagle Hotel, at the south end of Hellertown, was built in 1902 by a brewer, J. Widman and Company. It was later changed to the Hellertown Hotel, owned and operated by the Matey family.

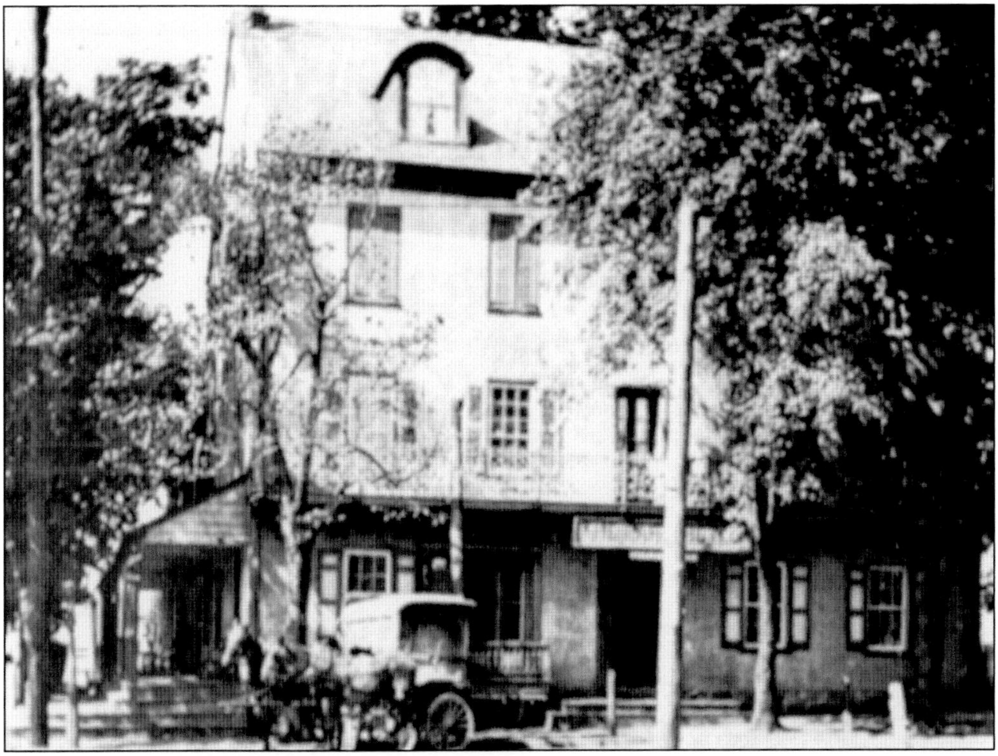

The Park Hotel was originally located across Main Street from the Weisel Harness Shop. In 1860, the hotel was operated by O.H. Desh. Today, it would be across from Detwiller Plaza.

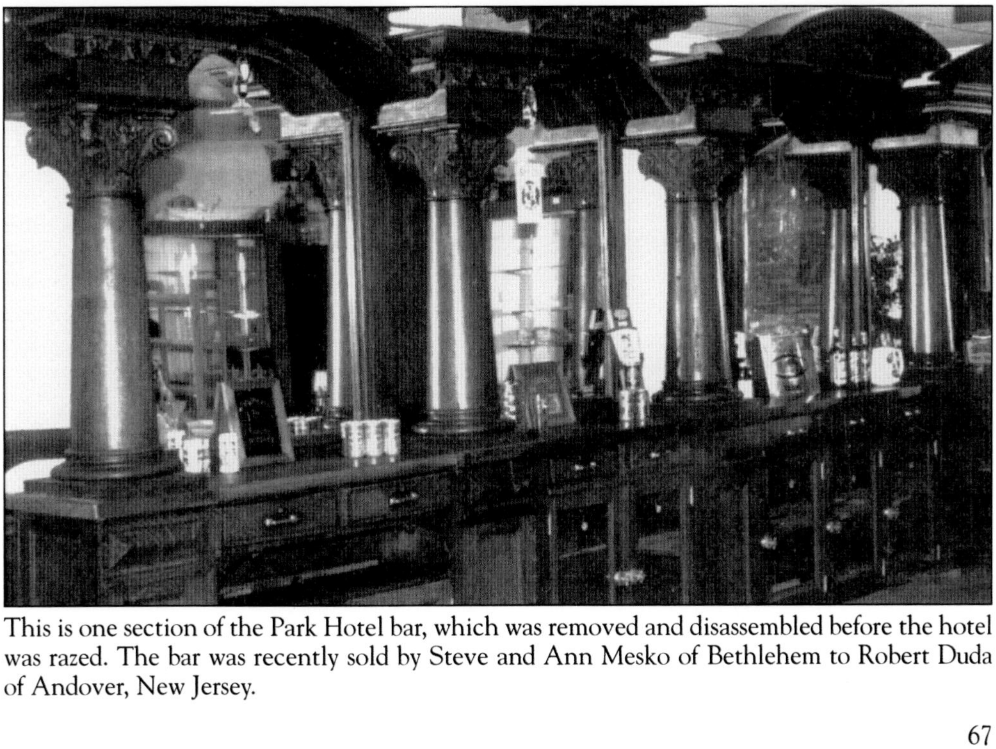

This is one section of the Park Hotel bar, which was removed and disassembled before the hotel was razed. The bar was recently sold by Steve and Ann Mesko of Bethlehem to Robert Duda of Andover, New Jersey.

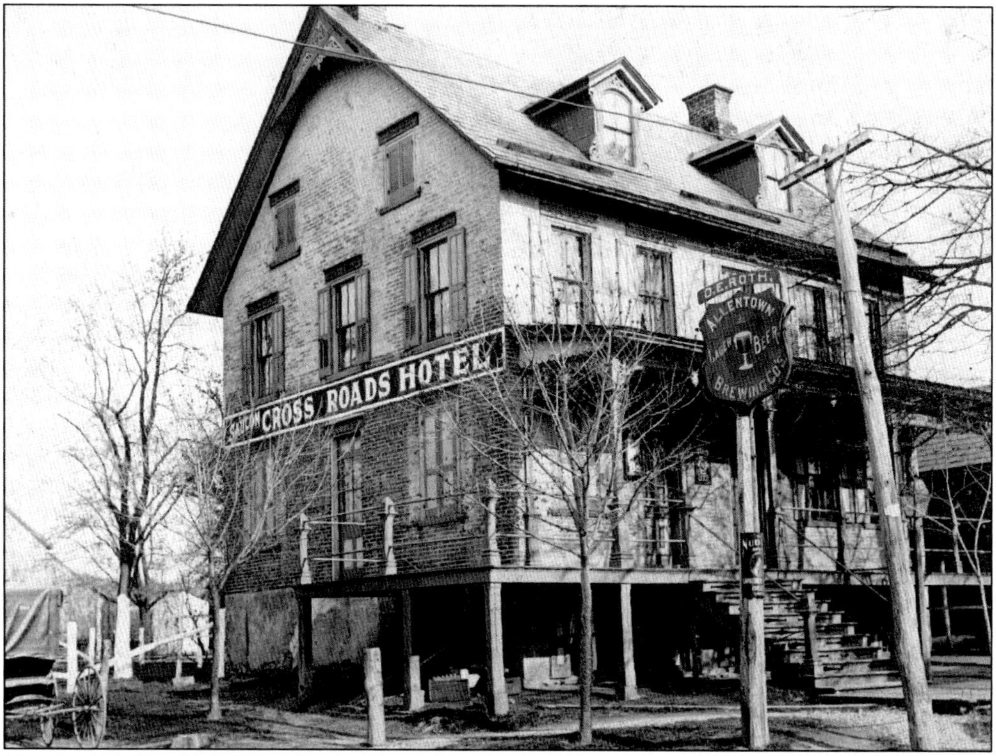

The Saucon Cross Roads Hotel, seen here on May 5, 1907, has occupied the southeast corner of Main and High Streets for more than a century. The sign in the front reads, "Ollie E. Roth, Allentown Lager Brewing Company." At that time, the hotel was within Lower Saucon Township.

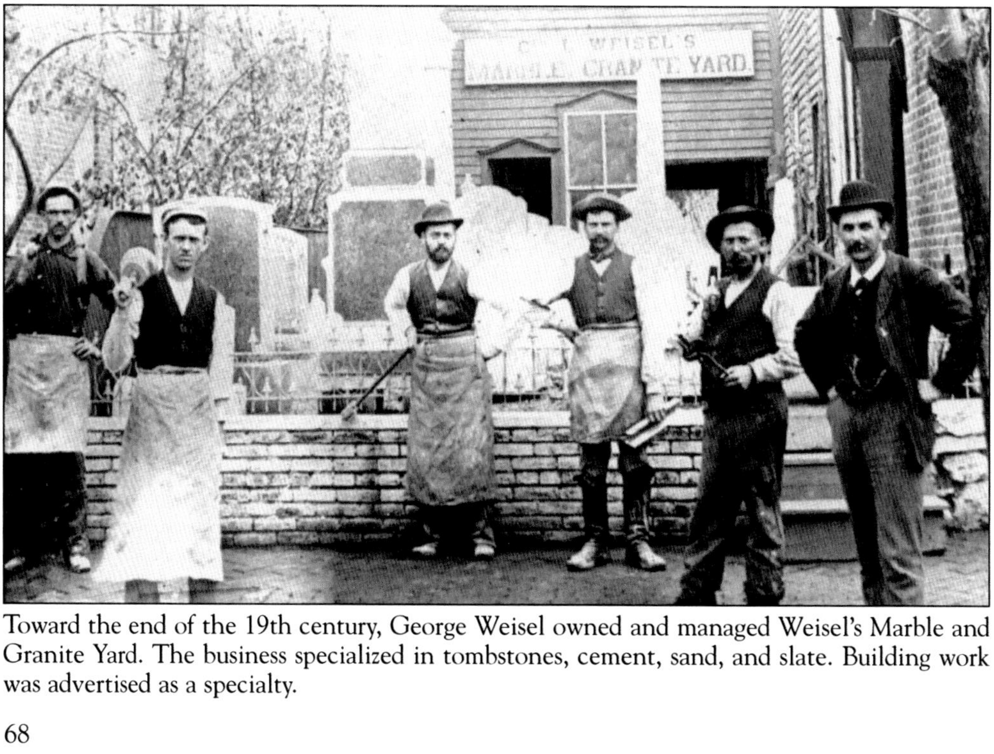

Toward the end of the 19th century, George Weisel owned and managed Weisel's Marble and Granite Yard. The business specialized in tombstones, cement, sand, and slate. Building work was advertised as a specialty.

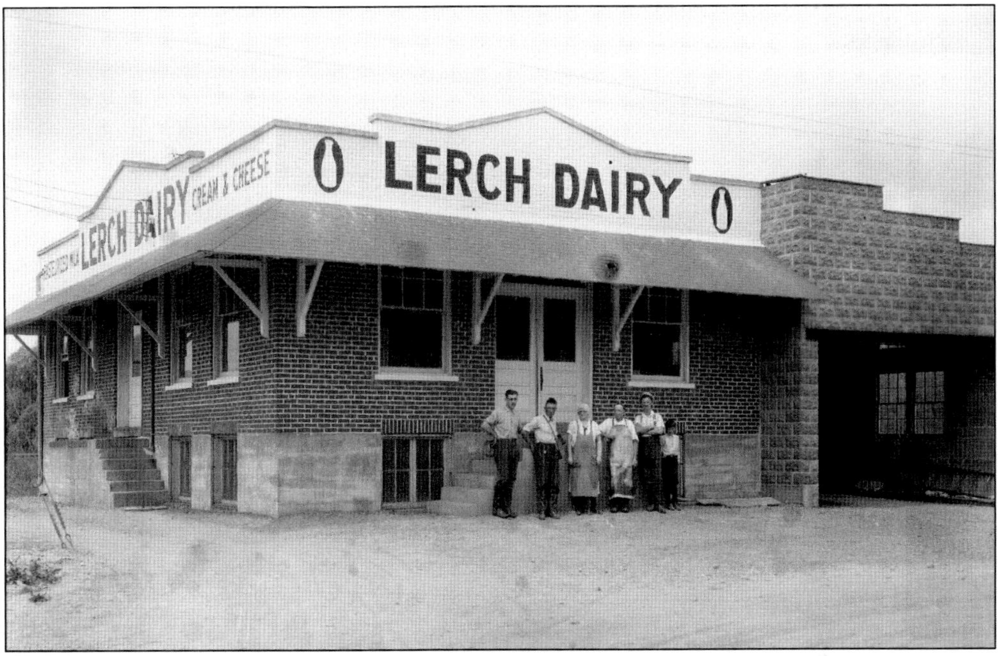

The Lerch Dairy was the forerunner of the Brookfield Dairy. Assorted milk products were available. The men's apparel suggests the times, the 1930s and 1940s. The building materials were most likely available locally.

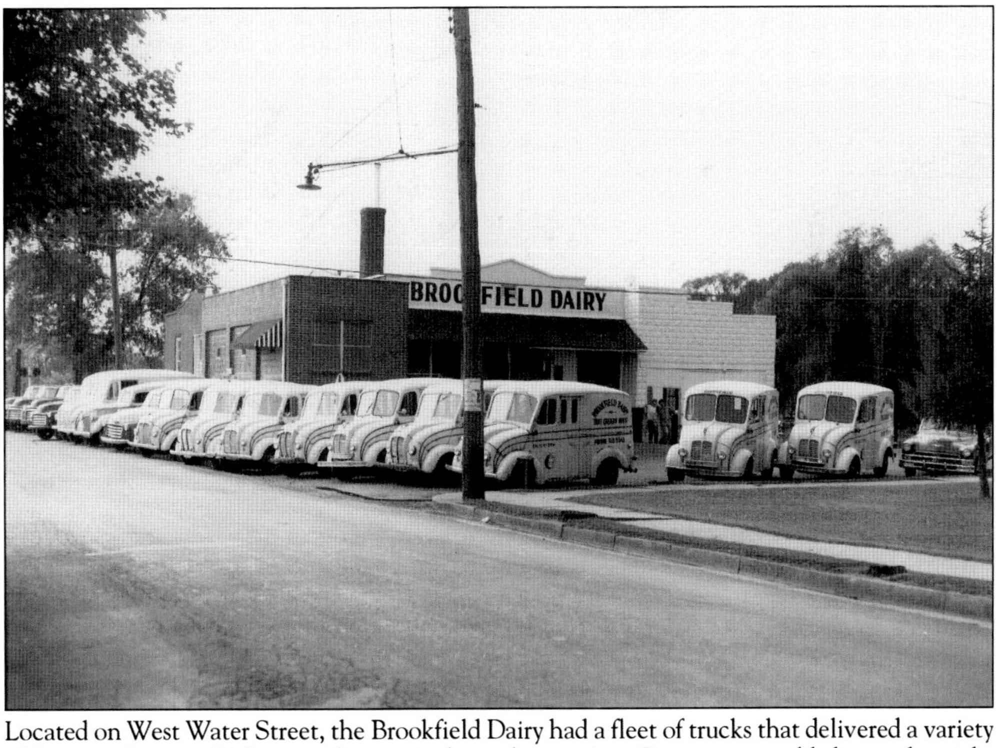

Located on West Water Street, the Brookfield Dairy had a fleet of trucks that delivered a variety of dairy products to Hellertown homes in the early morning. Customers would choose the night before and display the products desired on colored cardboard marking fingers.

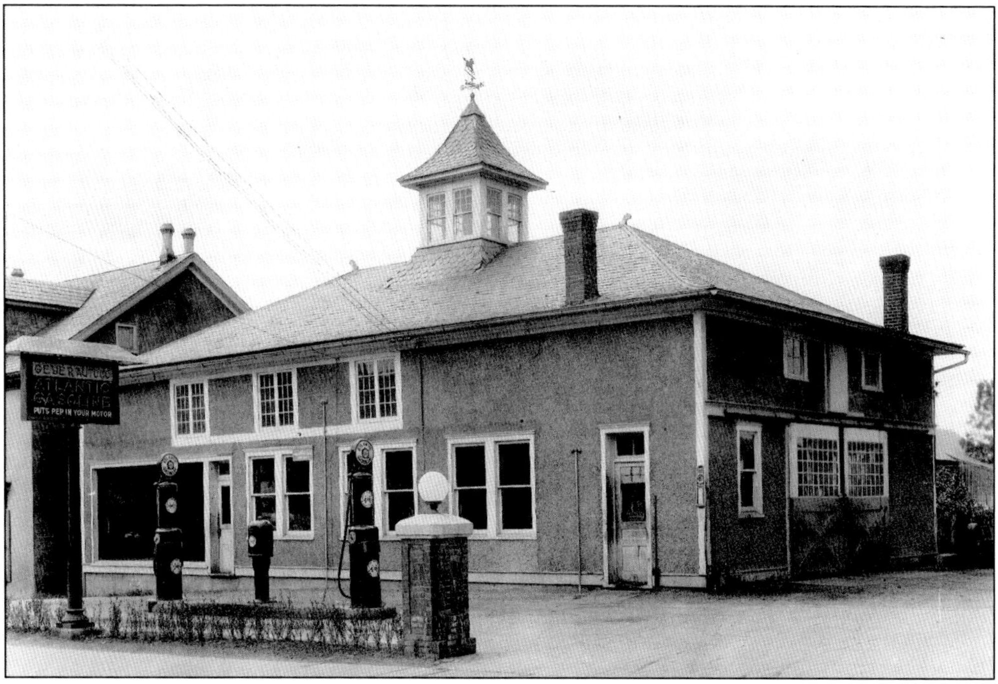

In the 700 block of Main Street, the Geyer service station served Hellertonians for many years. For several years in the 1930s, passersby would stop by in the evening to watch the Geyer quoit team compete.

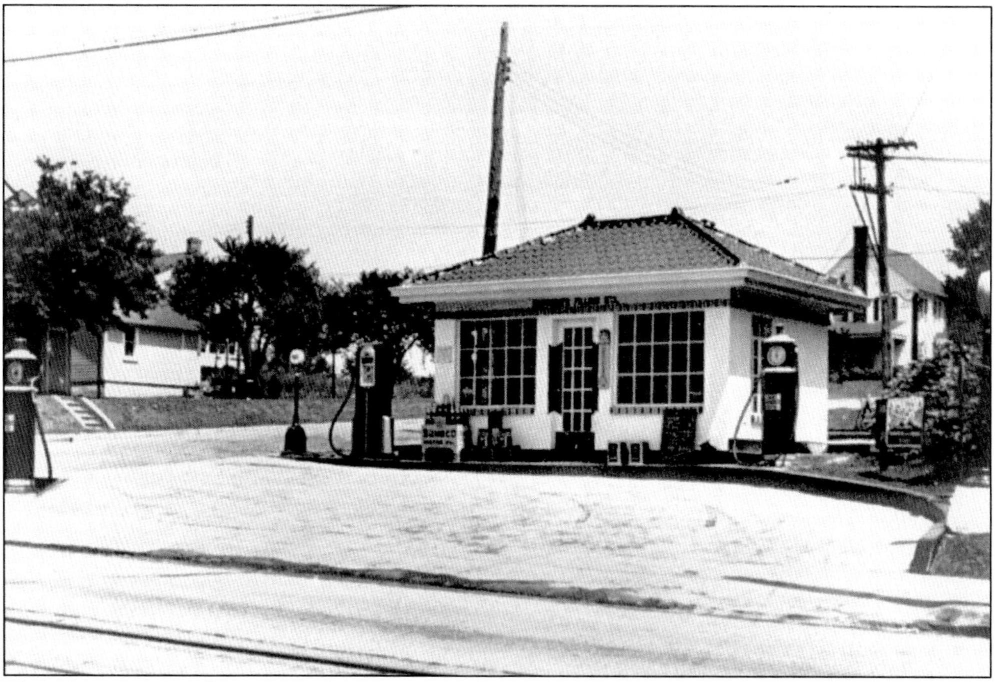
The Hartman Brothers service station was located at the southeast corner of Main Street and Wilson Avenue. Later, the Sunoco station became Pearson and Kies and, after that, Kies Sunoco, owned by Edward "Skip" Kies.

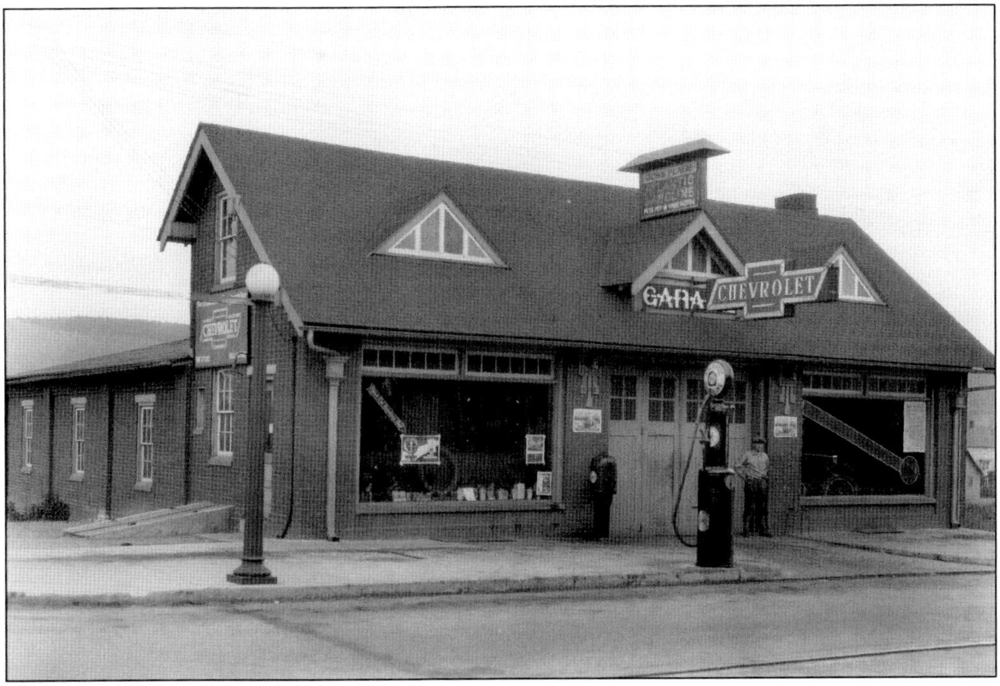

Robert Rickert worked at Bethlehem Shipbuilding in New Jersey for 13 years and was superintendent during World War I, when the plant set production records. Then, he entered business for himself in Hellertown when he opened a car dealership in 1920. He was soon the local Chevrolet dealer and Atlantic gasoline retailer. The sign on the roof reads, "Bob's Place / Atlantic Gasoline / Puts Pep in Your Engine."

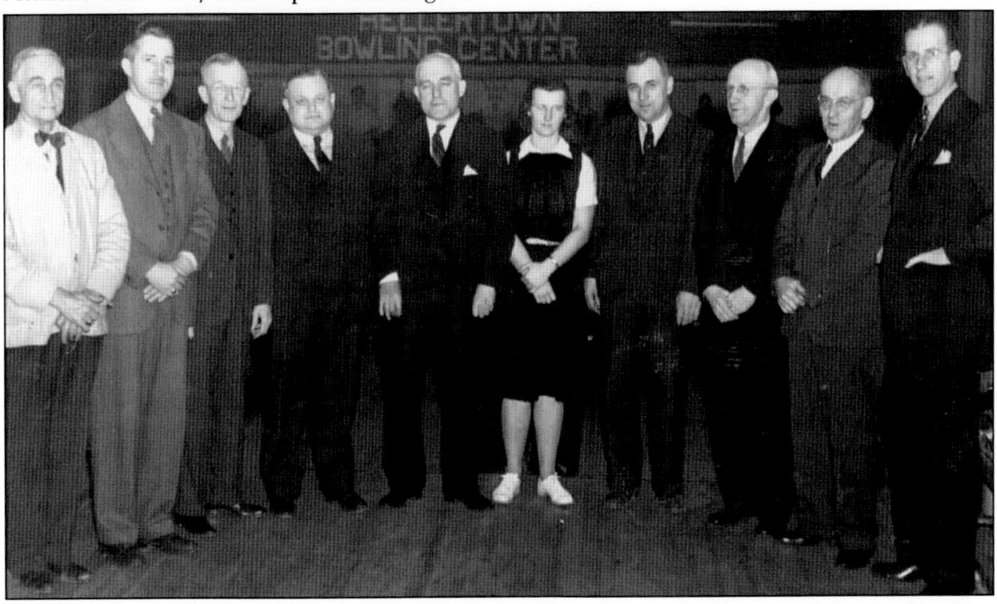

The Hellertown Bowling Alley was dedicated on February 1, 1941. Many locals remember their first bowling experiences that occurred on the second floor of Rauscher's Hardware Store. From left to right are an unidentified man, Harold Ward, Weg Peffer, Stanley Yeager, Morris Dimmick, Jeanette Scholl, William Buecher, Herb Hoffert, John Bergstresser, and Charles Bauder.

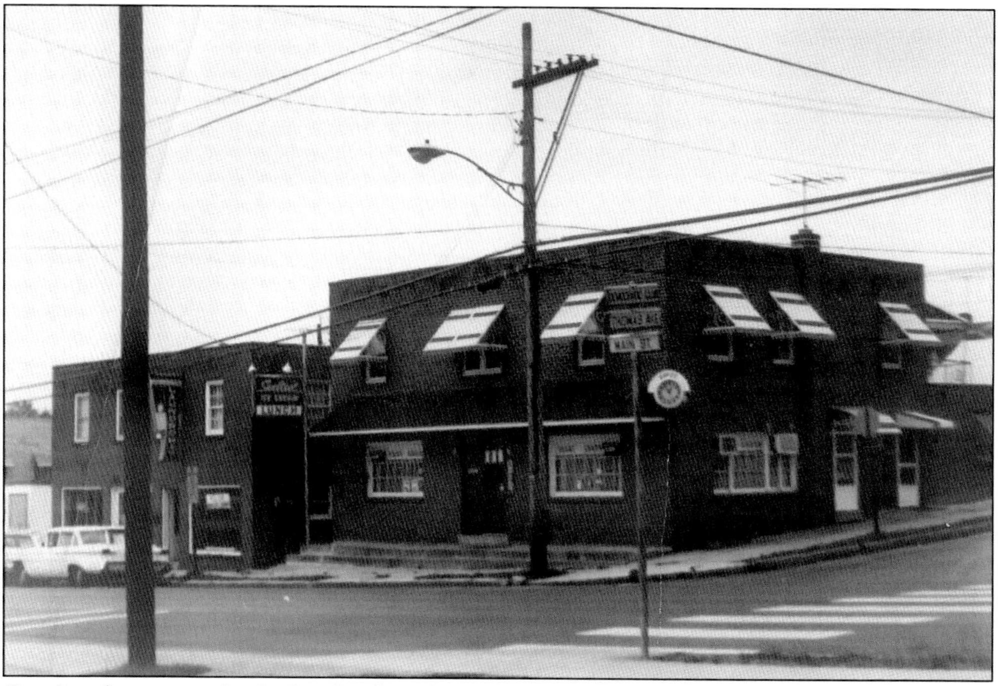

Guro's, adjacent to the high school on Main Street, was the place to hang out after school was out. The cool groups could be found there for rock and roll and the soda fountain during the 1950s.

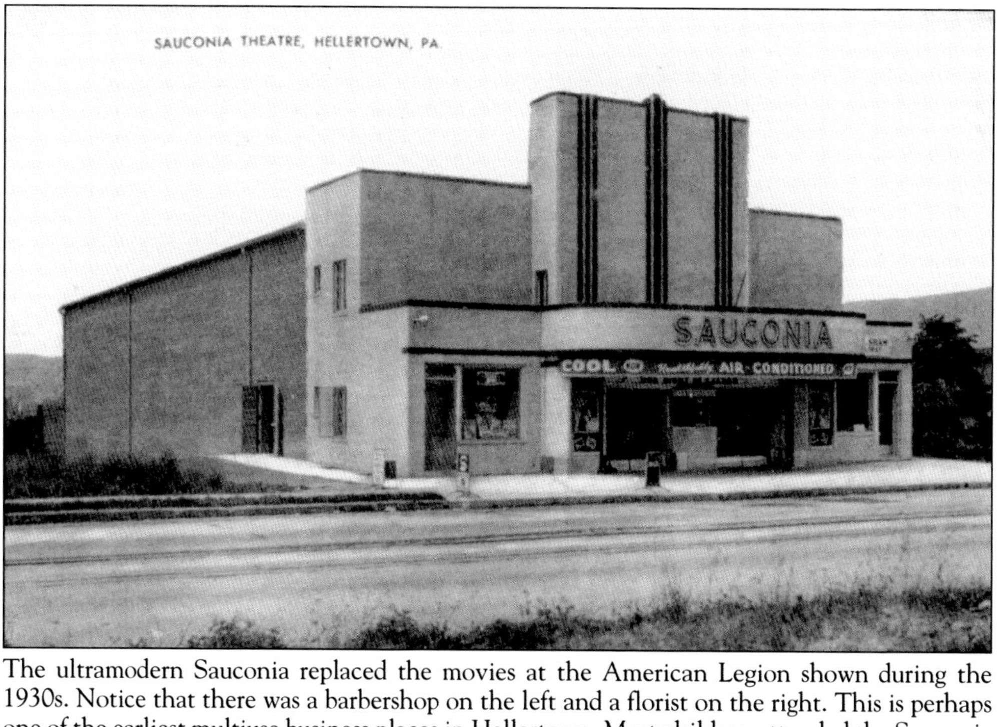

The ultramodern Sauconia replaced the movies at the American Legion shown during the 1930s. Notice that there was a barbershop on the left and a florist on the right. This is perhaps one of the earliest multiuse business places in Hellertown. Most children attended the Sauconia on Saturday afternoon for the matinee. The entry fee during the 1950s was 16¢.

The Gilmans of Hellertown have welcomed 25,000 tourists per year to Lost River Caverns for years. Not only do visitors tour the caverns, but they also have the opportunity to browse through the museum and gift shop.

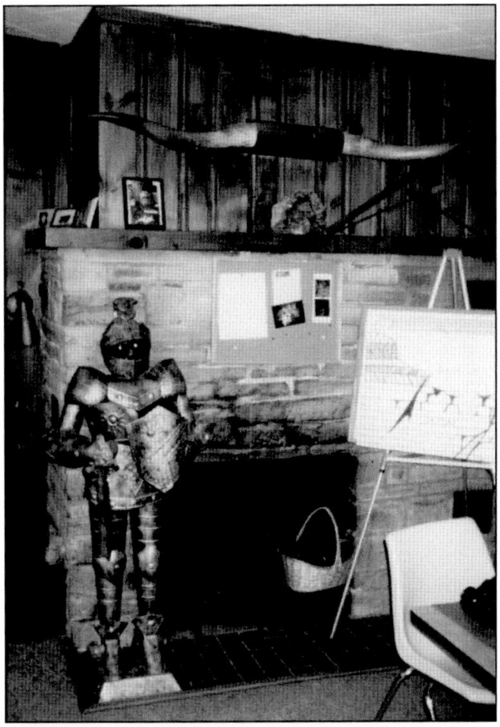

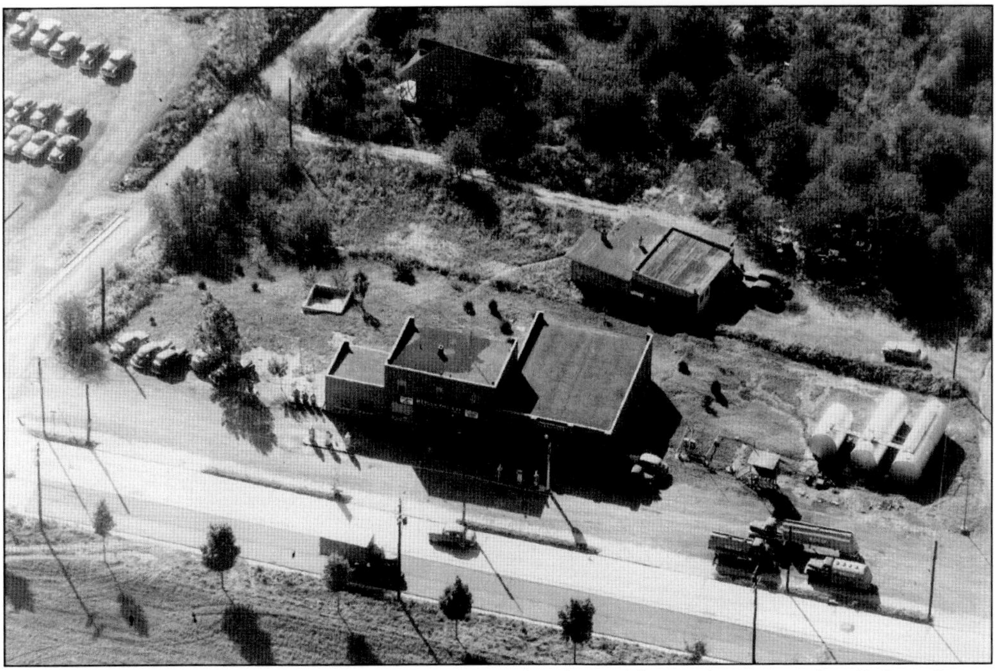

During the 1950s, the Reilly Oil Company was plainly visible on the west side of Main Street almost on the Hellertown-Bethlehem line. It was probably one of the two oil distributors in town, the other being Ward's. Many homeowners were in the process of converting from coal to oil furnaces.

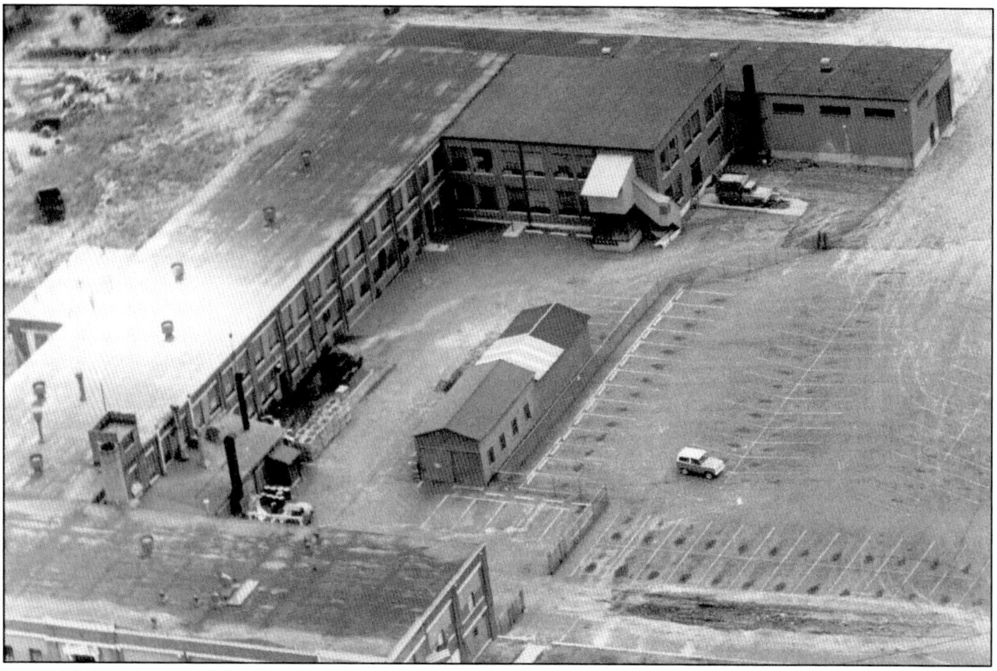

The Hellertown Manufacturing Company made Champion spark plugs in the mid-20th century. Many jobs were available, but unfortunately, toxic waste was disposed of improperly on the site over the years.

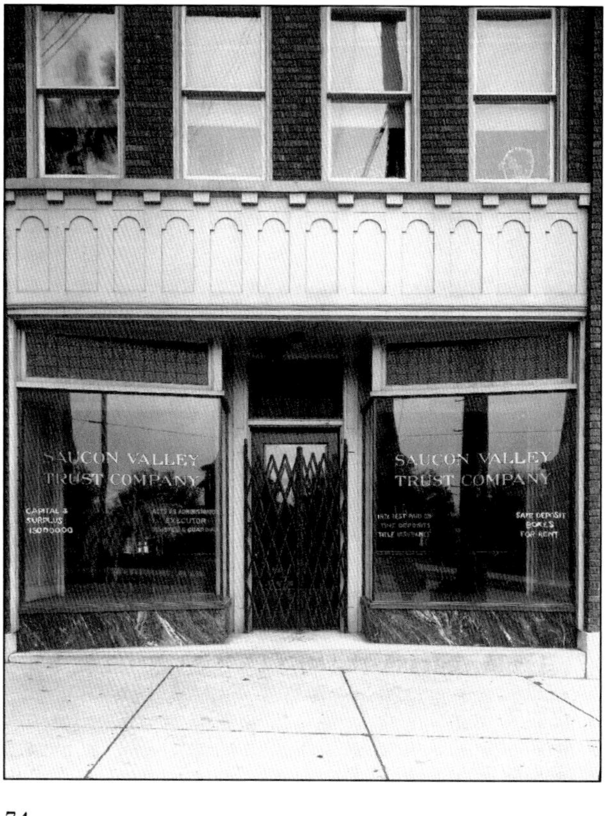

In the 600 block of Main Street, Saucon Valley Trust was squarely among the main "downtown" businesses during the 1950s. First-time depositors felt secure since the bank was only one block south of the police station within Hellertown Borough Hall.

Five

COMMUNITY

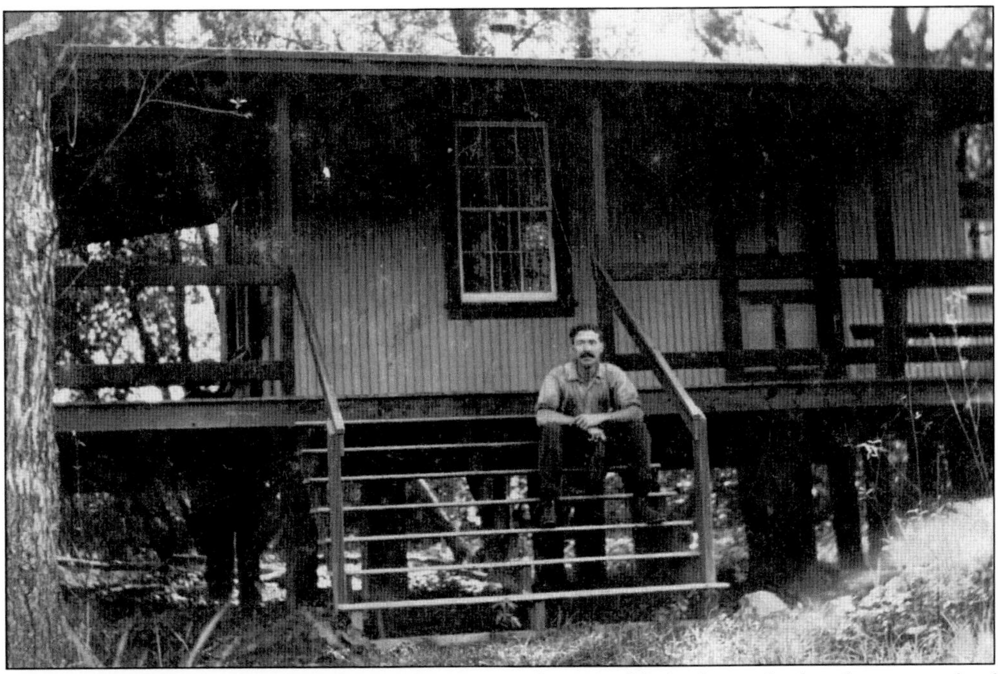

Taken during the first decade of the 20th century, this view likely shows the boathouse north of the Water Street Bridge, with Aaron Ward seated on the steps. Conjecture aside, this building was used jointly by a group of men who met socially and floated their rowboats on the Saucon, sometimes with large kegs inside.

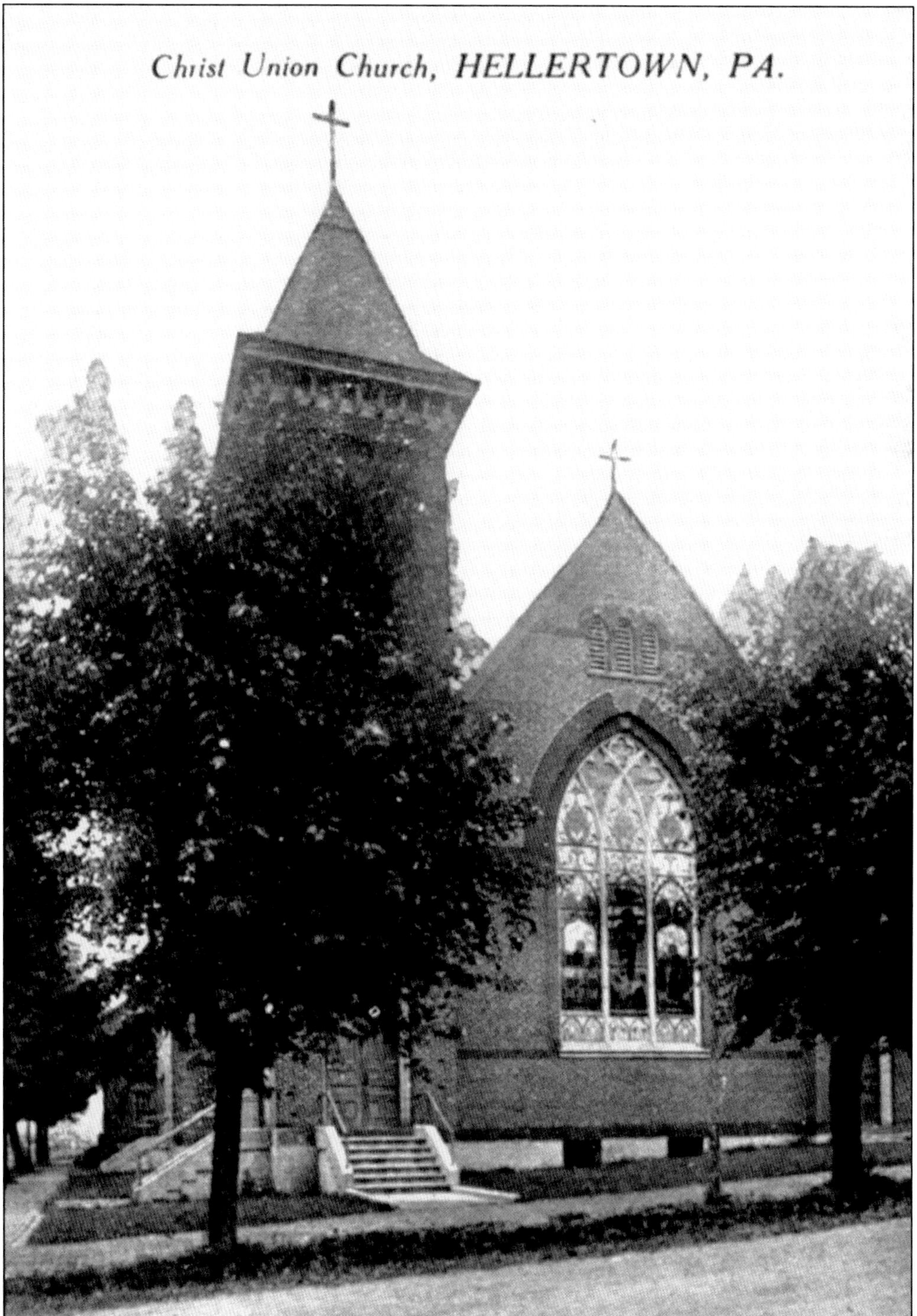

As a note on this image says, Christ Union burned after being struck by lightning. It was rebuilt in the same place, and the original stained-glass windows were recently sold at auction. After the fire, firefighters joined to design new firefighting strategies.

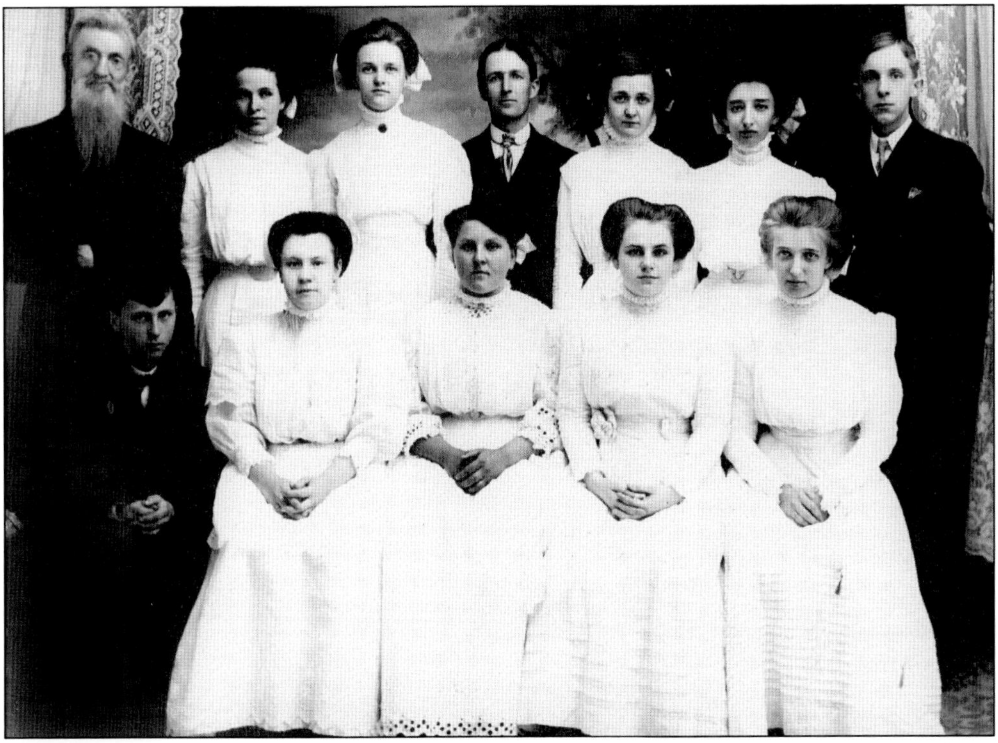

This group is one of A.B. Koplin's confirmation classes at Christ Union Church early in the 20th century.

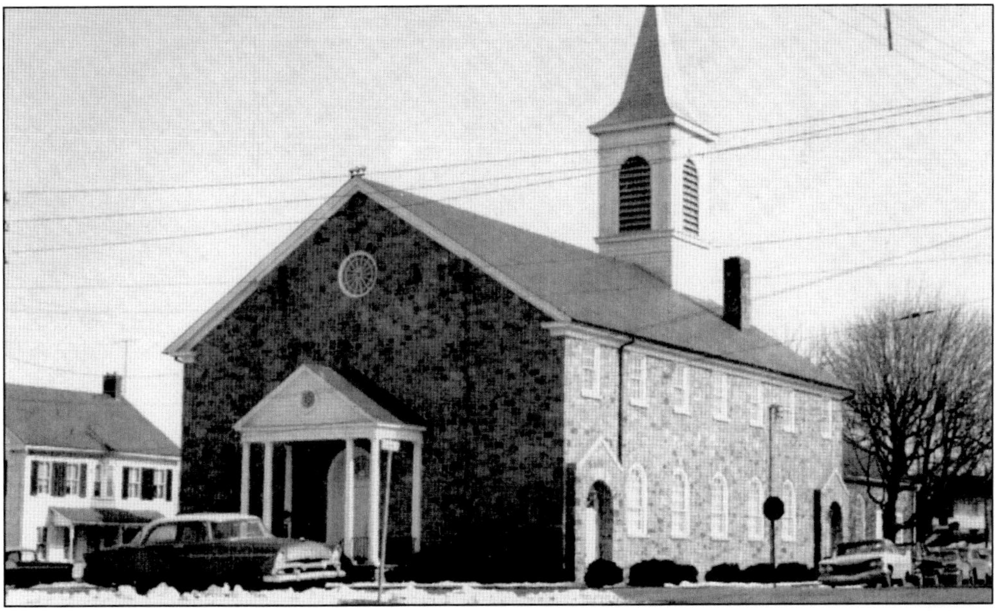

In the 1950s, First United Church of Christ experienced major population growth, as did the borough. This called for renovations to accommodate Sunday school classes. Rev. Theodore Haas and his wife, Norine (Hinckley) Haas, were spiritual leaders at the time.

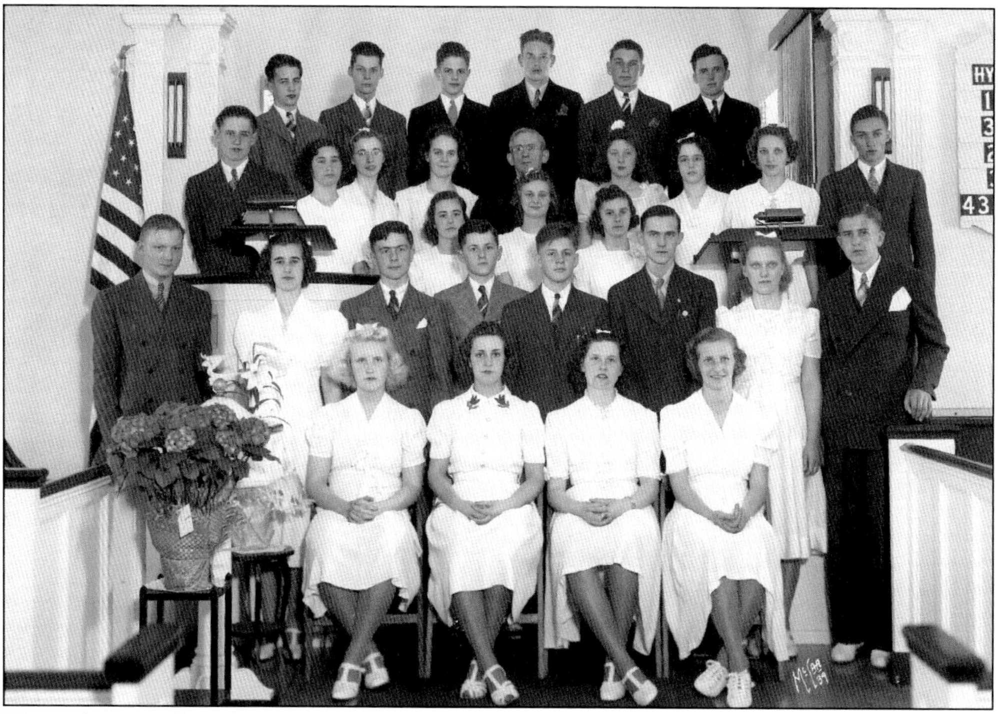

This is the typical confirmation class among Protestant churches in Hellertown. The Evangelical and Reformed Church on Northampton Street held this service here in 1939.

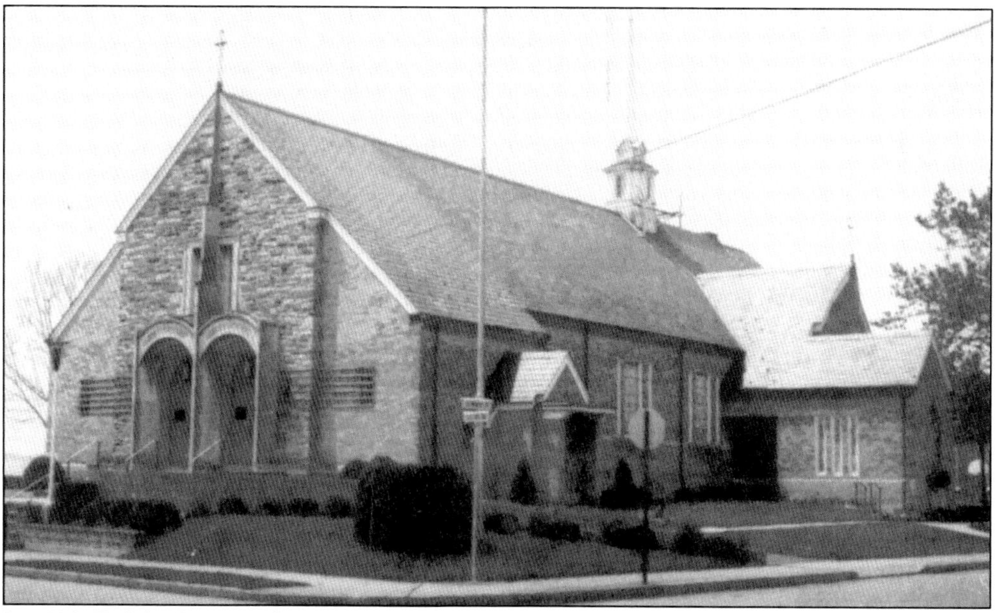

In 1923, Fr. John H. Trescak was assigned to lead a mission parish of the Roman Catholic Church to Hellertown. That year, Fr. George Check, a newly ordained priest, became administrator of the Hellertown mission. The property from Leonard Street to Easton Road was purchased for a permanent home of believers, known as St. Theresa of the Child Jesus.

First housing St. Paul's Evangelical Church and later the Methodist church, this is the site of the first school in Hellertown. Originally, some classes were held in this building and next door under the carriage shop. The Silver Creek ran beneath this building, and the pupils often had cold feet during those long winters. Before St. Paul's was built, the first school had been torn down.

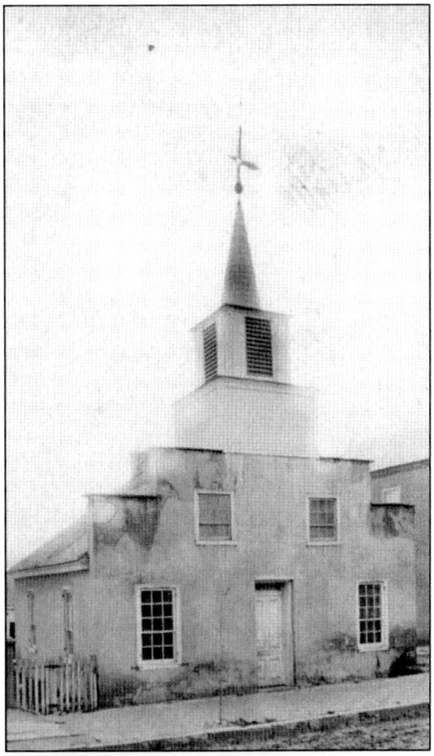

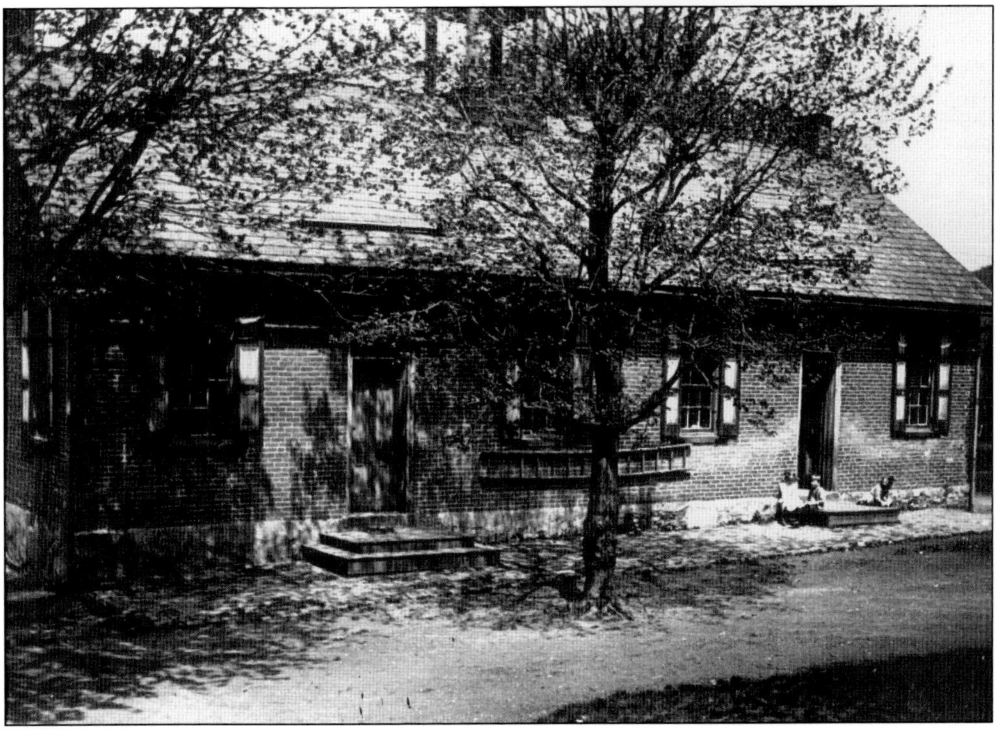

Built c. 1870, this was the first Reinhard School on Northampton Street. It was replaced c. 1910 by an eight-room structure.

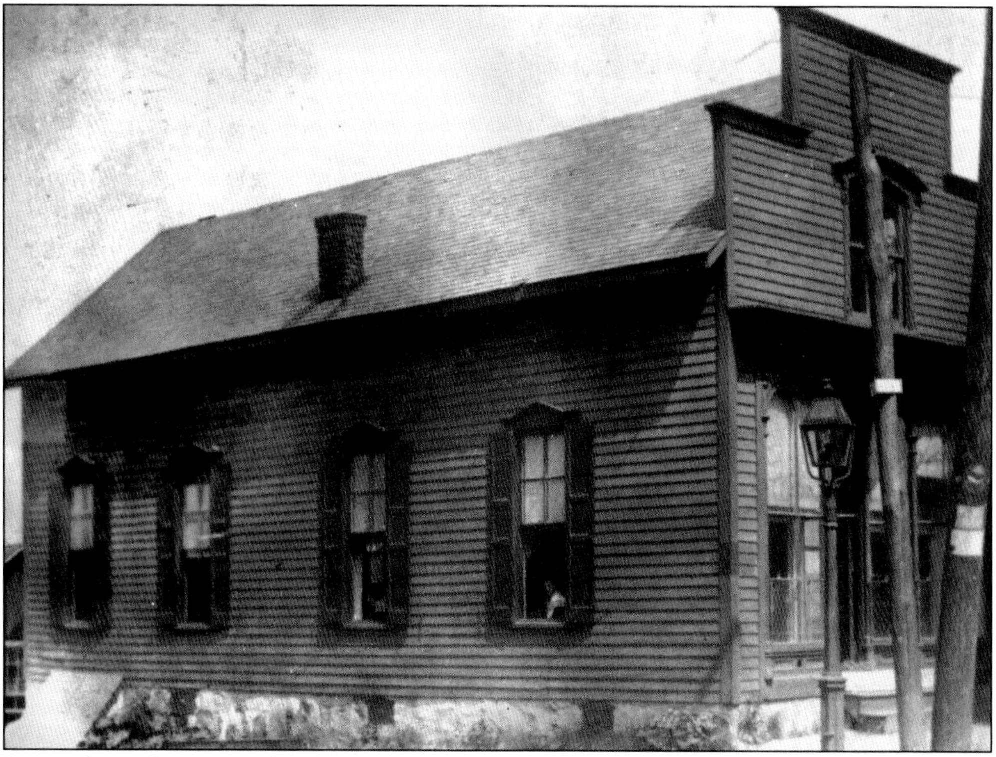

Situated on the west side of Main Street, the first Hellertown High School was in use between 1896 and 1910. The building served also as the office of Hess Lumber and later Brown and Borhek.

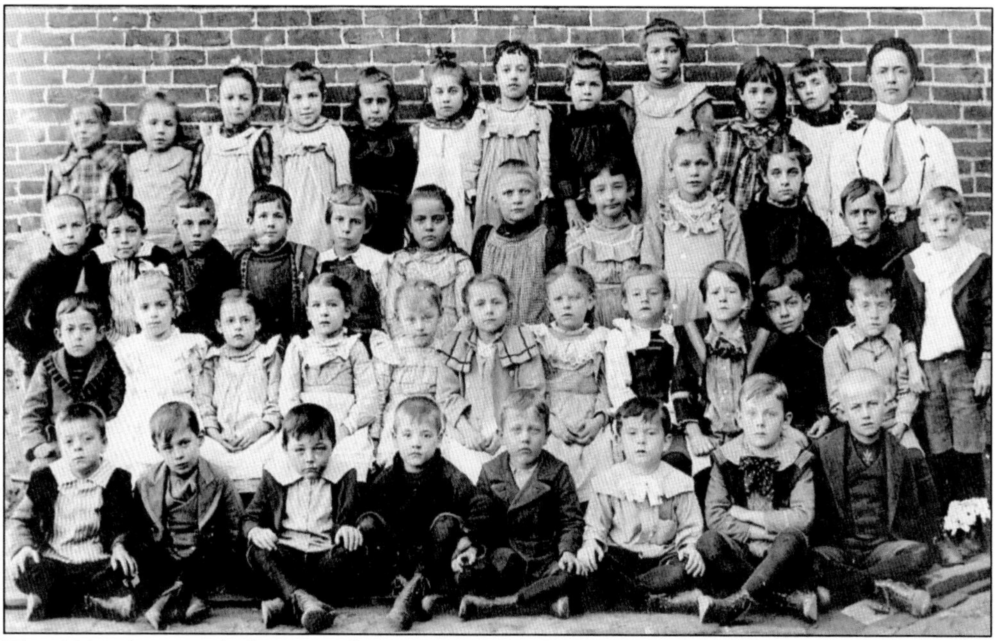

This 1901 photograph shows teacher Mary Hess and a primary class. Notice the teacher's stern expression. She probably had good discipline.

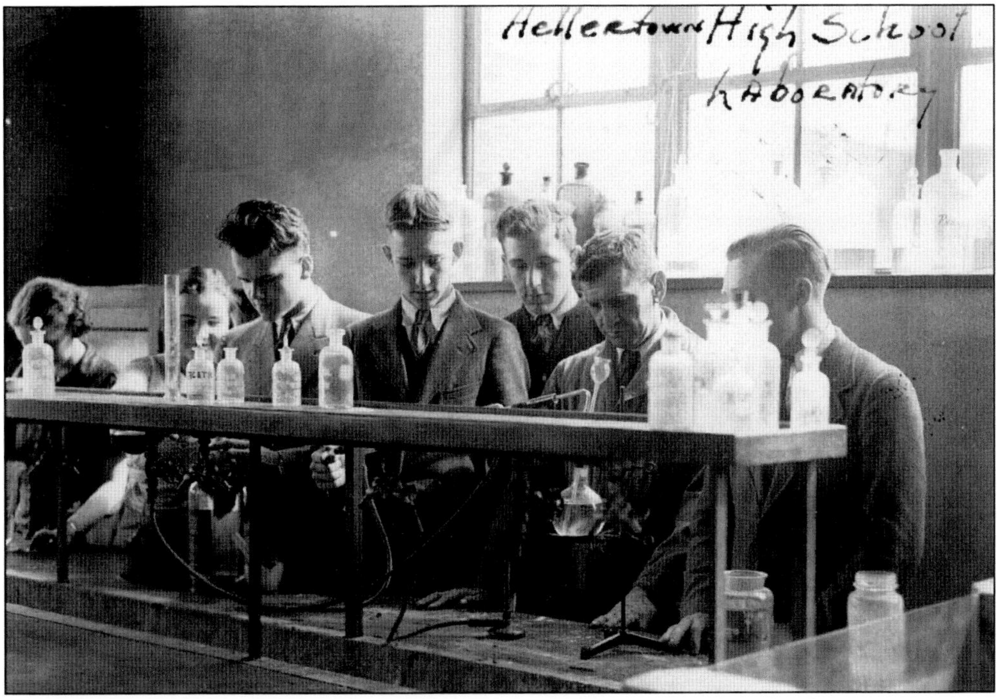

Pictured here is the original science laboratory in Hellertown High School on Main Street. From left to right are two unidentified students, Warren Achey, Charles Fluck, Edward Hess, Robert Hoppes (teacher), and an unidentified student.

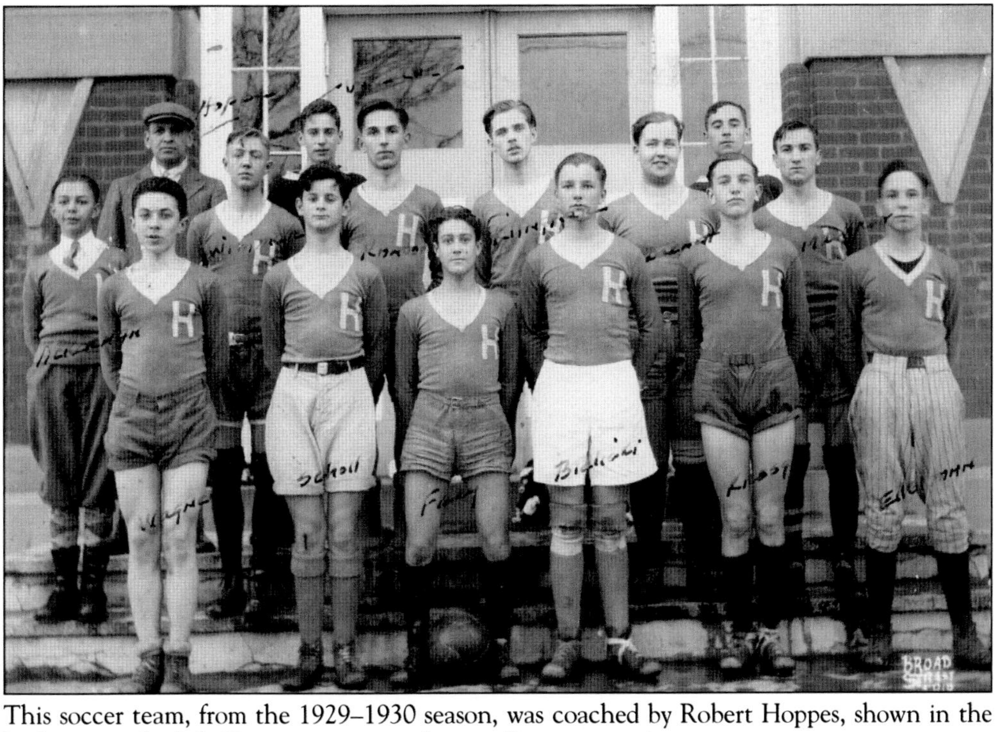

This soccer team, from the 1929–1930 season, was coached by Robert Hoppes, shown in the back row to the left. Everyone seems to be standing at attention.

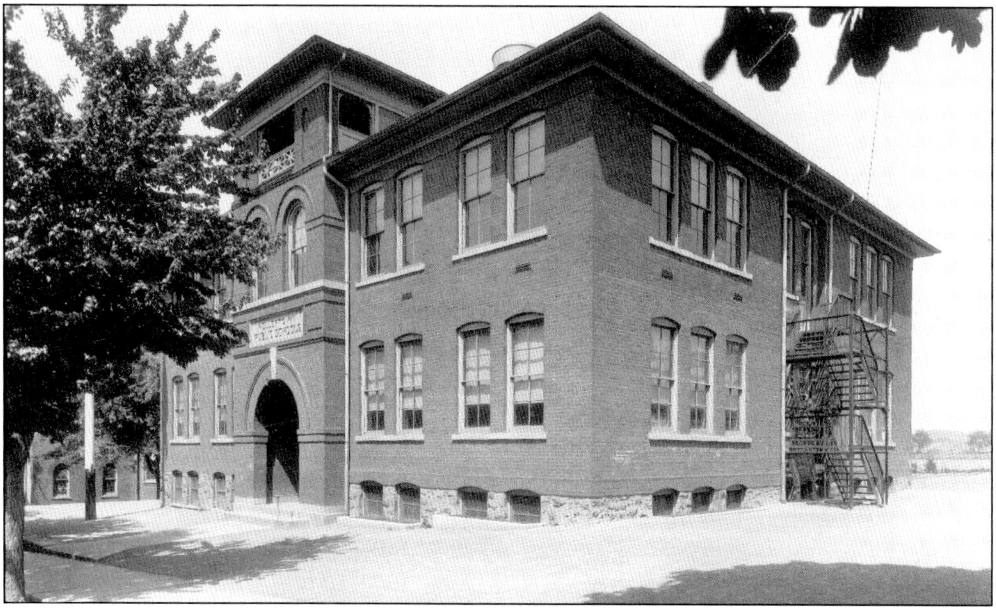

From 1910 to 1920, this school (in the Reinhard Building, on Northampton Street) served grades 1 to 11. Starting in 1920, it housed grades 1 to 8.

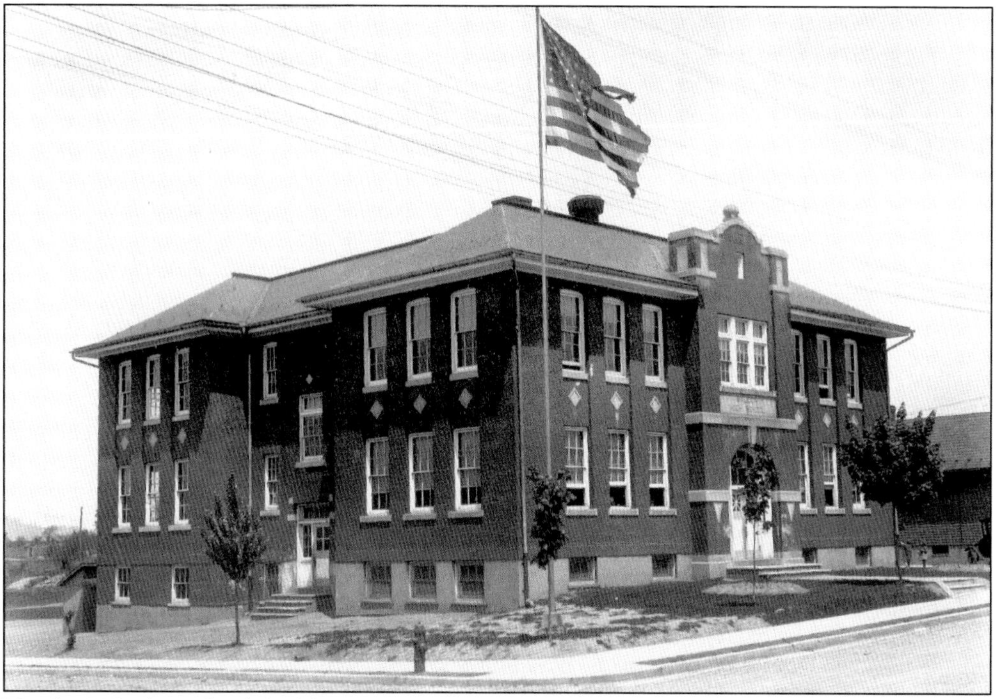

Until 1920, the school building on High Street was named Saucon High School. During the 20th century, the high school occupied various locations in town, the very first being at the south end of town on Main Street adjacent to the Hess family homestead. Mary Hess was one of the early high school teachers and later taught in Bethlehem. The Saucon High School pictured here later became the Wolf Elementary School, which housed students from kindergarten through sixth grade at the north end of the borough.

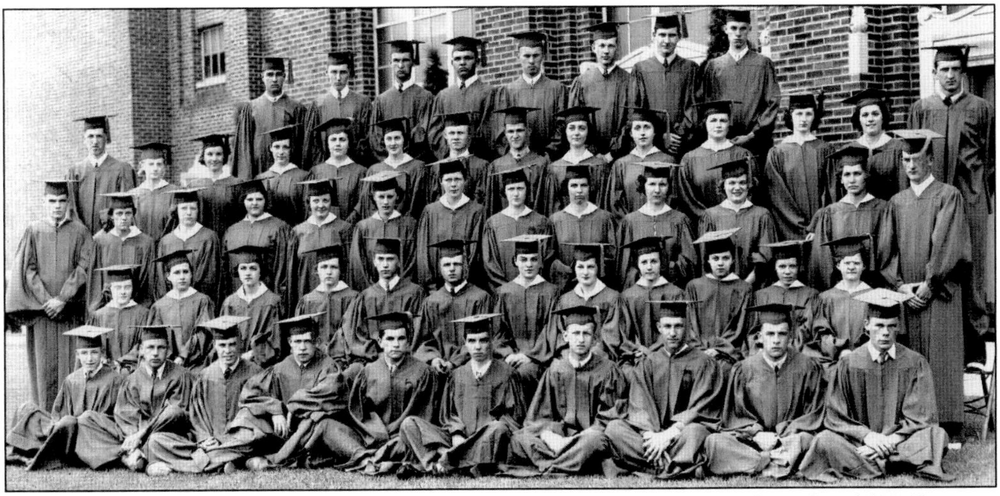

As representative of the many graduating classes, this is the Class of 1937 from the old Hellertown High School. From left to right are the following: (first row) Ernest Muschlitz, Edward Ruch, Charles Pastir, Frederick Angstadt, Earl Nicholas, Ralph Ganssle, Joseph Makoski, Charles Fluck, Zolton Szabo, and George Kish; (second row) Margaret Kemmerer, Norma Fetzer, Doris Stoneback, Althea Gorski, Paul Koplin, William Shimer, Beatrice Weisel, Sylva Barnett, Eva Hulak, Ruth Nixon, Margaret Franko, and Pauline Frankenfield; (third row) LeRoy Johnson, Caroline Fulmer, Leone Weidner, Lorraine Peters, Roberta Weidner, Lucy Pfeiffer, Margaret Heckert, Lucy Baker, Mary Munson, Alice Hagel, Verna Solomon, Mary Horwath, and Edward Kugler; (fourth row) John Specialny, Ruby Rogers, Olga Machkow, Vernetta Dimmick, Mildred Hoppes, Earl Mohn, David Weidner, James Rosenberger, Bernetta Fritchman, Pauline Ruch, Florence Gilman, Jean Schrantz, June Weaver, and John Kajmo; (fifth row) Chester Kubik, Maynard Fritchman, Michael Yamnicky, Walter Kresge, Joseph Pusch, Edward Judd, Albert Schuster, and Wilmer Huhn.

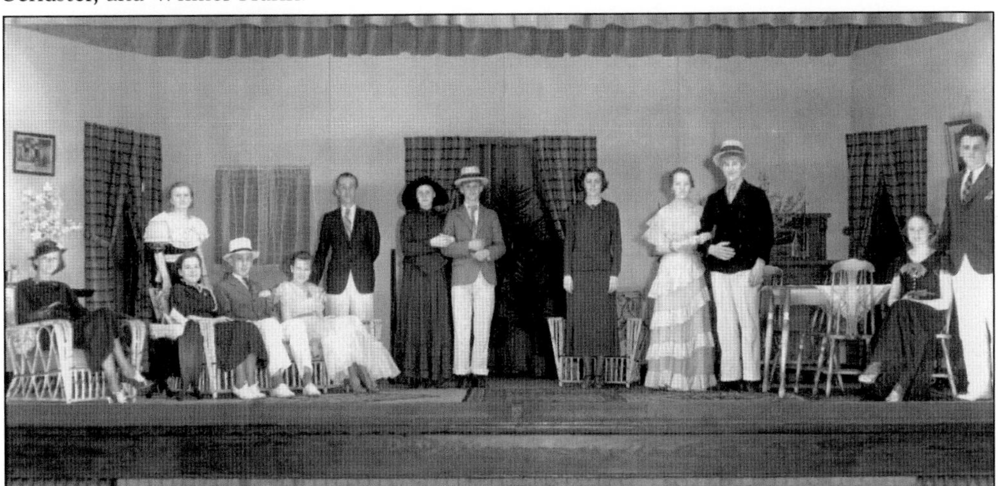

Apple Blossom Time, a play by Eugene Hafer, featured the junior class in 1935. The cast included, from left to right, Verna Weber as Mrs. Forrest, Margaret Martin as Loretta Harris, Ruth Thomas as Polly Biddle, Edward Hess as Cal Pickens, Virginia Henderson as Nancy Prescott, Charles Brown as Charlie Lawrence, Nancy Baker as Annabel Spriggins, John Scholl as Mickey McGuire, Marian Fritch as Coach, Pauline Skibo as Malvina Kurtz, Steve Macey as Spud McClosky, Frances Jacobs as Betty Ann Stewart, and Warren Ache as Bat Matthews.

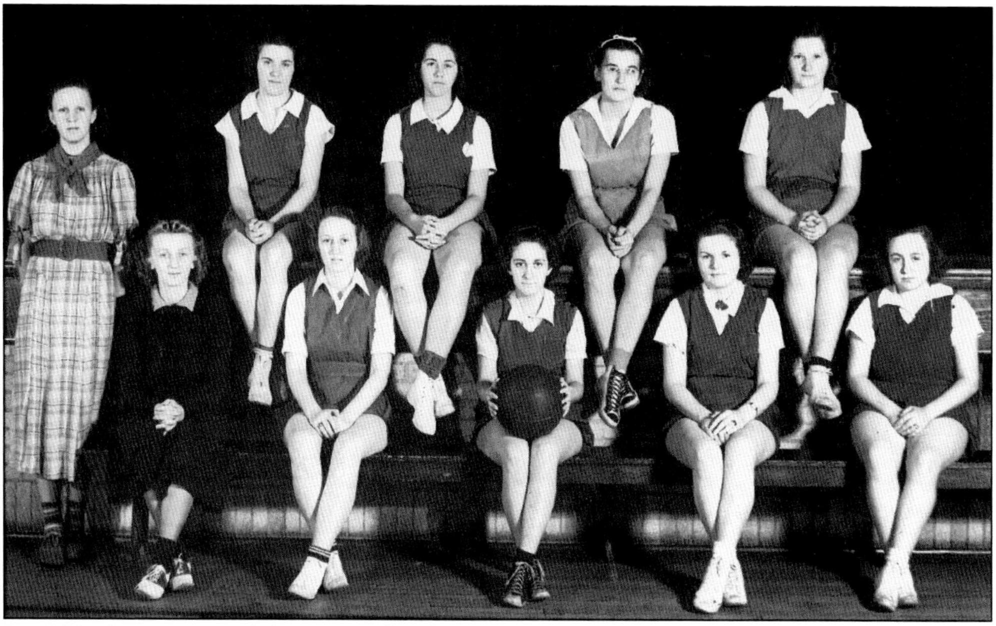

In 1938, this was one of the senior class basketball teams. From left to right are the following: (front row) Helen Bednar, Betty Fritchman, Isabel Boehm, Irene Horvath, and Dorothy Snyder; (back row) coach Dorothy Reiss, Velma Doncecz, Louisa Seifert, Jane Diehl, and Beatrice Bernhart.

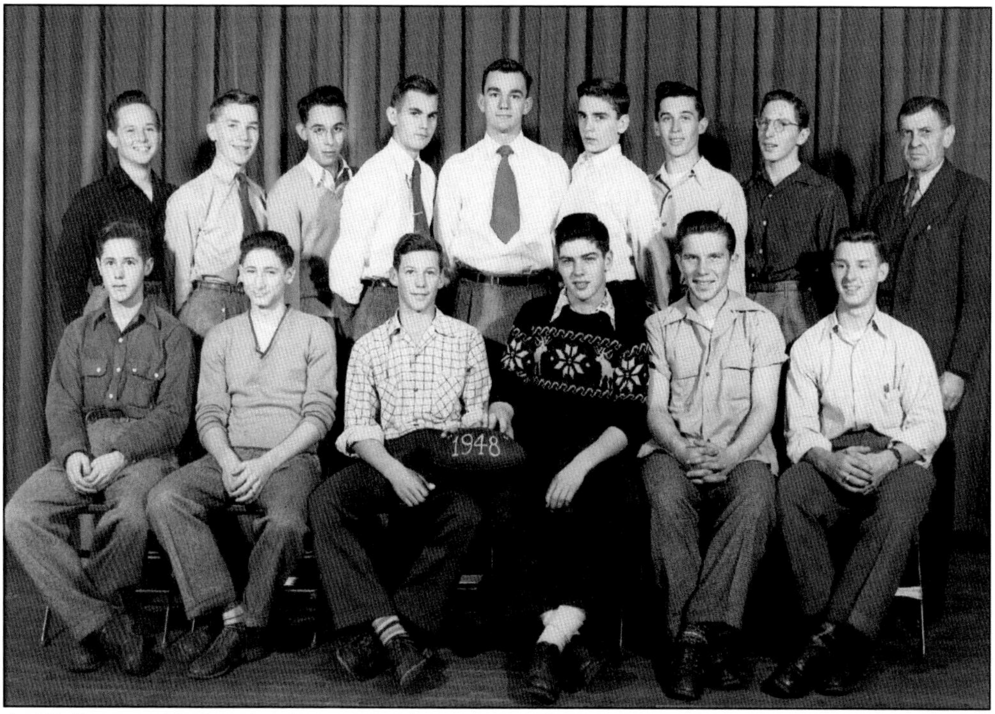

At Hellertown High School in 1948, there was no league for football. Pictured here is one of several in-house, intramural football teams. Pictured to the right is science teacher and team sponsor Robert Hoppes.

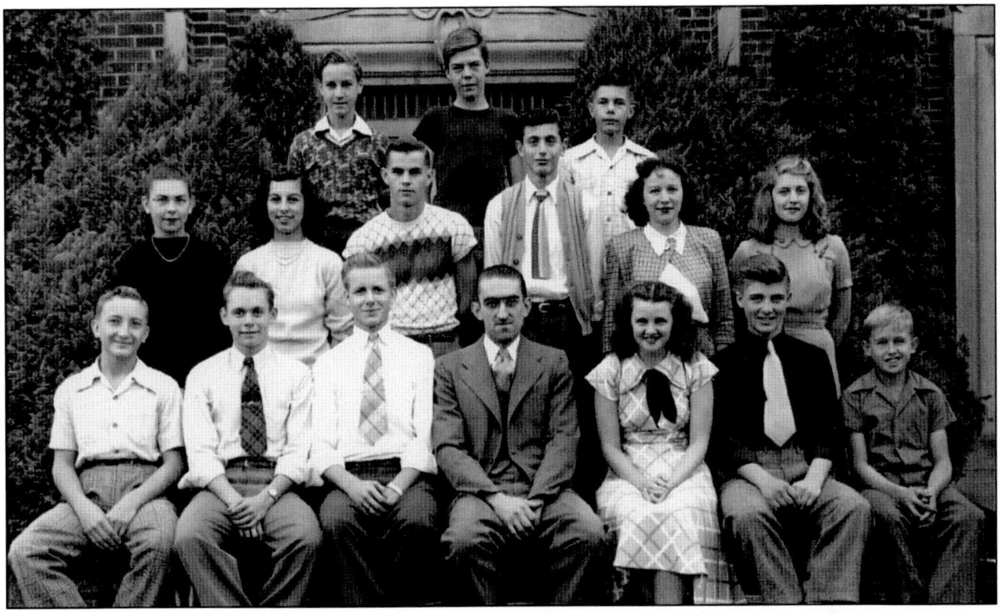

In 1949, the high school athletic council consisted of these students. From left to right are the following: (front row) Frederick Eckert, Paul Hoffner, Howard Gibson, Frank Meyers (the advisor), Lorraine Mindler, Brent Finken, and Robert Bauder; (middle row) Lucille Boehm, Mary Julio, David Barton, Karl Bauder, Janet Ward, and Shirley Beil; (back row) Monroe Fabian, Julius Aszli, and Carl Laub.

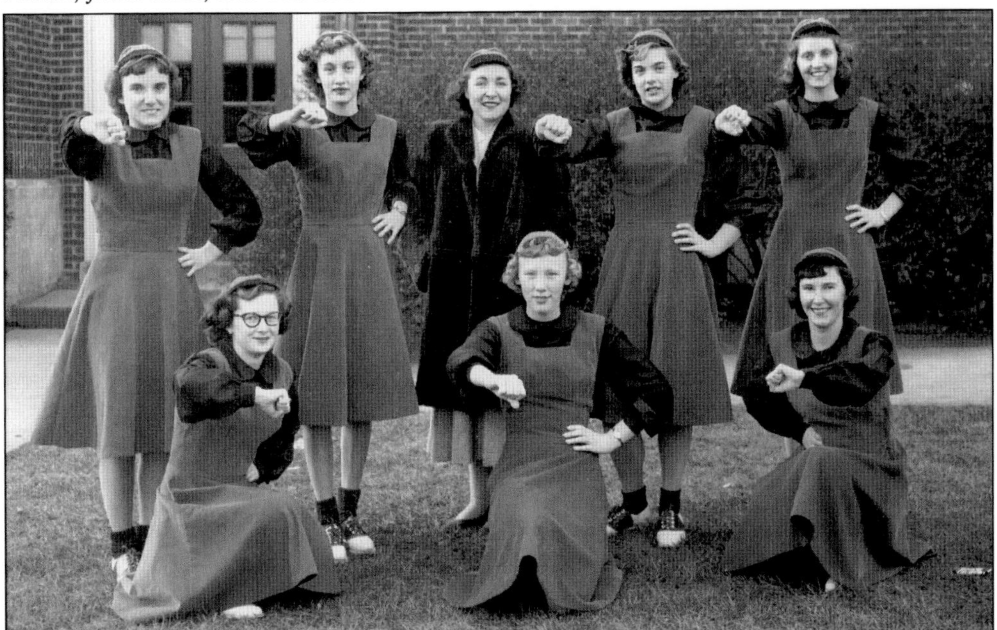

Hellertown High School cheerleaders pose in 1950. From left to right are the following: (front row) Marilyn Reichard, Geraldine Toggert, and Jeanette Frey (captain); (back row) Martha Tapajcik, Olga Grozdanoff, Helyn Farrell (advisor), Barbara Findon, and Peggy Gozzard. Cheerleaders at that time wore red corduroy jumpers, black blouses, saddle shoes, and red caps with black visors.

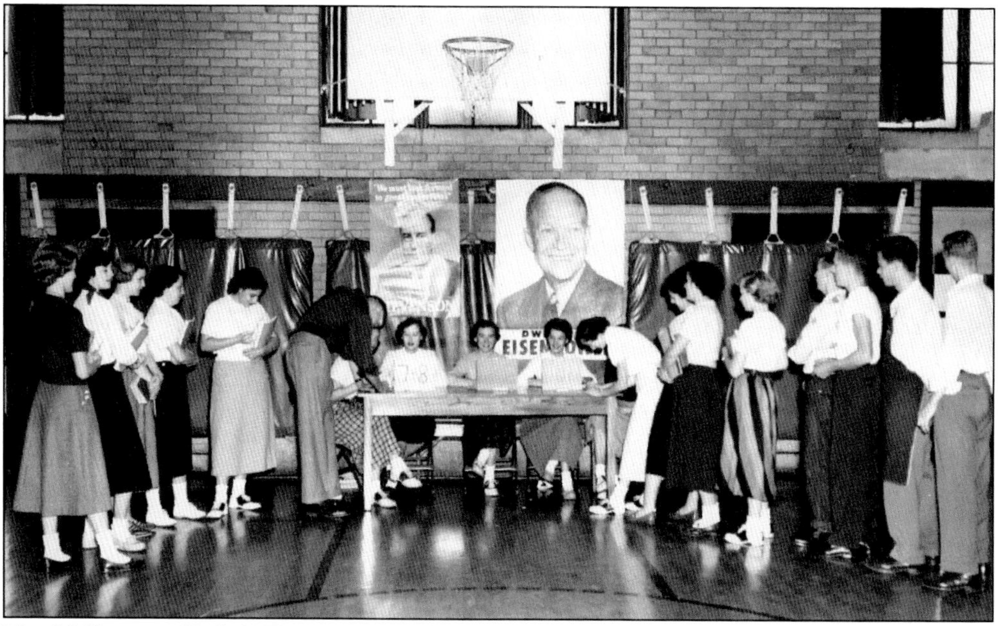

The Hellertown High Y-Teens sponsored a mock election in November 1952. Many students wore campaign pins reading, "I Like Ike."

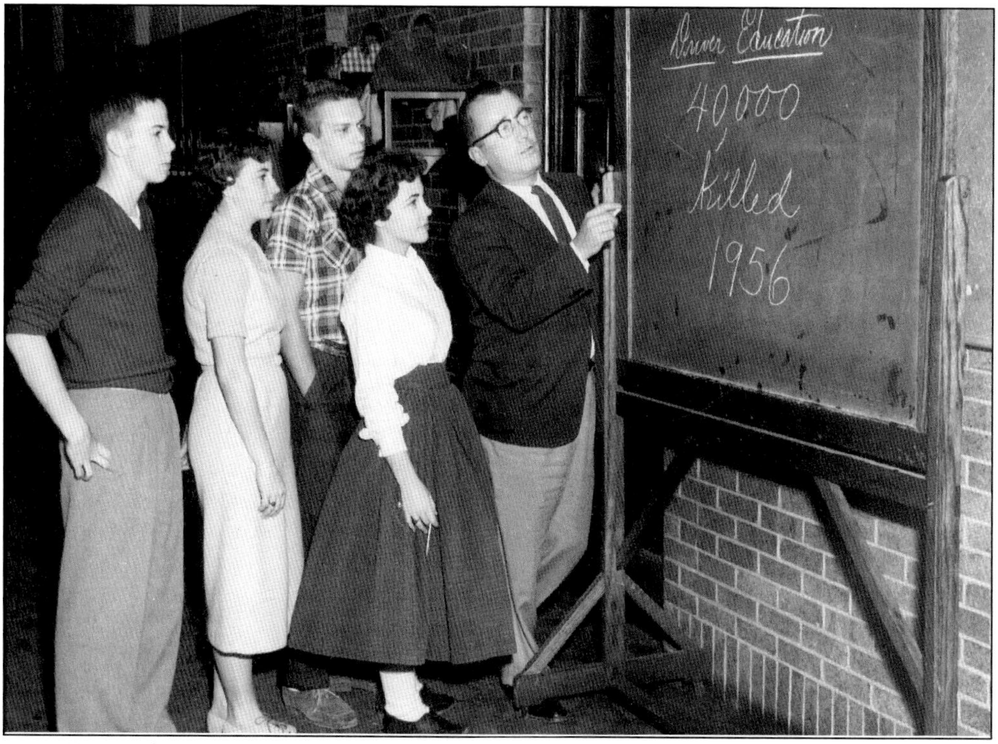

Leon Brown, longtime math teacher and, later, a driver education instructor, is shown here with students. Notice that the hallway is being used for discussion. Soon after this photograph was taken, renovations took place and the old Hellertown High School became the new Hellertown-Lower Saucon High School.

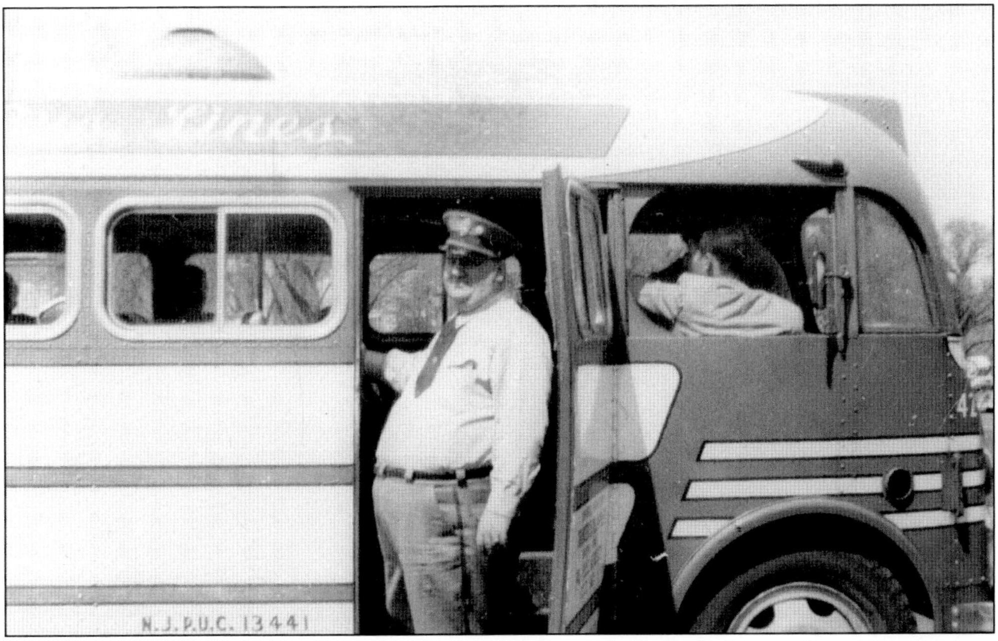

During the late 1930s and early 1940s, Klipple Bus Lines from Bath was used to carry all teams to away games. At that time, Hellertown Borough had given exclusive rights to and from Hellertown to Lehigh Valley Transit, so teams using a Klipple bus had to walk across Water Street into Lower Saucon Township.

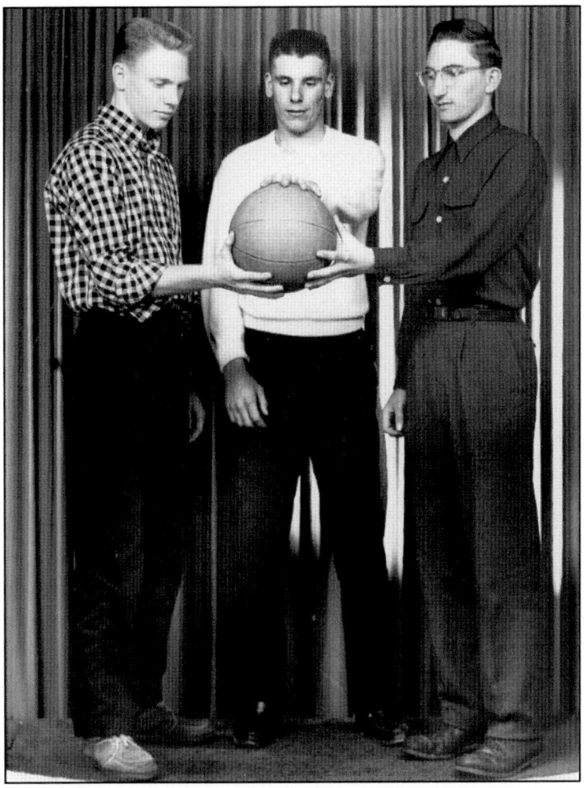

These basketball players on stage are wearing the boys' fashions of the 1950s. The two on the left have a haircut then known as the "wiffle." Perhaps that is where the inventor of the Wiffle Ball got the name. The boys are not wearing jeans or athletic shoes, which would have been against the dress code. They are, from left to right, Ricky Wartman, Doc Fenstermacher, and Jeff Lightner.

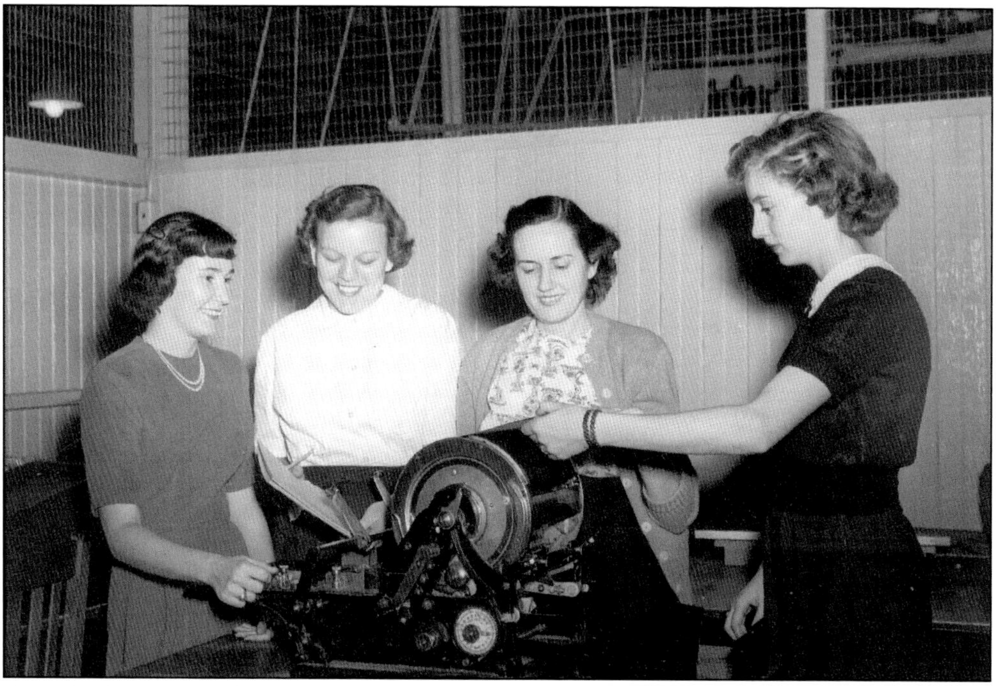

These high school workers are preparing the *Hive*, the school's literary periodical. From left to right are Jeanette Frey, Eleanor Gori, Irene Towey, and Olga Grozdanoff.

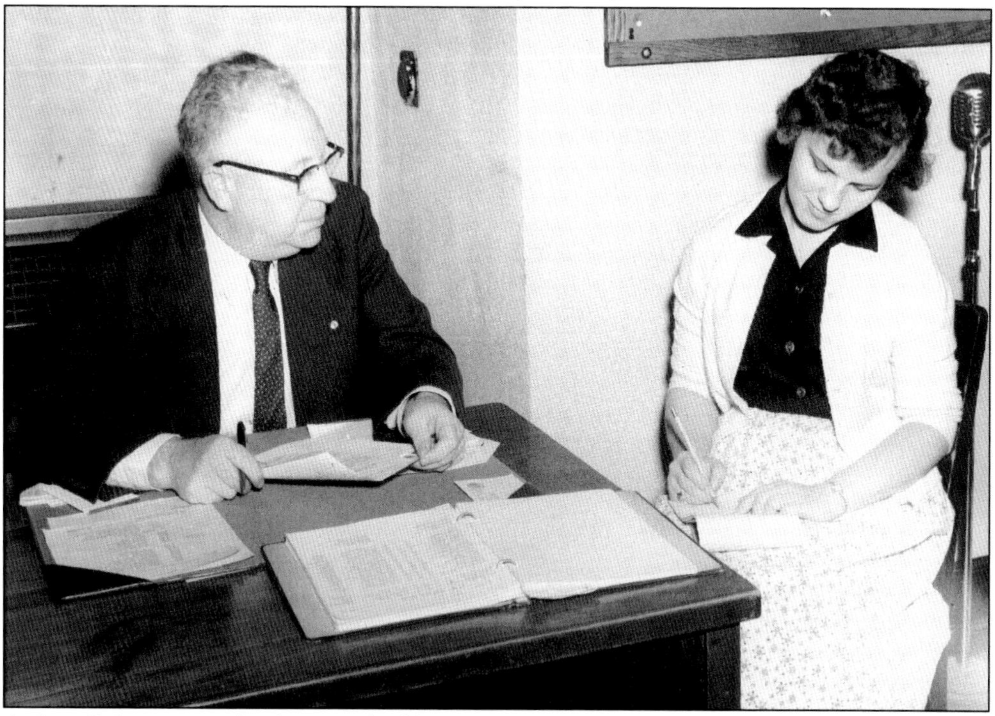

Arthur Oplinger was the distinguished longtime principal at Hellertown High School. When the school was transformed through renovations in 1958, half-day sessions were held. Here, he confers with Barbara Frey.

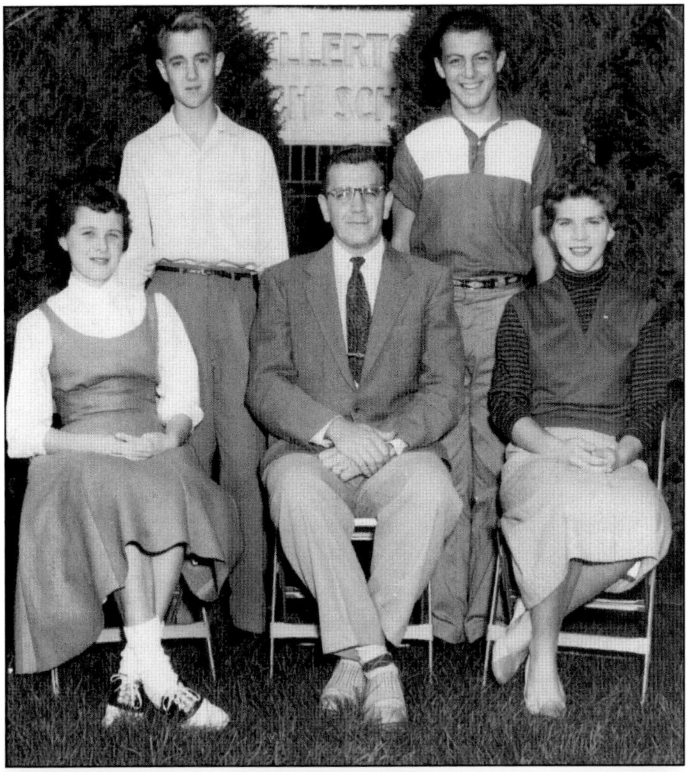

Albert Hoppes taught science and was class advisor at the high school. He is surrounded by Karen Reichard (seated, left), Nancy Marish, John Chegwidden (standing, left), and Edward Stauffer. Hoppes also was active in sponsoring various activities, such as the Science Club and Hi-Y, as well as coaching.

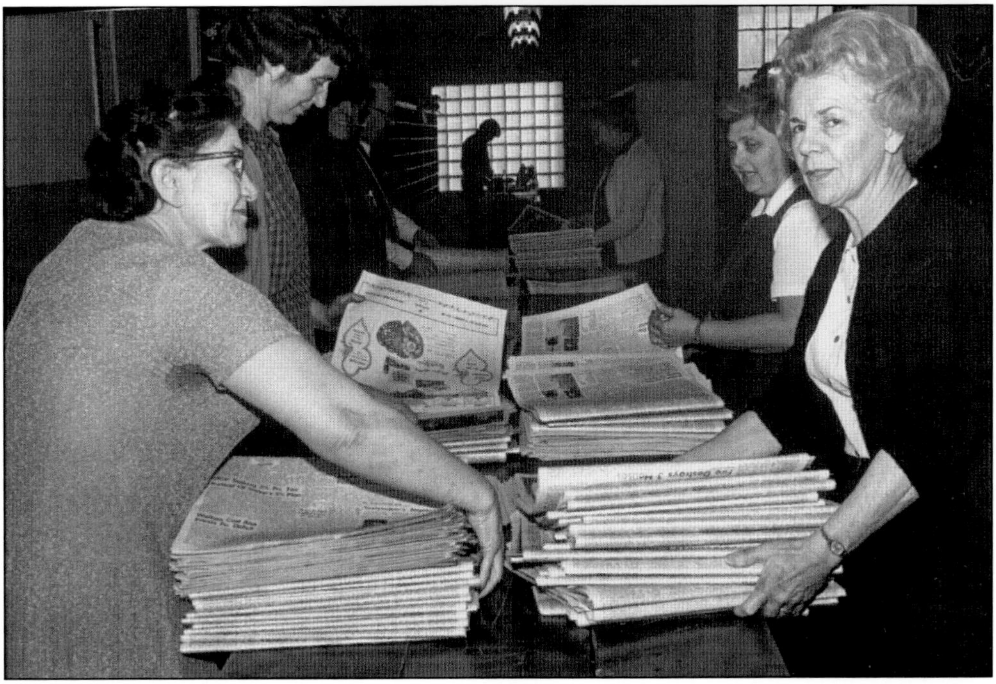

Placing inserts into the Sunday edition of the *Bethlehem Globe Times* yielded proceeds that went into the band uniform fund. Shown sorting papers are, from left to right, band parents Mrs. Harry Green, Mrs. Louis Pagats, and Mrs. Ray Dimmick with teacher Edith Kantor.

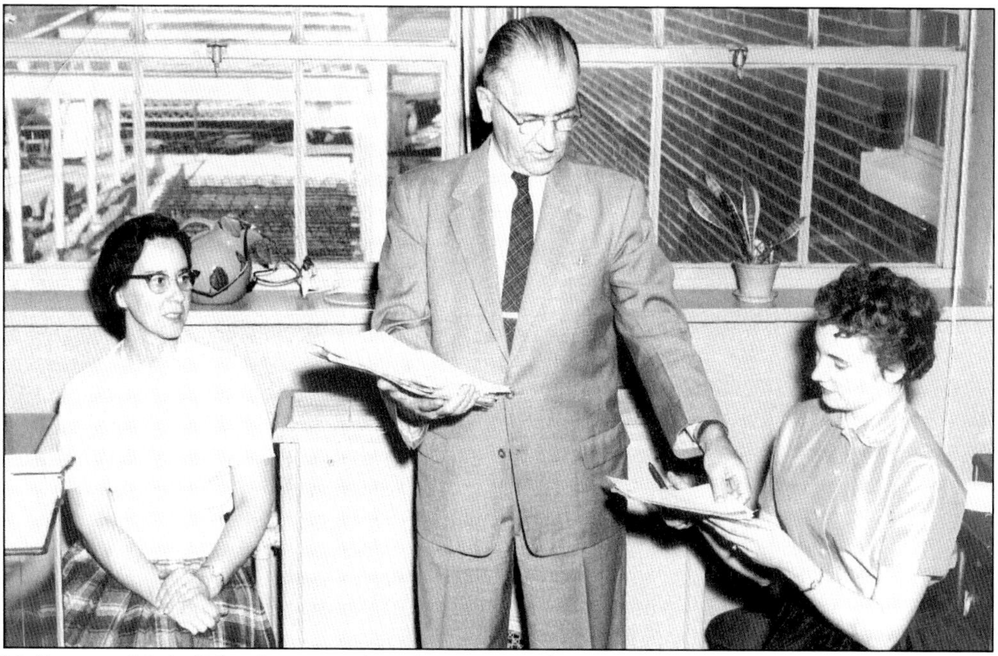

Hellertown High School principal and superintendent Montford Illick was a well-respected administrator for many years. Illick also took an active part in the community. He served a term on the town council and was a gentleman in the truest sense of the word.

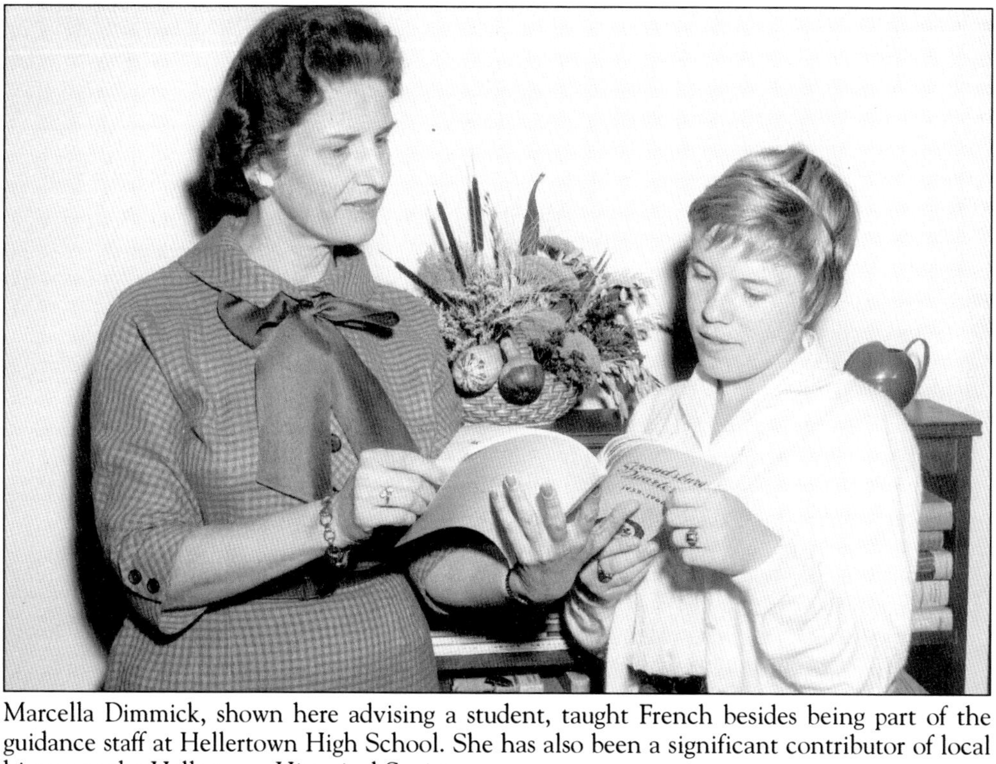

Marcella Dimmick, shown here advising a student, taught French besides being part of the guidance staff at Hellertown High School. She has also been a significant contributor of local history to the Hellertown Historical Society.

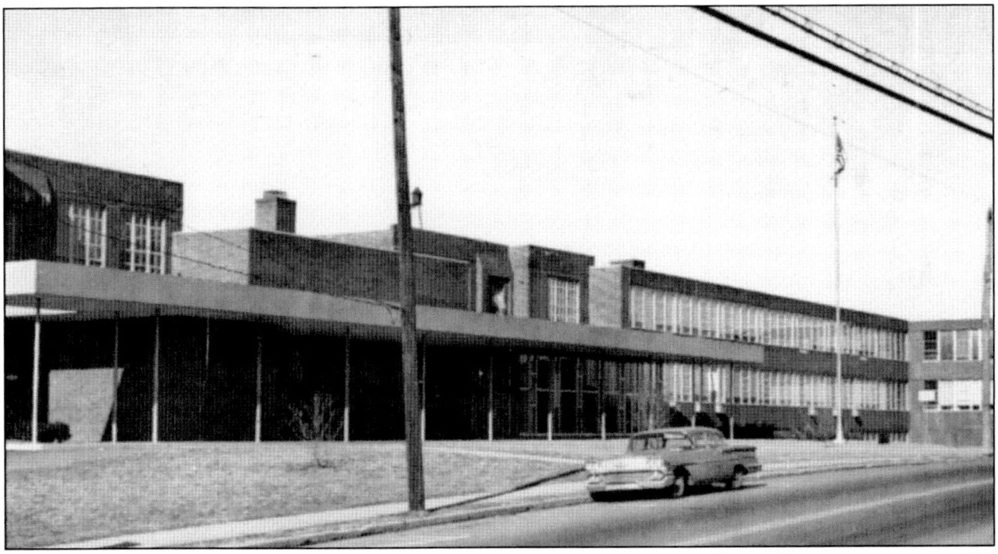

The newly completed high school and junior high housed grades 7 through 12 starting in 1958 after major renovations had been completed. At this time, the term Hellertown High had slipped into the past. Later, this building was changed to the Saucon Valley Middle School.

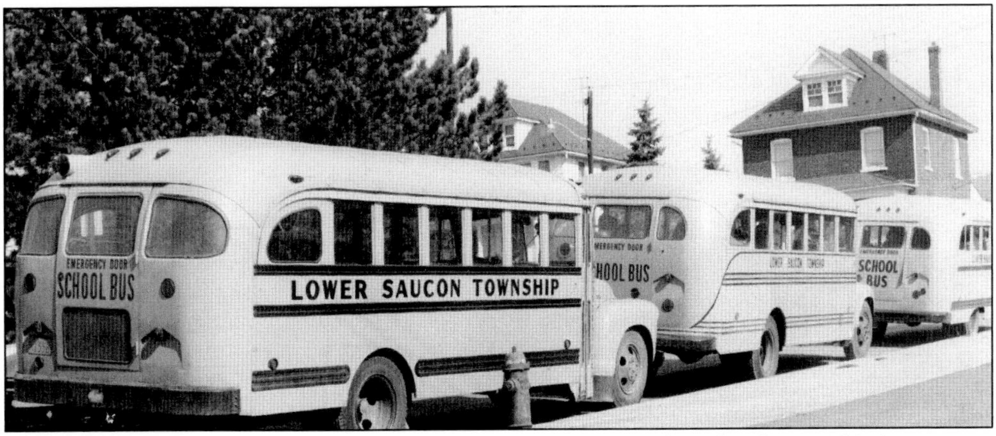

With the advent of the new Hellertown-Lower Saucon High School in 1958, buses were provided for Lower Saucon students' transportation.

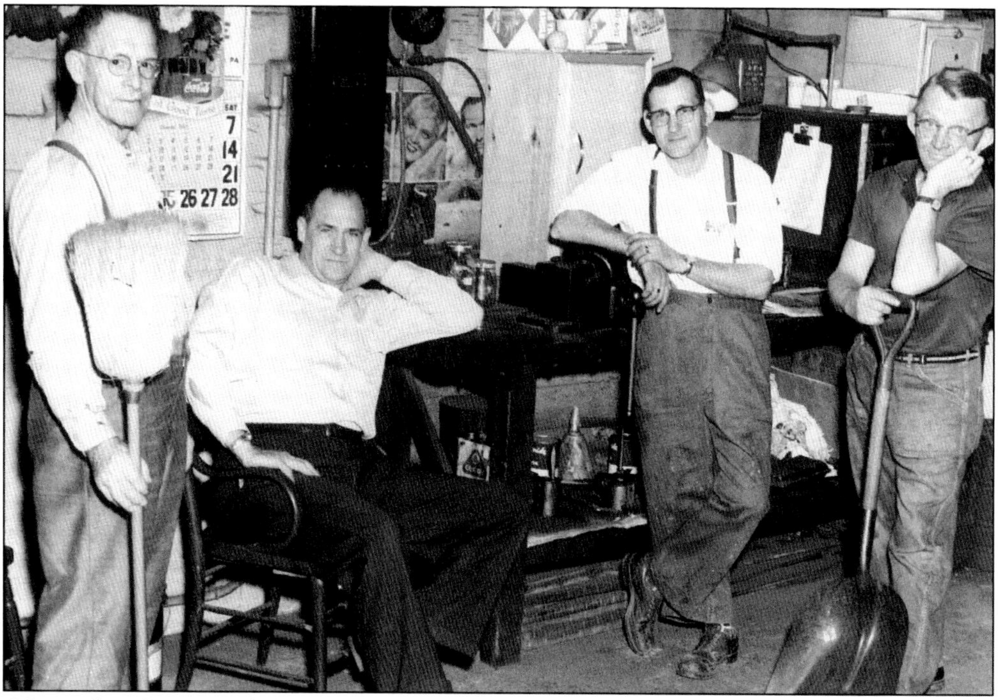
Often taken for granted, these Hellertown High School custodians are pictured in their shop area. They are, from left to right, John Long, Earl Seifert, Preston Sloyer, and George Riegel.

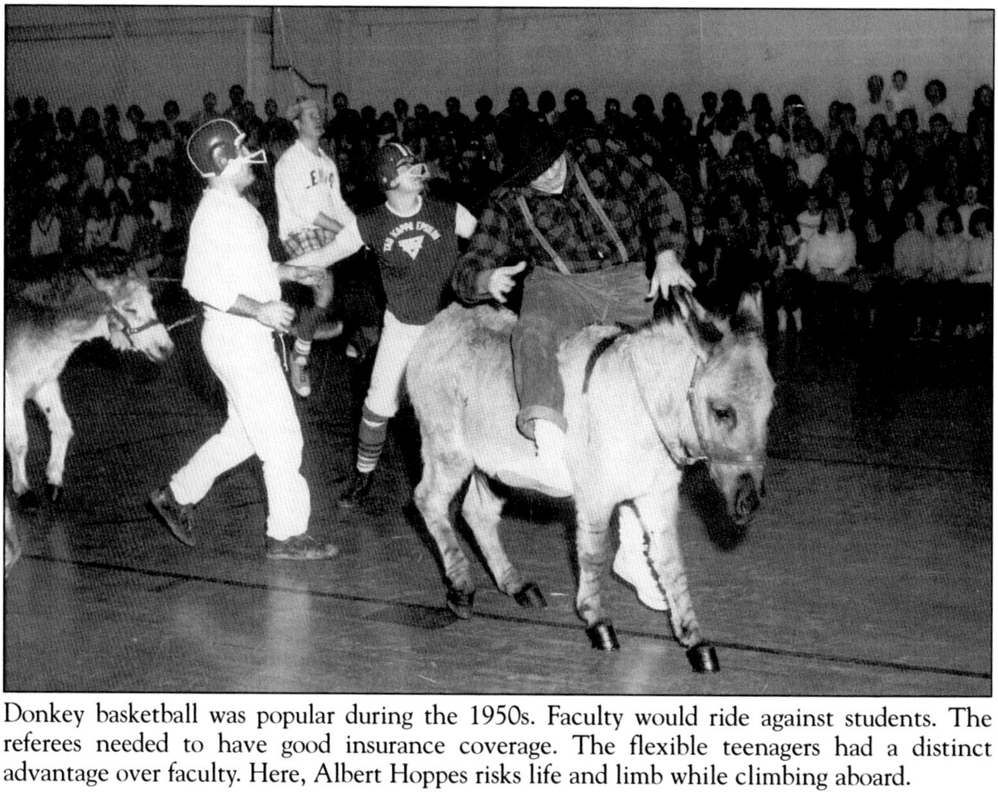
Donkey basketball was popular during the 1950s. Faculty would ride against students. The referees needed to have good insurance coverage. The flexible teenagers had a distinct advantage over faculty. Here, Albert Hoppes risks life and limb while climbing aboard.

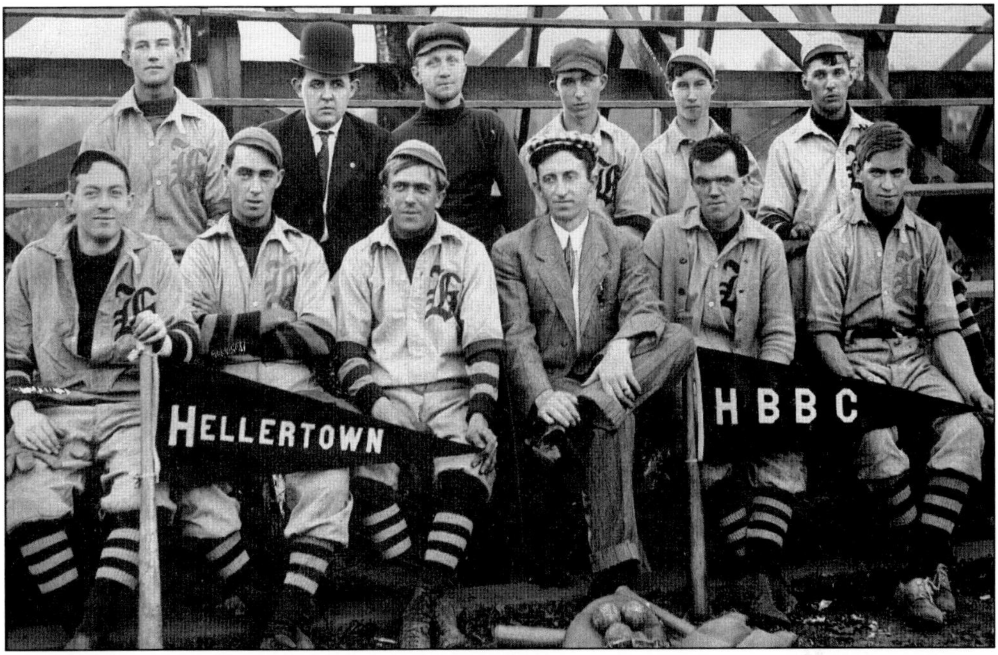

Pictured here are the team members of the 1910 Hellertown baseball team. From left to right are the following: (front row) Kenny Fritchman, unidentified, Bill Snyder, "Doc" Eckert, Bill Diehl, and unidentified; (back row) Ted Hagey, "Sheriff" Heft, Herb Hoffert, and three unidentified.

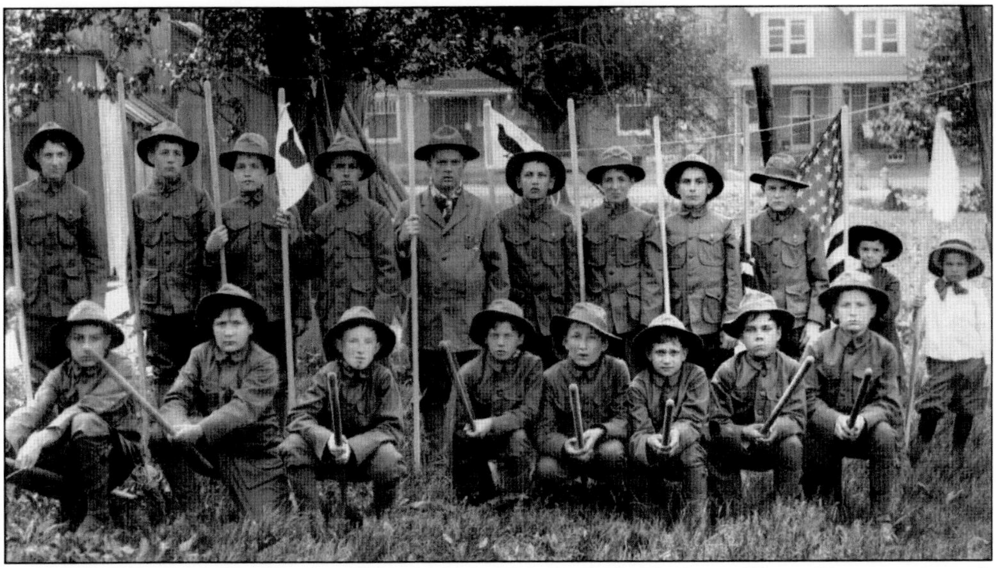

In April 1914, through efforts of Christ Union Sunday School, Scout Troop 13 was organized. Jeremiah Hess and Titus Ruch were of particular help. Harry Ache became the first scoutmaster, to be followed by Robert Hoppes and Charles Wasser. Pictured, from left to right, are the following: (front row) Elroy Harwi, Norman Diehl, Ralph Rothrock, Austin Guth, Warren Ziegenfuss, Titus Bergstresser, Warren Zimpher, and Russell Frey; (back row) Elton Eisenhart, Clifford Frey, Herbert Potter, Norman Boehm, Harry Achey, Robert Diehl, Horace Diehl, Wilbur Harwi, and Clifford Koch. Joseph Ruch's and Harry Achey's sons (back row, 10th and 11th from left, respectively) were mascots.

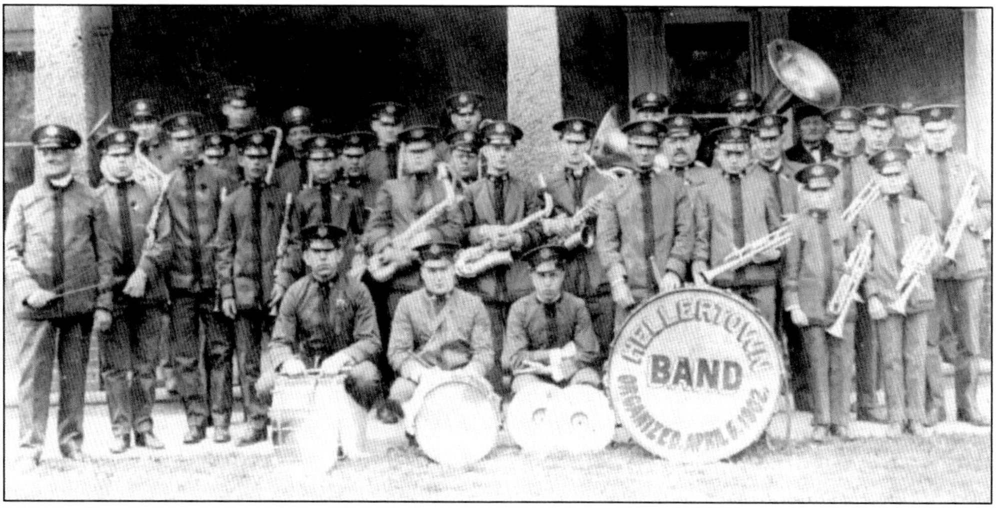

The Hellertown Municipal Band was organized on April 6, 1902, with Milton Warmkessel as director. From left to right are the following: (front row, kneeling) Jay Arnold, Ed Fritchman, and Philip Fritchman; (middle row) Milton Warmkessel, Ralph Warnke, Frank and Albert Stern, Benett Arnold, Herb Seifert, Al Knauss, Harold Gross, and the rest unidentified; (back row) Charles Fritchman, John Rice, and ? Stackhouse, and the rest unidentified.

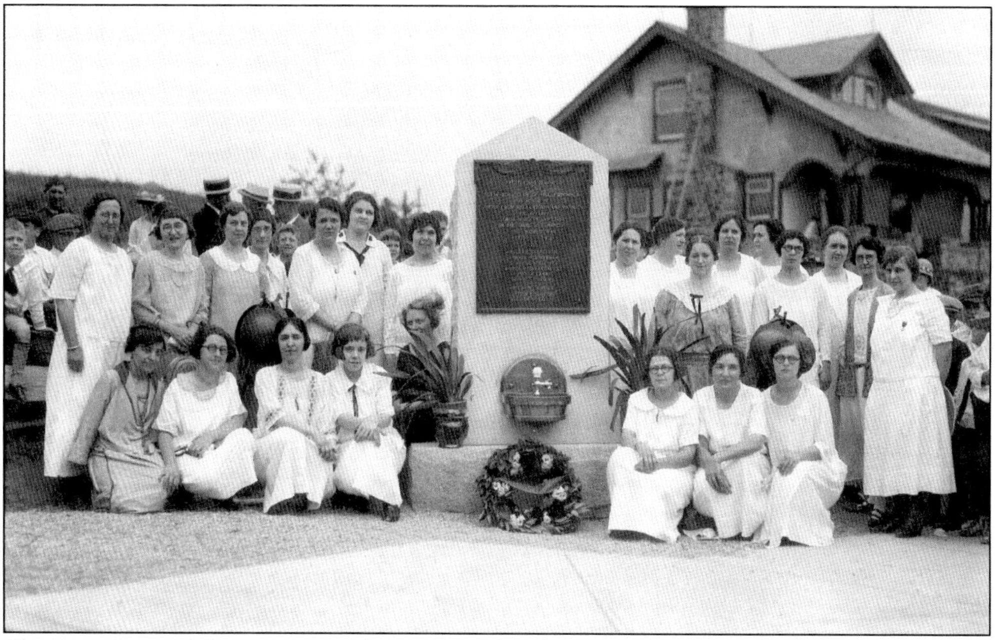

The Betsy Ross Club was organized in 1917 to be of assistance to American soldiers in Europe during World War I. Clara Hess led the club in activities such as knitting socks, making bandages, and sending shipments of candy and other items. After the war, the club donated the memorial fountain to the local American Legion post. The Hellertonians who died during wartime included Edward H. Ackerman, Henry H. Schaeffer, Austin W. Frankenfield, John W. Leary, Howard L. Strohl, Titus E. Sloyer, and William M. Balliet. The dedication occurred on June 21, 1924.

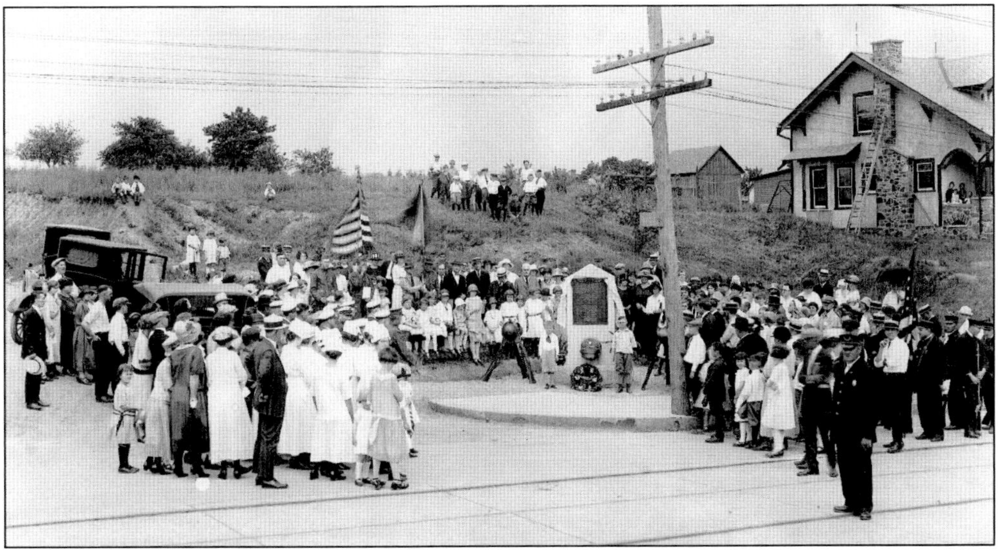

The plaque dedication was in memory of Howard Strohl and Russell Ackerman, who had lost their lives during World War I. Notice the young boys, Howard R. Strohl and Russ Ackerman (right). They were sons of the lost soldiers.

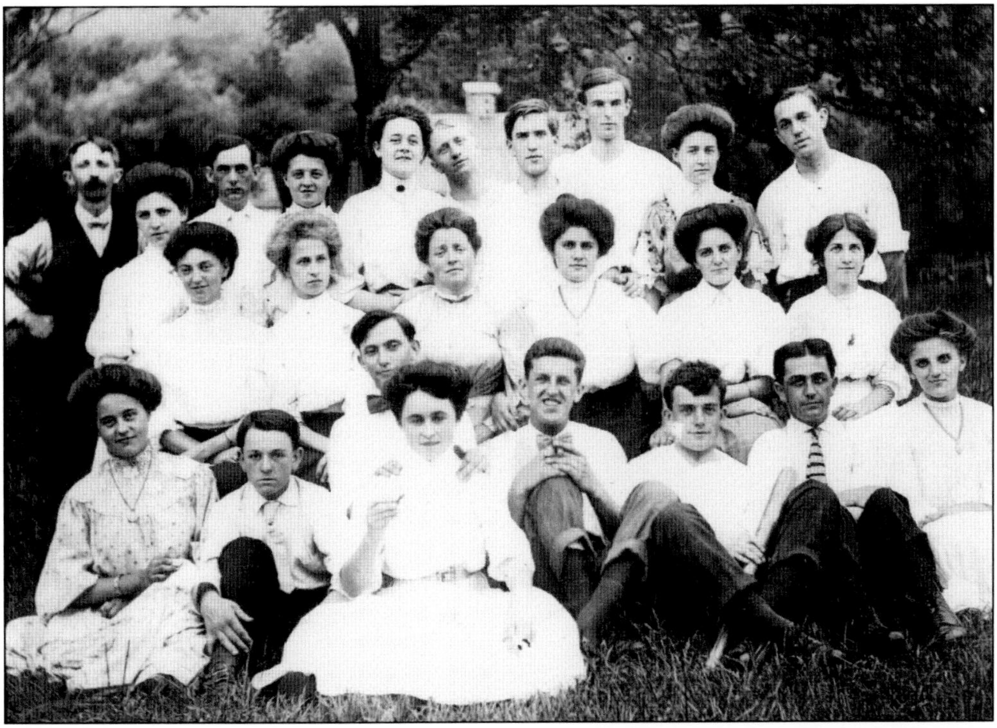

This photograph shows a picnic chaperoned by Pete and Mame Boehm. The apparel seems to be much more formal than that of today. From left to right are the following: (front row) ? Appel, Frank Boehm, Irma Wasser, Jane Schaeffer, Howard Eckert, Morris Dimmick, Howard Boehm, and unidentified; (middle row) Ella Schaeffer, Florence Abel, Mame Boehm, Eva Hilliard, Laura Raub, and Carrie Boehm; (back row) Pete Boehm, two unidentified, ? Appel, ? Appel, Herb Hoffert, unidentified, Victor Abel, unidentified, and Charles Fluck.

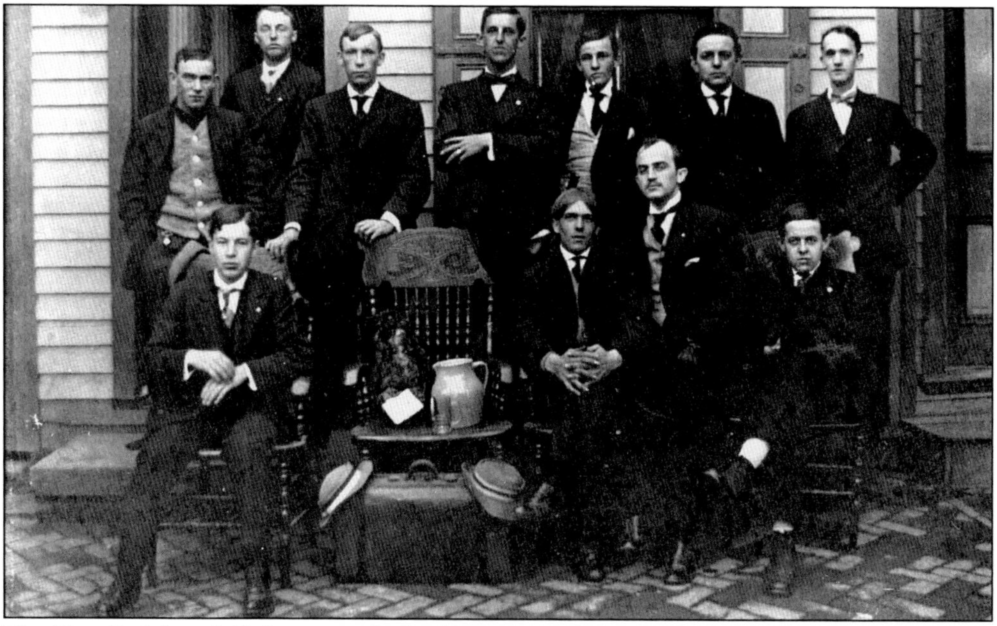

The Nite Owl Social Club occupied a building across the street from Carson's Hardware. Only three of these Owls are identified: Walter Barnett (front row, second from left), Warren Koch (middle row, center), and Howard Eckert (back row, right). Unfortunately, the club was noted for fighting, and one member was fatally wounded.

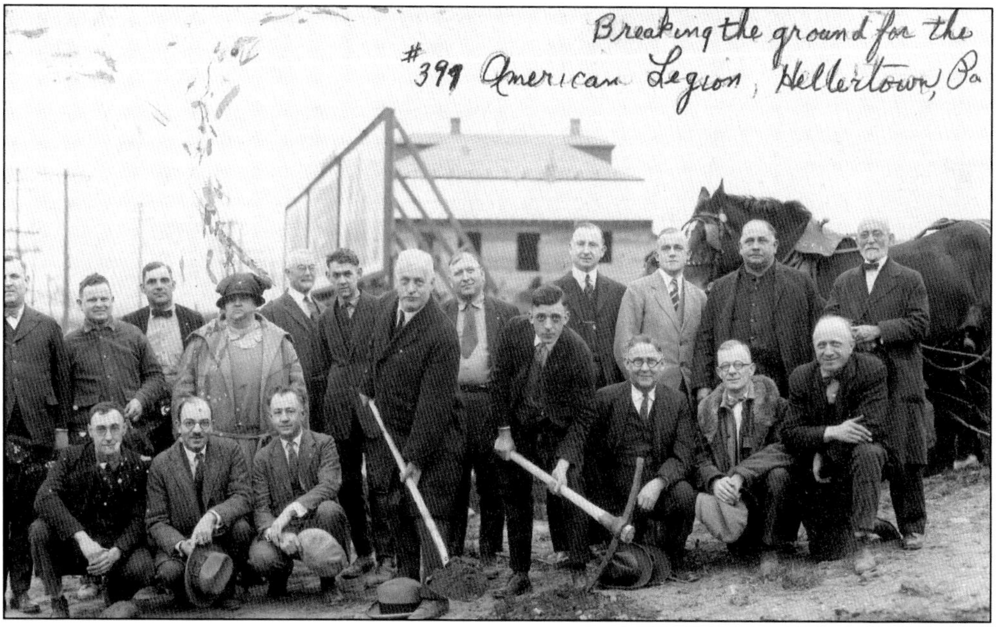

After meeting to discuss plans for a community building, the Edward Ackerman American Legion Post 397 groundbreaking occurred in 1924. From left to right are the following: (front row) Charles Heft, Herb Weisel, Art Anders, Titus Ruch, Web Peffer, and Herb Hoffert; (back row) Woody Eckert, Stan Yeager, Clarence Clark, Hattie Hager, George Deemer, Stuart Ziegenfuss, A.J. Welker, Frank Weidner, Howard Ache, Morris Dimmick, Charles Kichline, and Dr. W.H. Rentzheimer.

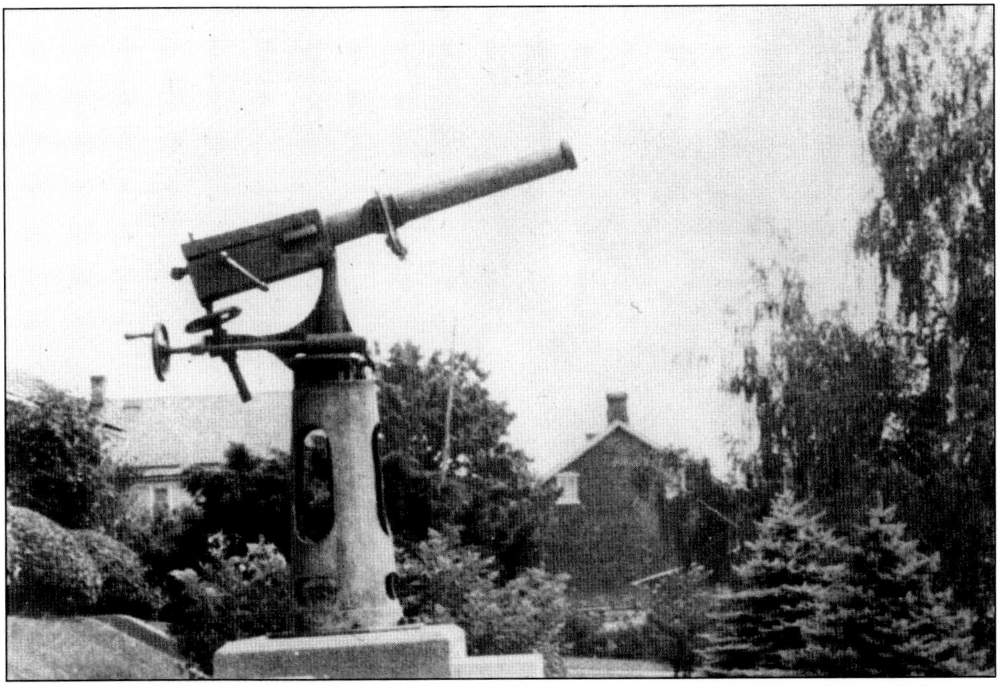

At one time following World War I, this machine gun monument stood in front of the new American Legion building. On April 16, 1917, Congress declared war on Germany. The American Expeditionary Forces (AEF) were led by Gen. John "Black Jack" Pershing. The Allies eventually gained victory, and the armistice was signed on November 11, 1918.

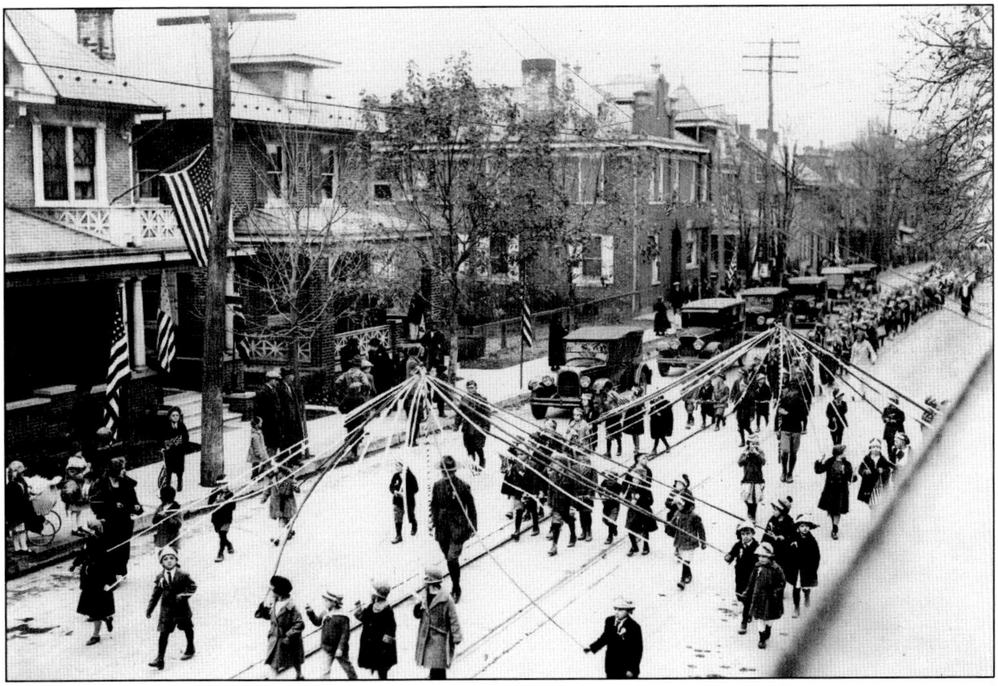

At the south end of town can be seen a group of children marching in the Legion Memorial Parade on June 21, 1924.

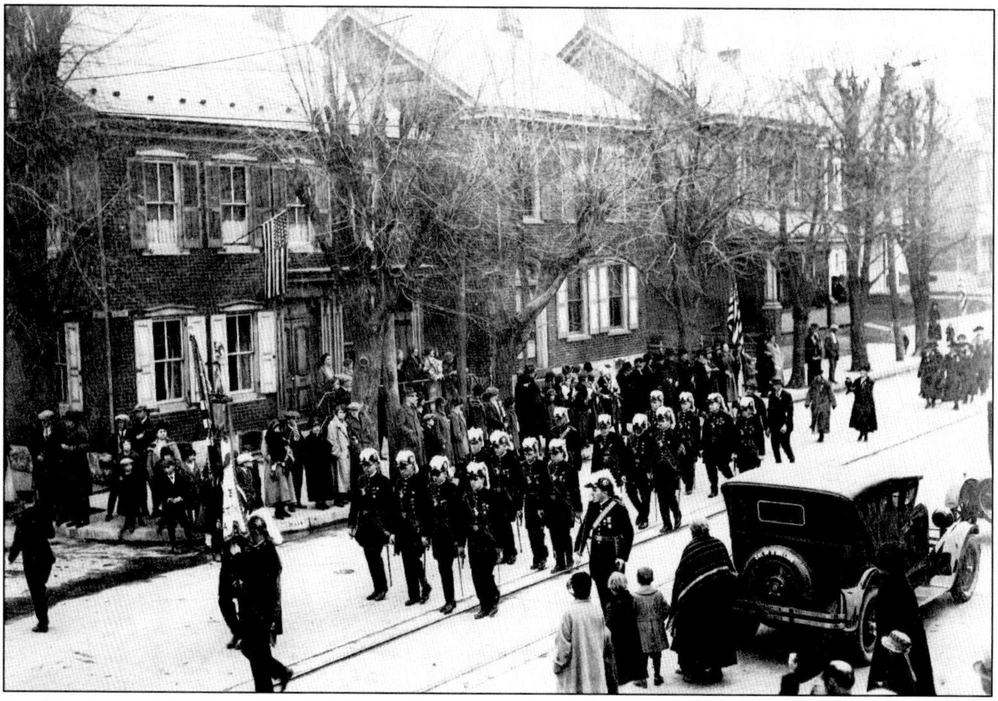

In this view of the June 21, 1924 parade, notice the fashions of the time. Most viewers, both male and female, have a head covering of some kind.

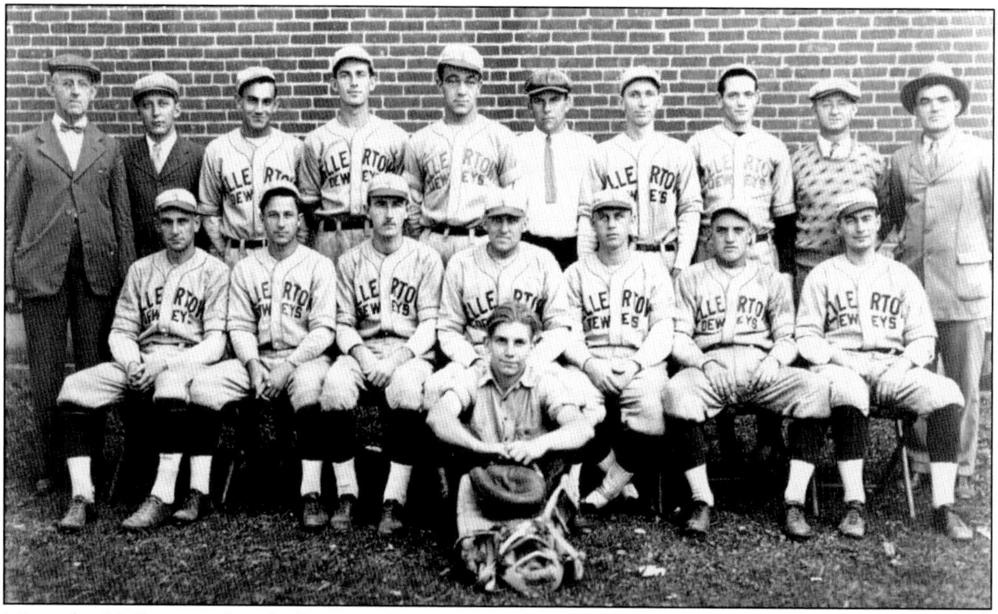

Meet the Hellertown baseball team, the Bucks County league champions of 1930. Sitting in the front is bat boy Willis Leidich. The others are, from left to right, as follows: (front row) Arch Simmons, Ken "Buckeye" Fritchman, Le Roy Everett, Warren Eckert, Gilbert Raudenbush, Orville Grube, and Howard Hess; (back row) Elmer Eckert, Dewey Fritchman, Jake Simmons, Kenneth Dimmick, Gilbert "Moxie" Eisenhart, Charles "Sheriff" Heft, George Koplin, Bill Lembach, Tim Spillane, and William Diehl.

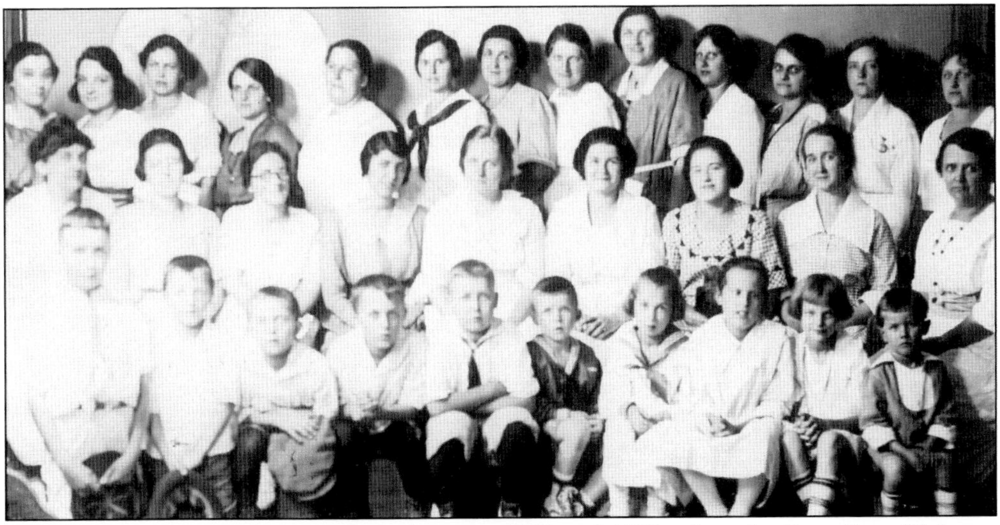

This photograph was taken sometime between 1920 and 1930, when the Betsy Ross Club was interested in preserving the Boehm Homestead as a library and museum. From left to right are the following: (front row) James Barnett, Paul Brown, Elmer Brown, unidentified, Robert Barnett, Charles Mauch, Meryl Mauch, Josephine Prosser, unidentified, and Kermit Judd; (middle row) May Rentzheimer, two unidentified, Margaret Altoeffer, Katie Weidner, Bess Mauch, Katherine Lerch, Lizzie Barnett, and Kate Hess; (third row) Elizabeth Weisel, two unidentified, Edna Bergey, Elsie Prosser, unidentified, Lottie Trumbower, Erma Eckert, Marion Baker, Daisy Judd, Kate Keiper, and unidentified.

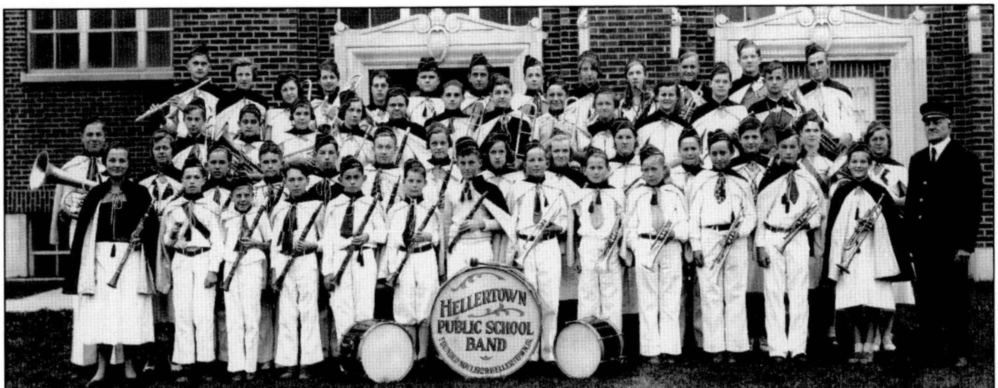

According to the drum, the Hellertown Public School Band was organized on November 1, 1929. Judging from the photograph, the band consisted of children from elementary school through senior high school. From left to right are the following: (first row) Ina Fehr, Carl Loux, Albert Hoppes, Maynard Fritchman, Granvil Strauss, Robert McKiven, LeRoy Wagner, Harold Fritchman, George Fritchman, Frederick Angstadt, Austin Kunsman, Michael Yamnicky, Sylvia Barnett, and Milton Warmkessel (director); (second row) Robert Hoppes, Marion Judd, Earl Solliday, Earl Nicholas, Harvey Laubach, David Keiper, Jenny Pfeifer, Hazel Koplin, Althea Nagorski, Gladys Ward, Austin Kunsman, Betty Kaufman, Betty Trumbower, and Martha Judd; (third row) Paul Koplin, Isabel Boehm, Mildred Hoppes, Irene Fritchman, Estella Werst, Leo Pondo, Barry Grubb, Walter Schreiber, Louisa Eisenhart, Jeanette Scholl, Anna Keck, and Edward Kies; (fourth row) Henry Laubach, Virginia Henderson, Anna Moyer, Barbara Henderson, Rachel Derr, Warren Ache, Bertram Schmell, Howard Strohl, Ruth Gangawere, Emma Statler, Lyman Rice, Kermit Judd, and Merritt Sloyer.

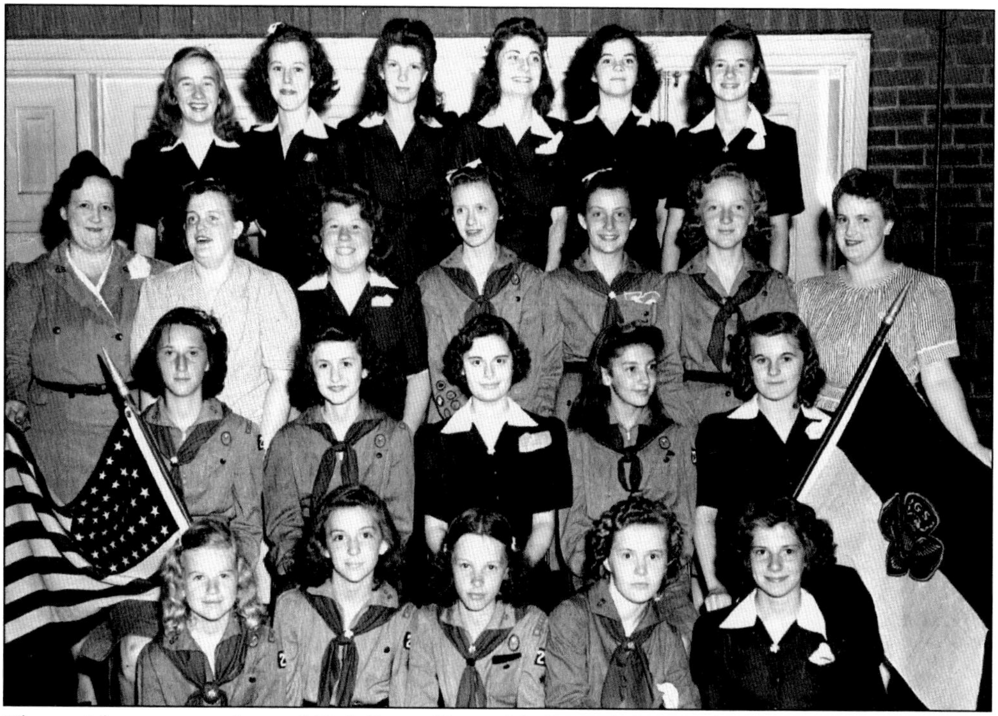

These girls were members of Girl Scout Troop 30. From left to right are the following: (first row) Rosemarie Ansbach, Jean Illick, Onalee Altoeffer, Elaine Bealer, and Claire Kichline; (second row) Majorie Fluck, Marjorie Illick, Phyliss Hess, Lois Martin, and Shirley Shimer; (third row) leader Evelyn Lipsky, unidentified, Frances Spillane, Jean Achey, Pat Barker, and MaryAnn Lipsky; (fourth row) Joann Morton, Catherine Simmons, Janet Ruch, Dorothy Hess, Jean Reilly, and Hazel Clarke.

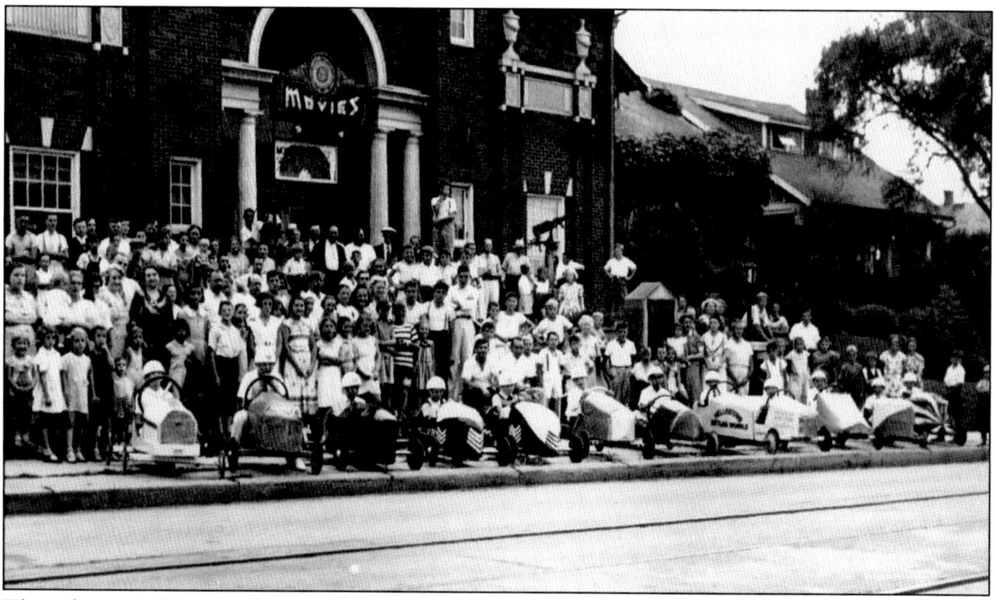

This photograph was taken *c.* 1937 in front of the American Legion. The entrants into the annual soapbox derby are poised behind their steering wheels.

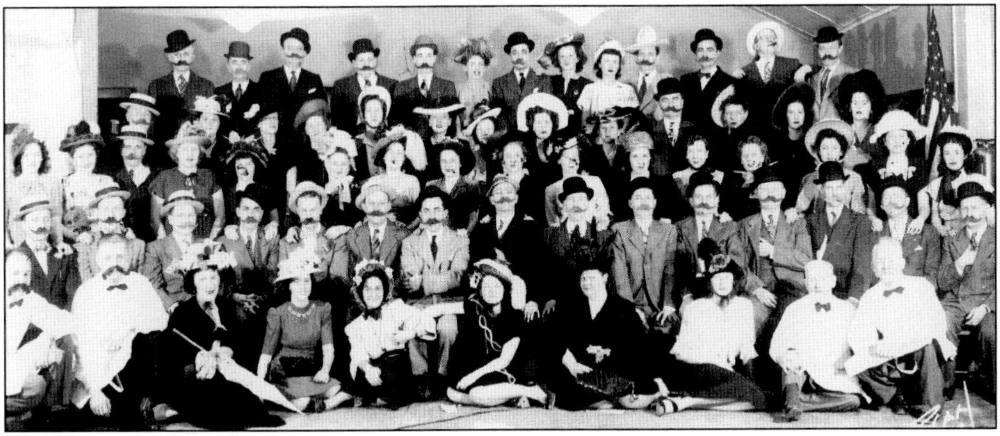

These thespians appeared on stage *c.* 1947 in a Hellertown Woman's Club production. From left to right are the following: (first row) two unidentified, Ethel Medve, Arlene Barnett, Isabel Zimpher, unidentified, Estella Werst, Ethel Weirbach, and two unidentified; (second row) Harold Gates, Elmer Brown, two unidentified, Bernard Pfeiffer, unidentified, John Wagner, unidentified, Owen McCall, Bill Lewis, Reuben Ruth, Clarence Templeton, Ray Wallender, and Walter Wimmer; (third row) Dolly Gates, Mary Brown, Bill Frey, Irene Frey, unidentified, Helen Pfeiffer, unidentified, Dot Wagner, unidentified, Loretta McCall, Fran Lewis, Maizie Ruth, Freda Templeton, Tida Wallender, and Barbara Wimmer; (fourth row) Bob Barnett, Grace Barnett, unidentified, Lillian Ruch, Ruth Frey, Bea Deibert, two unidentified, Quedel Nicholas, Chet Nicholas, Helen Reynolds, Emily Wright, and Bonnie Komich; (fifth row) unidentified, Bill Diehl, two unidentified, Francis Williams, Jean Williams, Walter Sterner, Verna Sterner, Arlene Behler, Wilmer Behler, unidentified, June Reynolds, and Bill Komich.

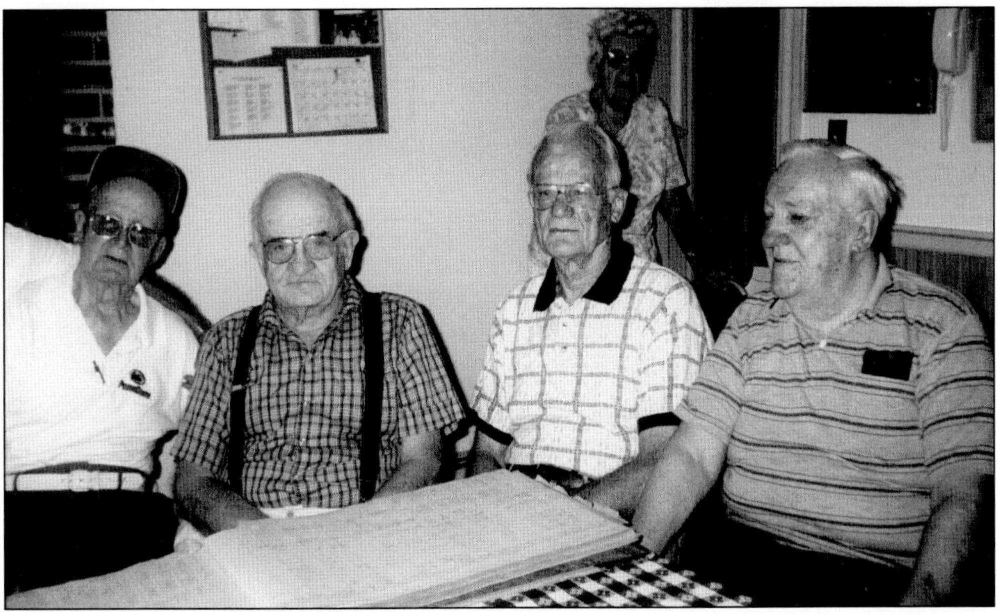

From January 20, 1942, to August 6, 1943, during World War II, hundreds of Hellertown volunteers manned the Civil Defense Observatory for spotting aircraft. Verna Calahan and Claire Rauscher were among the first observers to log in aircraft sightings. They had been instructed by teacher Mary Hess. Pictured here with the original logbook are, from left to right, former spotters Leo Stern, Ray Dimmick, Joe Kugler, and Bob Lipsky.

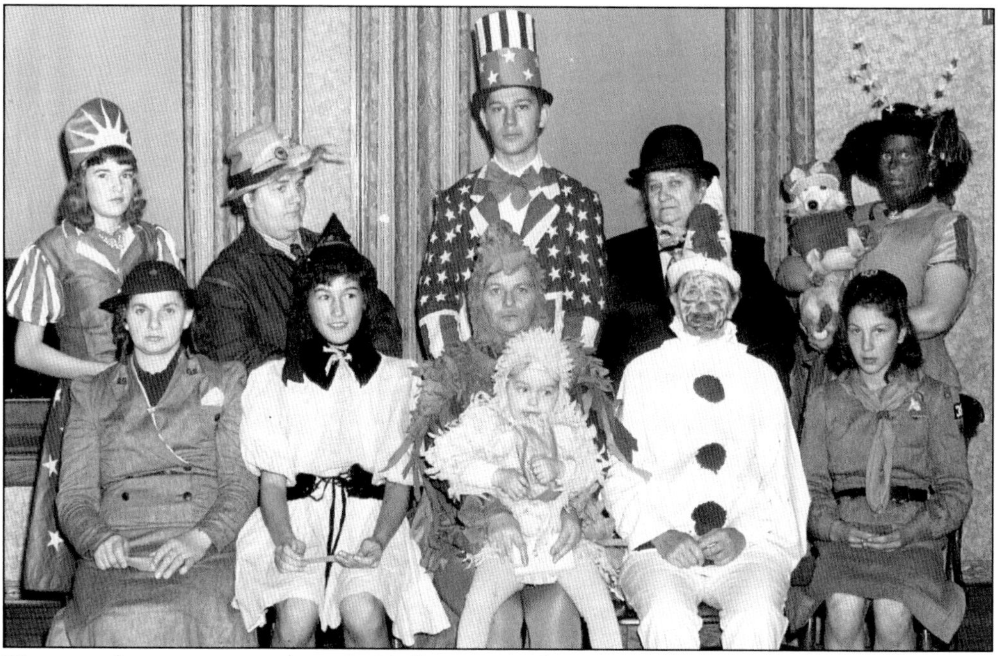

These are the prizewinners from the Hellertown Halloween parade on November 3, 1941. From left to right are the following: (front row) Mrs. Stephen Yambor, leader of Girl Scout Troop 39; Kathleen Hanner, best decorated girls' bicycle; Mrs. John Schlener and granddaughter, Barbara, most original marchers; Mrs. William Diehl, best clown; and Jeanne Schrader, from Troop 30; (back row) Pearl Stork, best decorated girls' bike; Florence Simmons, Ladies Auxiliary, First Evangelical and Reformed Church; Ted Fritchman, most patriotic; Helen Grube, most comical; Mrs. John Brown, holding Mrs. John Grogg's dog, second best decorated live animal.

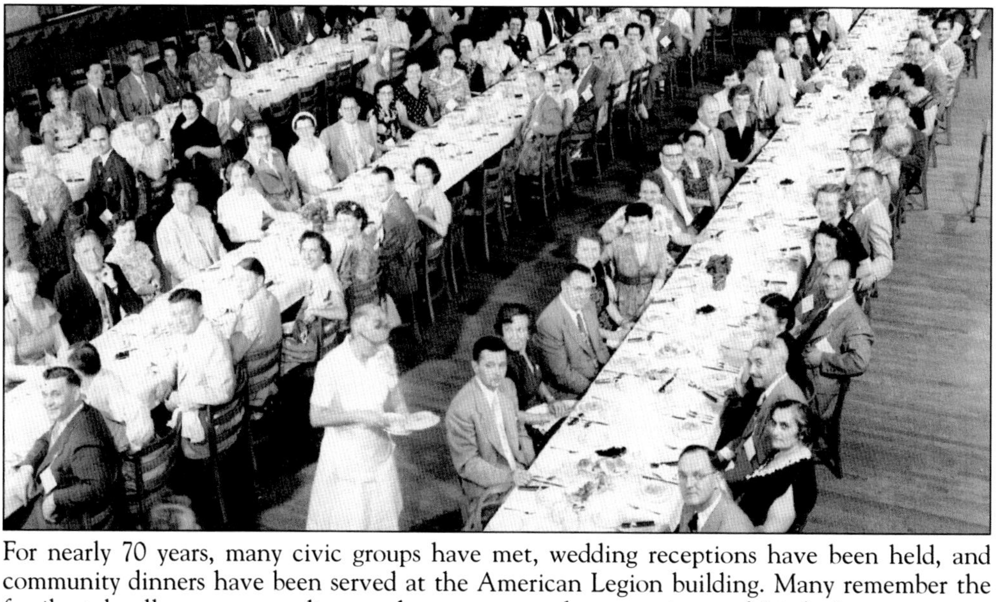

For nearly 70 years, many civic groups have met, wedding receptions have been held, and community dinners have been served at the American Legion building. Many remember the family-style all-you-can-eat dinners that were served at scouting and Little League events. The meat, potatoes, and gravy were plentiful, and the words "Pass the ———, please," have resounded hundreds of thousands of times.

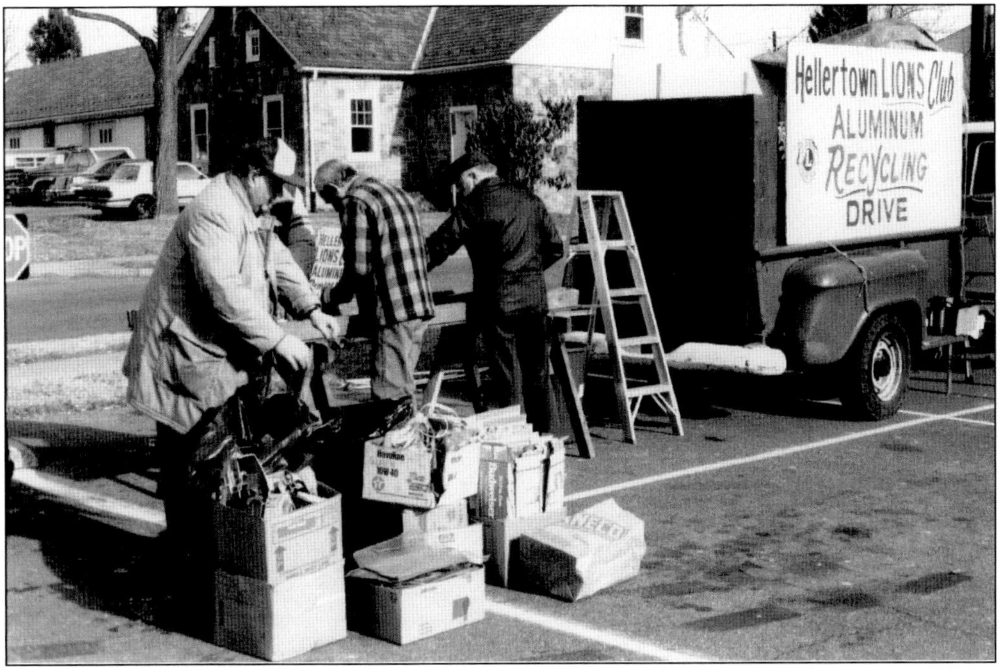

In the late 1950s, Vince Makoski and others became active members of the Lions Club in service to the borough of Hellertown. They helped build an extension on the pavilion roof at the reservoir and constructed a charcoal pit. They also assisted with the club's recycling program long before nearby communities. The Lions assisted at Halloween parades long ago by carrying kerosene torches so that the children could see.

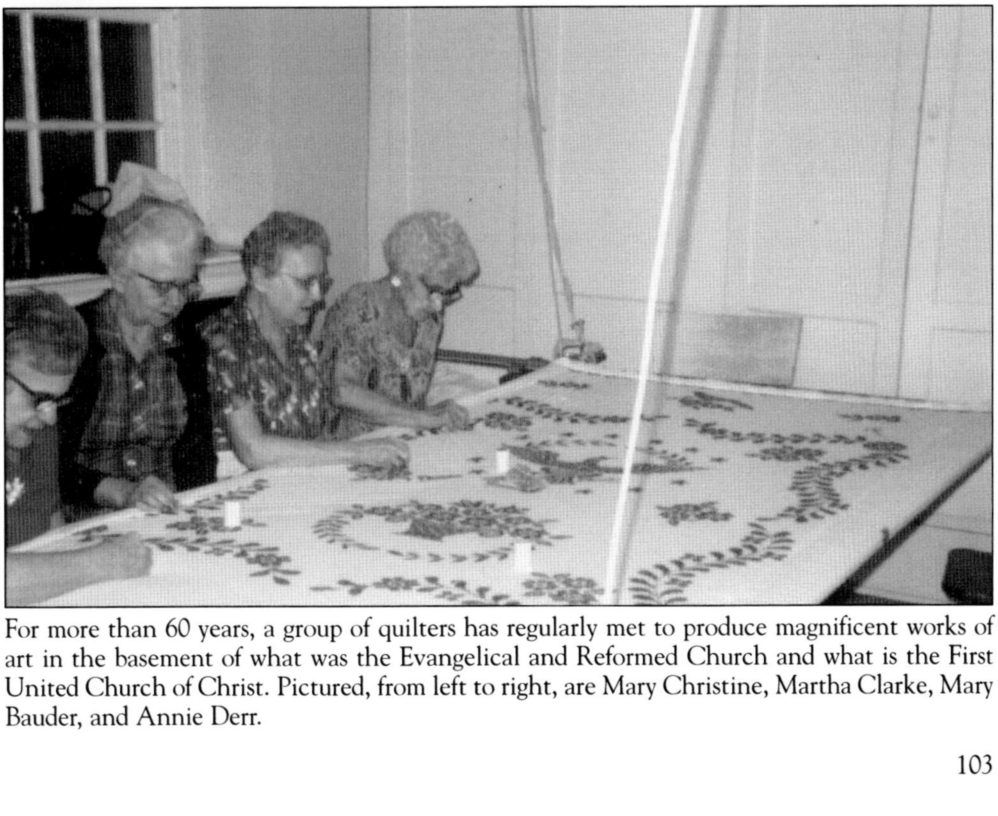

For more than 60 years, a group of quilters has regularly met to produce magnificent works of art in the basement of what was the Evangelical and Reformed Church and what is the First United Church of Christ. Pictured, from left to right, are Mary Christine, Martha Clarke, Mary Bauder, and Annie Derr.

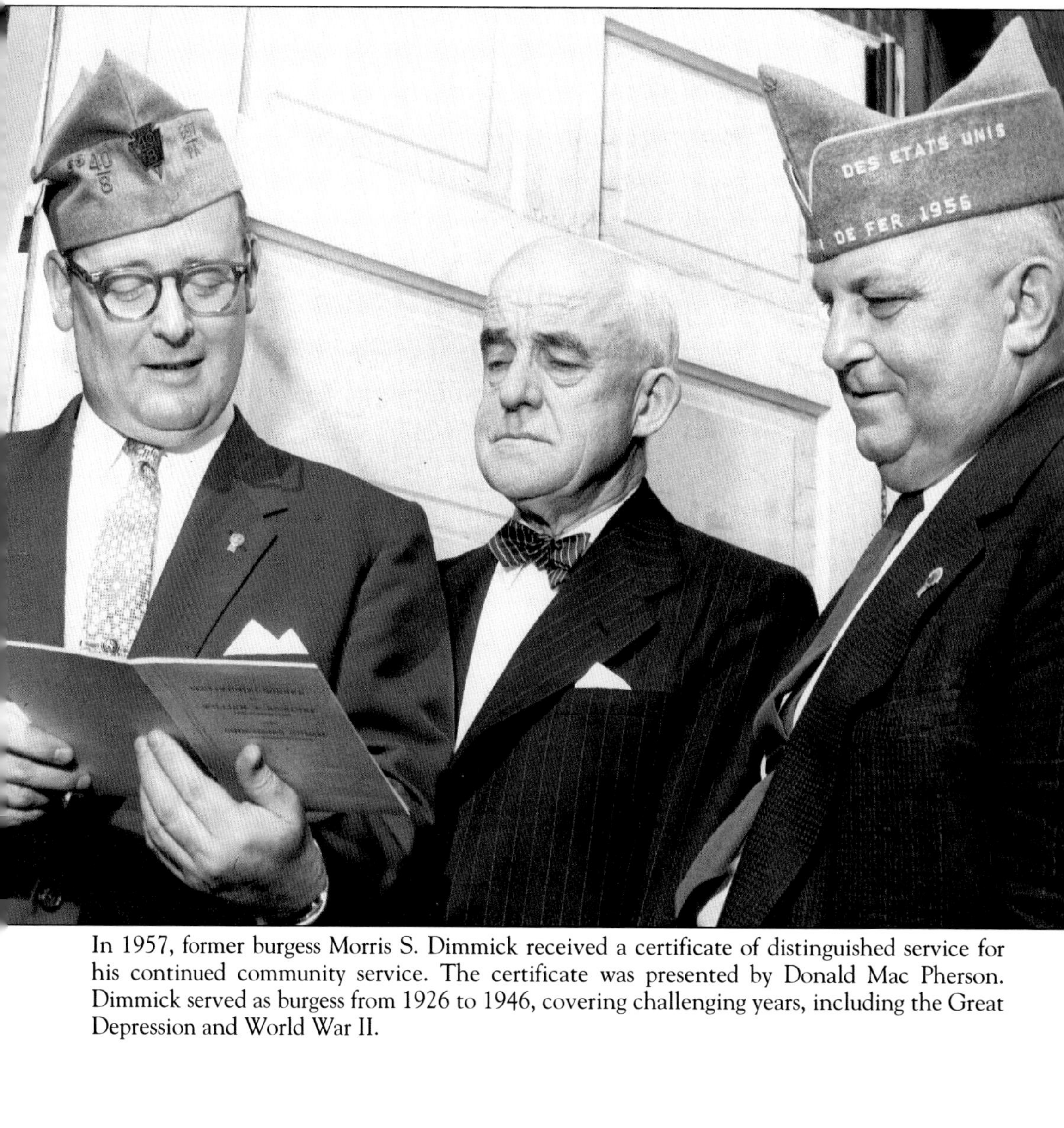

In 1957, former burgess Morris S. Dimmick received a certificate of distinguished service for his continued community service. The certificate was presented by Donald Mac Pherson. Dimmick served as burgess from 1926 to 1946, covering challenging years, including the Great Depression and World War II.

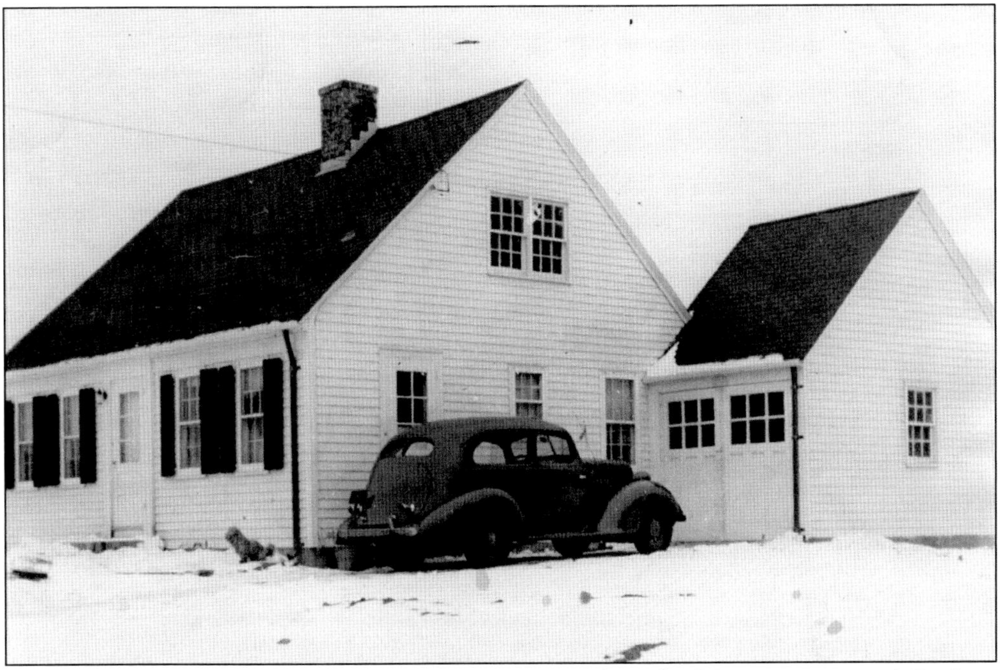

During the 1940s, many Sears homes were constructed in the Mountainview and Durham Terrace sections of town. They would often house families from whom came steelworkers. Bethlehem Steel was working full blast at the time during and after the war effort.

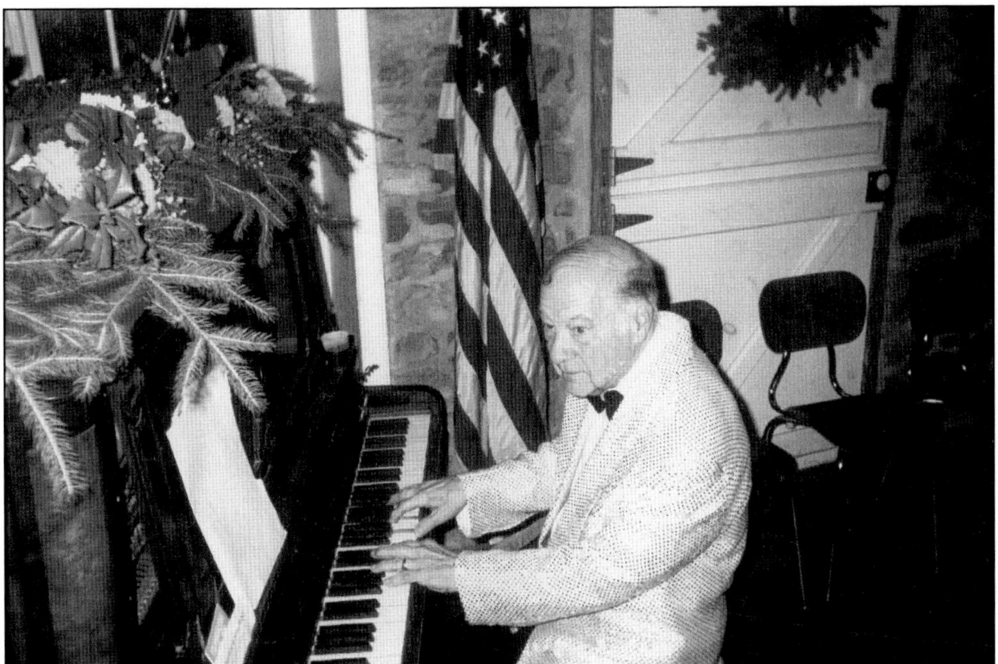

The Hellertown Historical Society holds its holiday open house during the first week of December. Here, Rodney Nickum plays holiday tunes on the Steinway donated by Ed and Karyl Laub.

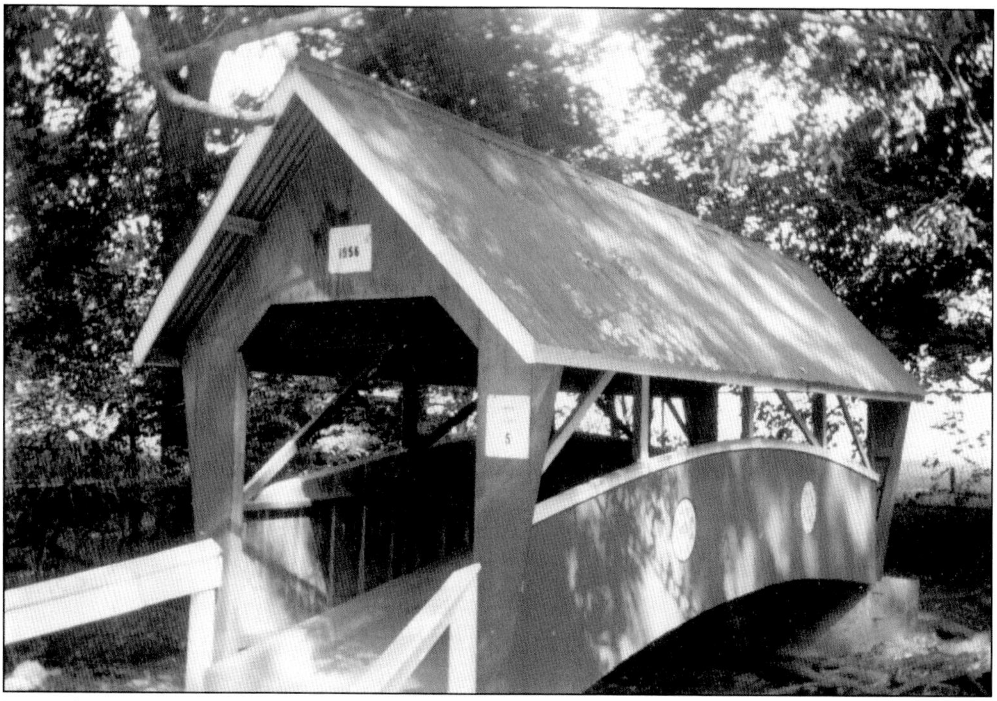

Near the picnic area across the street from Lost Cave, visitors view this miniature covered bridge built in 1956.

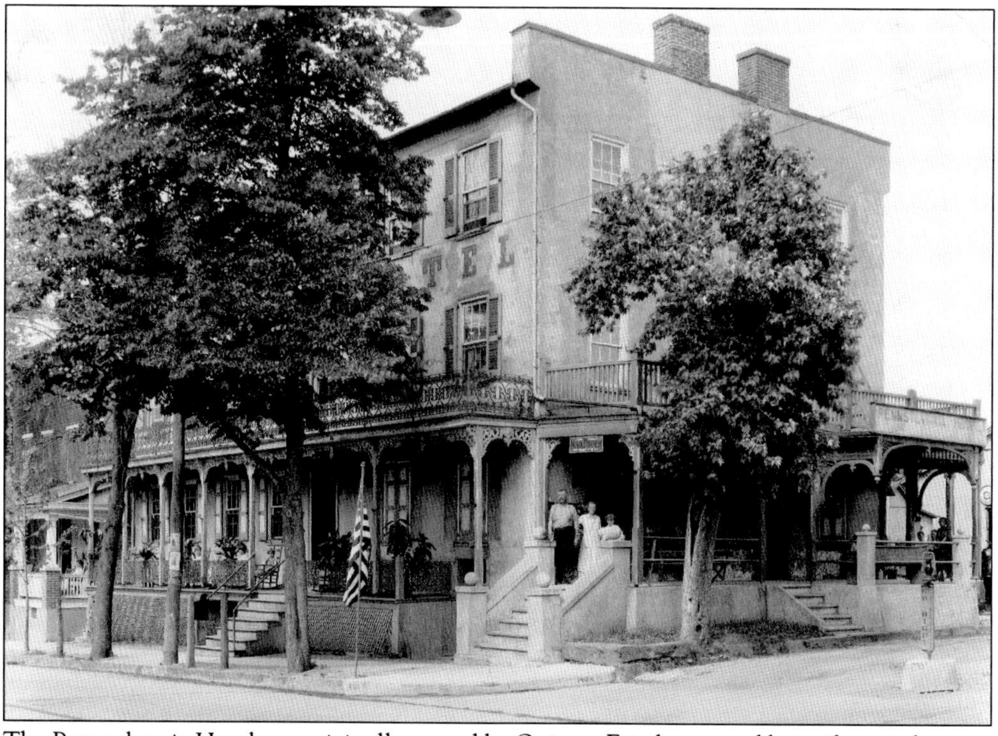
The Pennsylvania Hotel was originally owned by Quintus Fritchman and his wife, seen here on the porch in 1925. Other family owners would be Berger, Pondo, and Rodriguez.

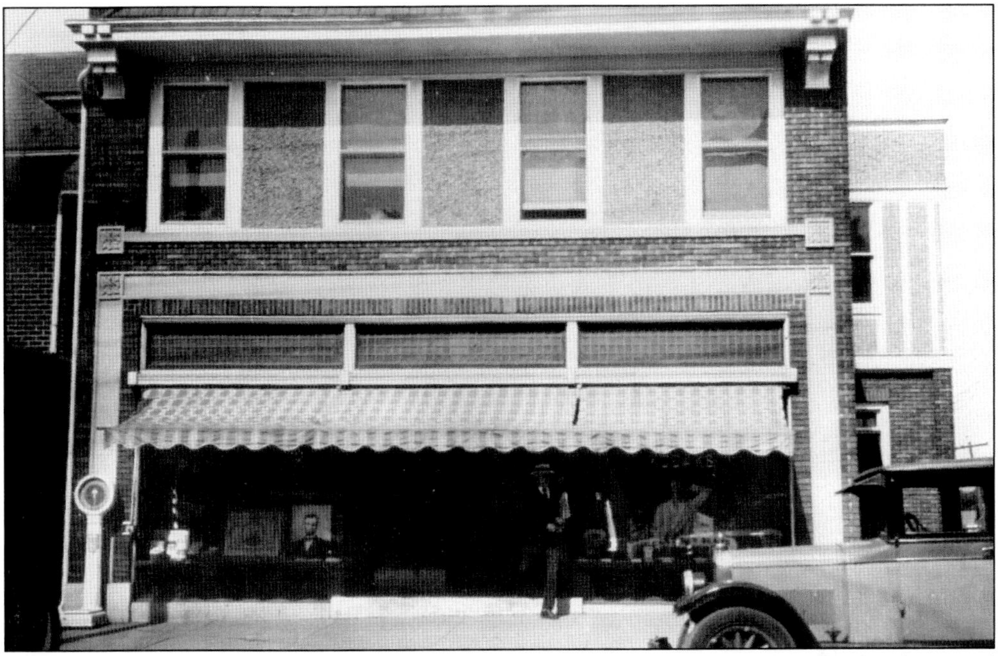

Built originally as a notions store by Dan Peffer, Prosser's would become one of the two family-owned pharmacies in Hellertown. This business was located on the southwest corner of Main and Depot Streets. Notice the 1929 Essex parked at the curb and the emerging straw-hatted customer.

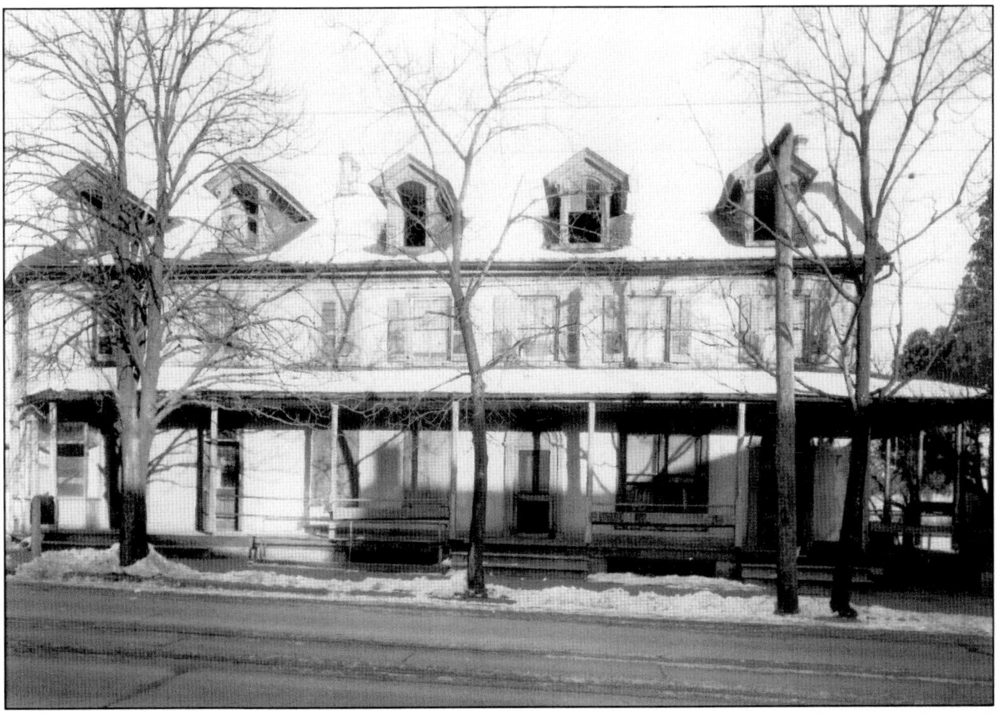

This is a winter view of the Dr. Henry Detwiller home, which later became the Central Hotel and, finally, Hellertown Borough Hall.

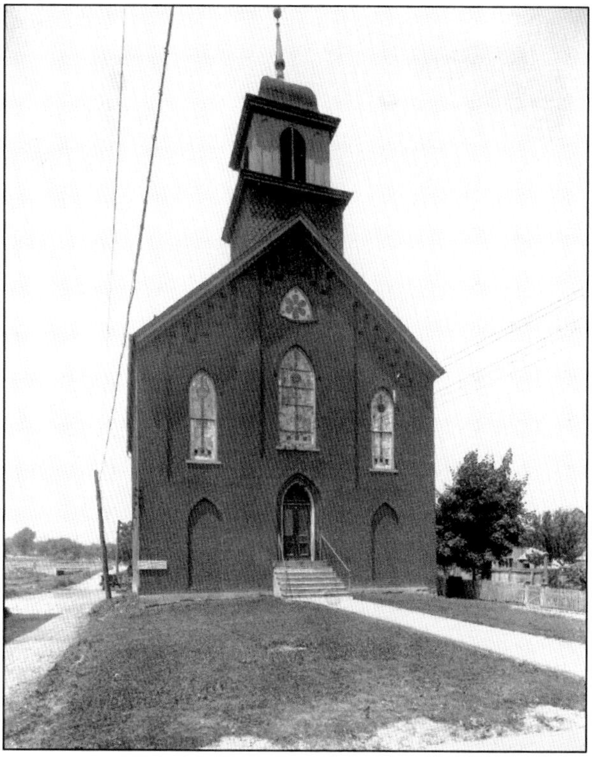

In the location of Hellertown's first school stood St. Paul's Evangelical Church and, later, the Methodist church.

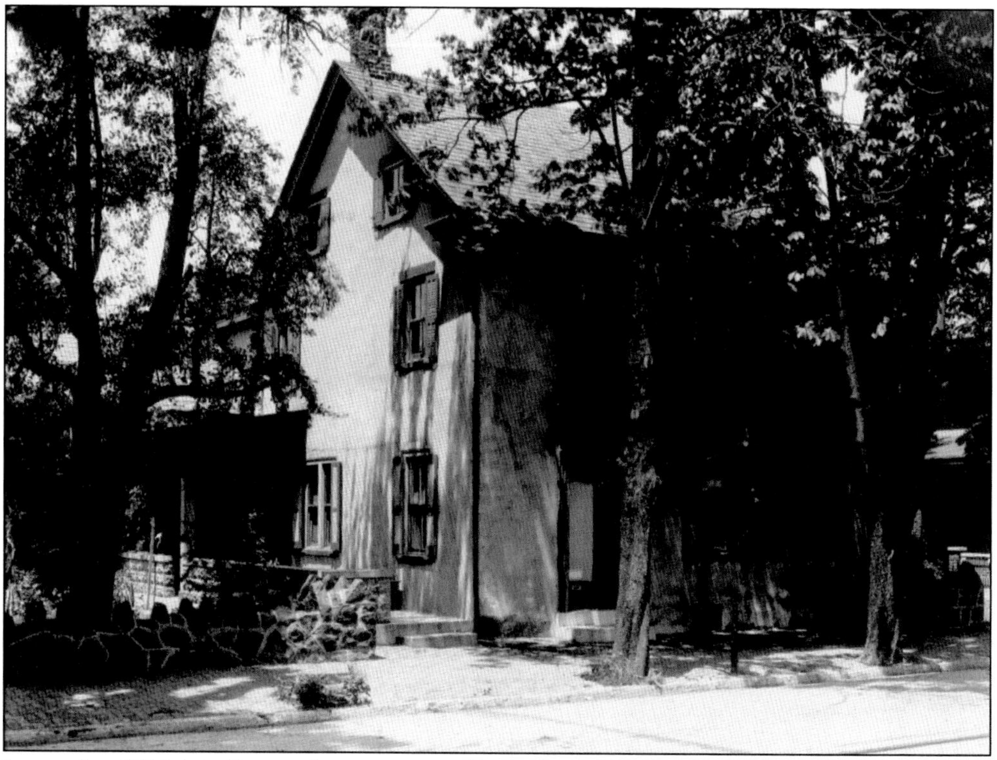

Located at 186 Main Street, this was originally the home of Rev. Samuel Hess.

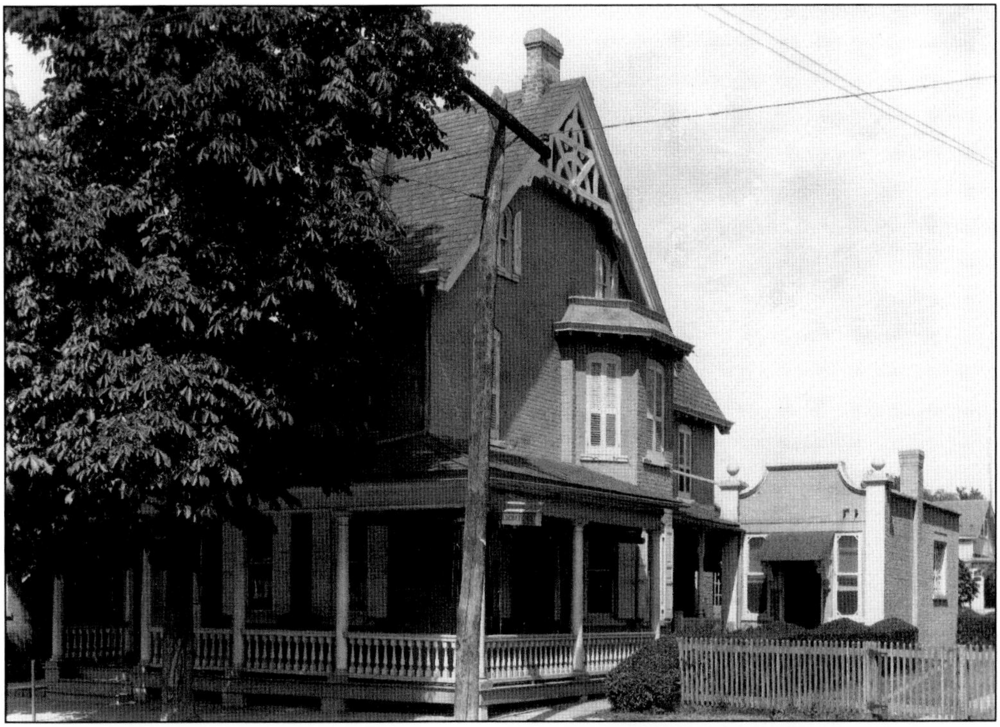

Dr. Edward Deibert's home, at 411 Main Street, provided easy access to patients and is another classic example of the architecture of the day, complete with ornamental latticework.

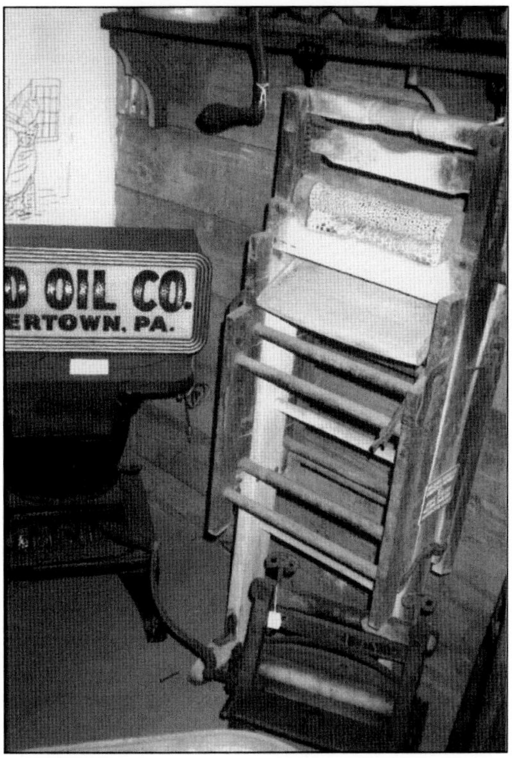

Relics now, these "new" appliances were welcomed by early-20th-century women in Hellertown, especially on Monday, which was traditionally washday.

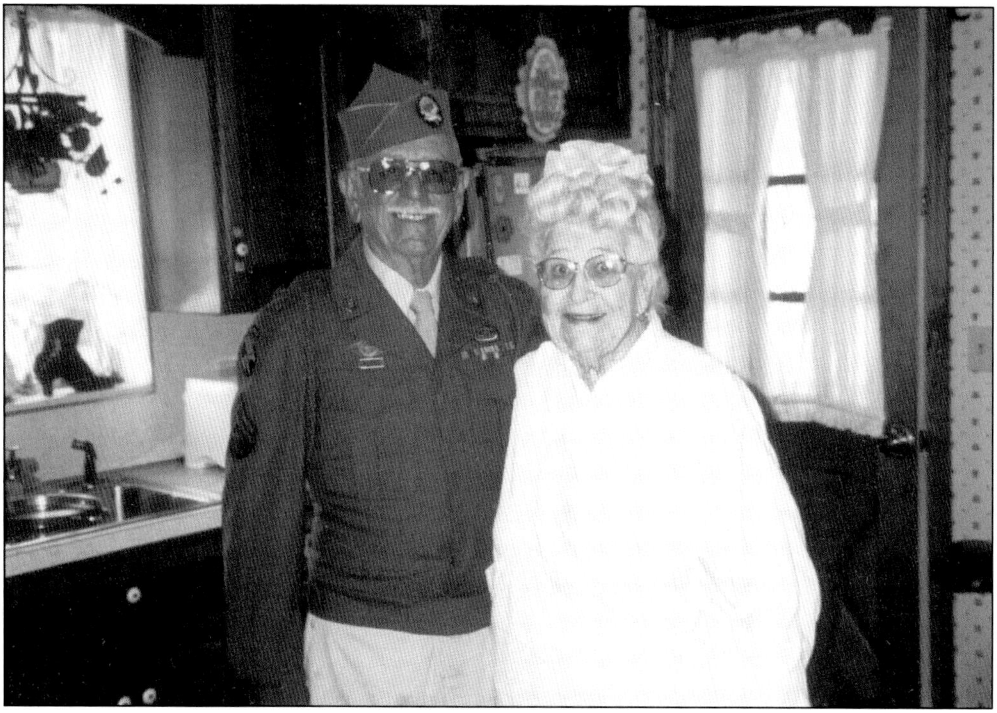

Bill and Irene Frey, longtime members of the Hellertown Historical Society, spend Tuesday and Saturday mornings volunteering often from spring to fall.

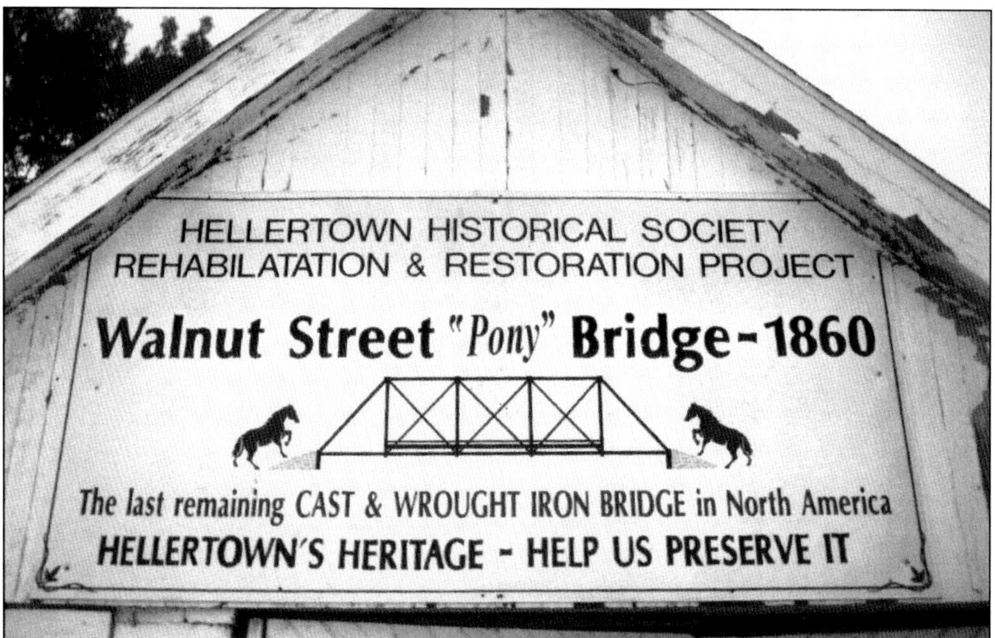

This sign near the renewed Pony Bridge speaks for itself. The bridge is a result of six years of intensive work.

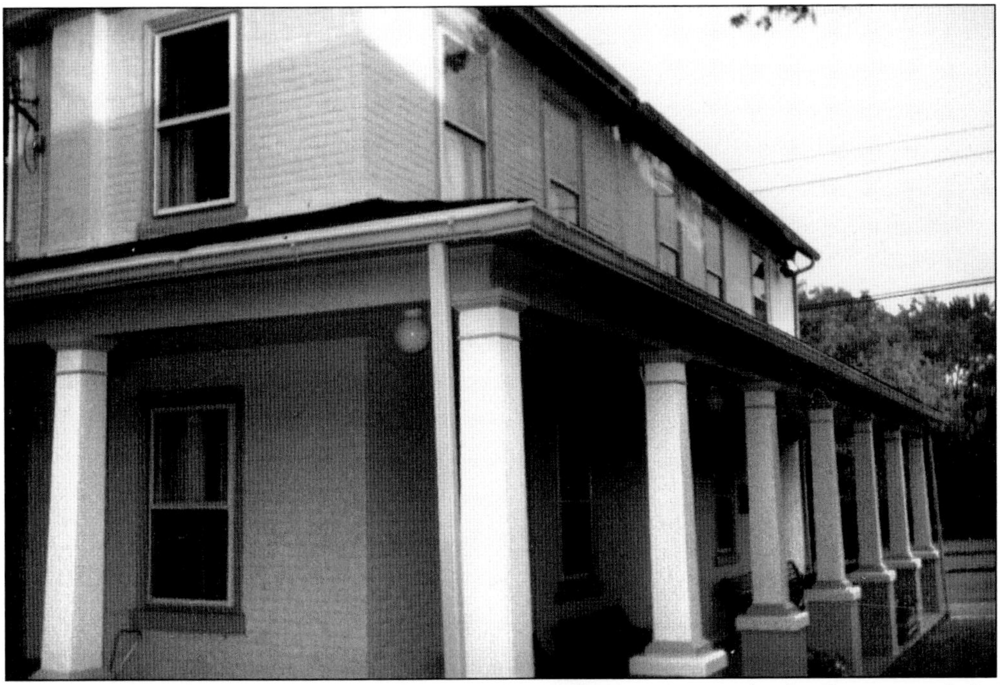

The early-morning sun has not entirely hit the Miller's House at the headquarters of the Hellertown Historical Society. In 1812, the will of Christopher Wagner stipulated that his heir, grandson Jacob Wagner, allow a decent dwelling house for John Wagner and wife, parents of Jacob Wagner. In 1841, after the death of Jacob, his second wife, Susanna, was granted the right to live rent-free in the Miller's House. The original home had been built c. 1800.

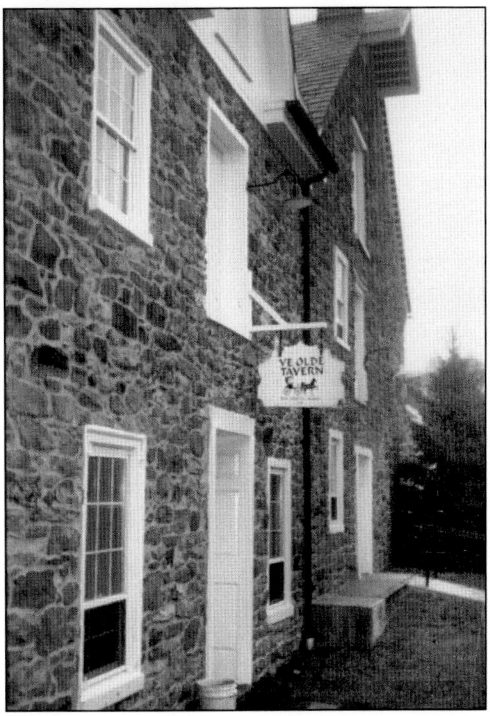

During the late 1700s, travelers were welcomed to the Tavern Room for liquid refreshment. It was a convenient stop for those traveling north or south along the King's Highway. Today, volunteers are needed to keep the environs of the mill in mint condition.

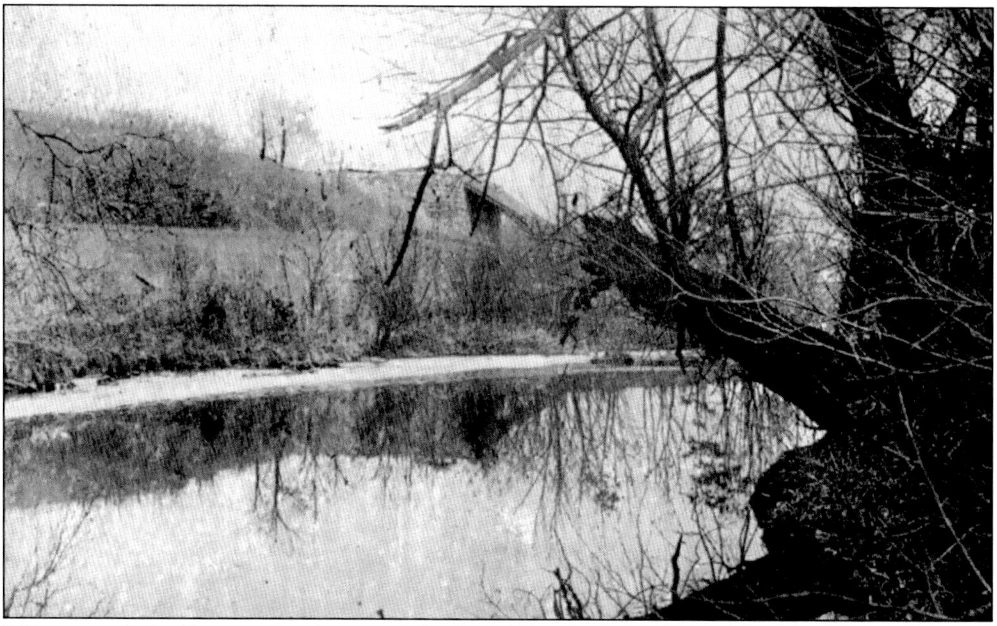

This view of the Saucon Creek is near the famed Bingen Naval Academy of the 1930s.

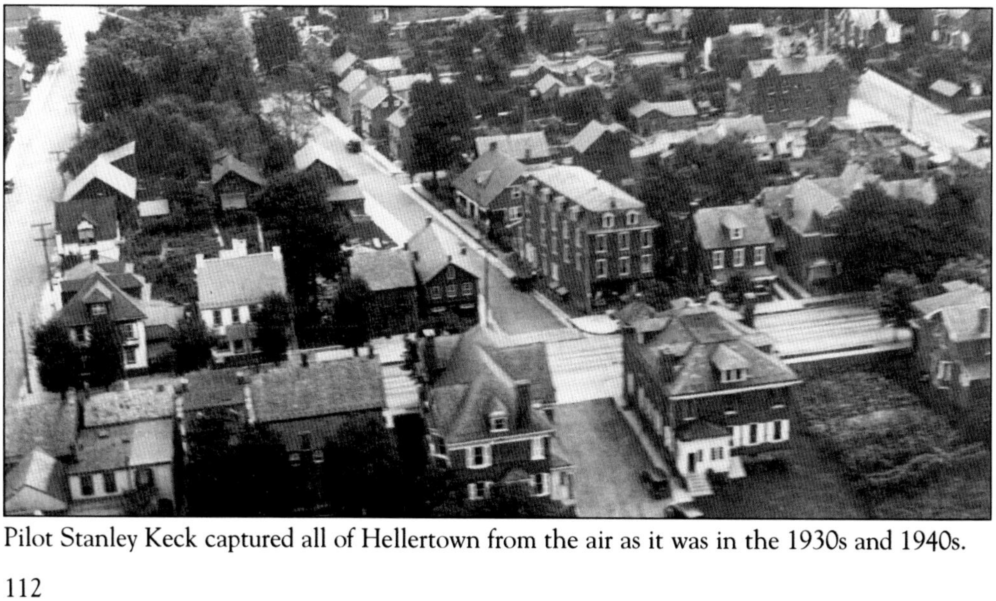

Pilot Stanley Keck captured all of Hellertown from the air as it was in the 1930s and 1940s.

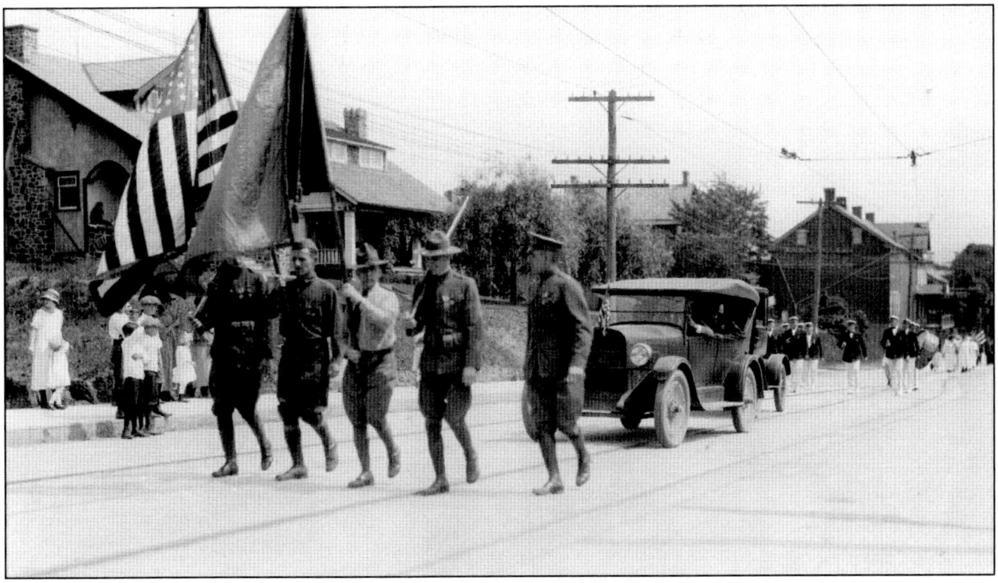

These young men in the Honor Guard on June 21, 1924, are frozen in time while in perfect step.

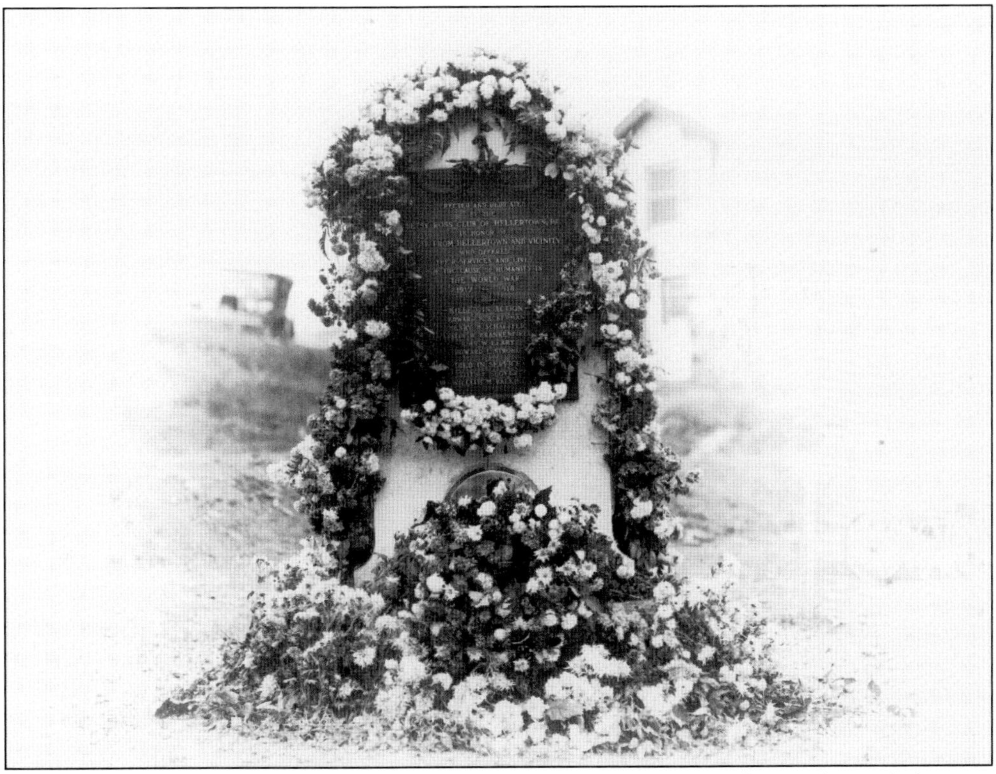

This World War I memorial plaque is seen clothed in a multitude of flowers for its dedication on June 21, 1924. The past merges with the present at the historical society.

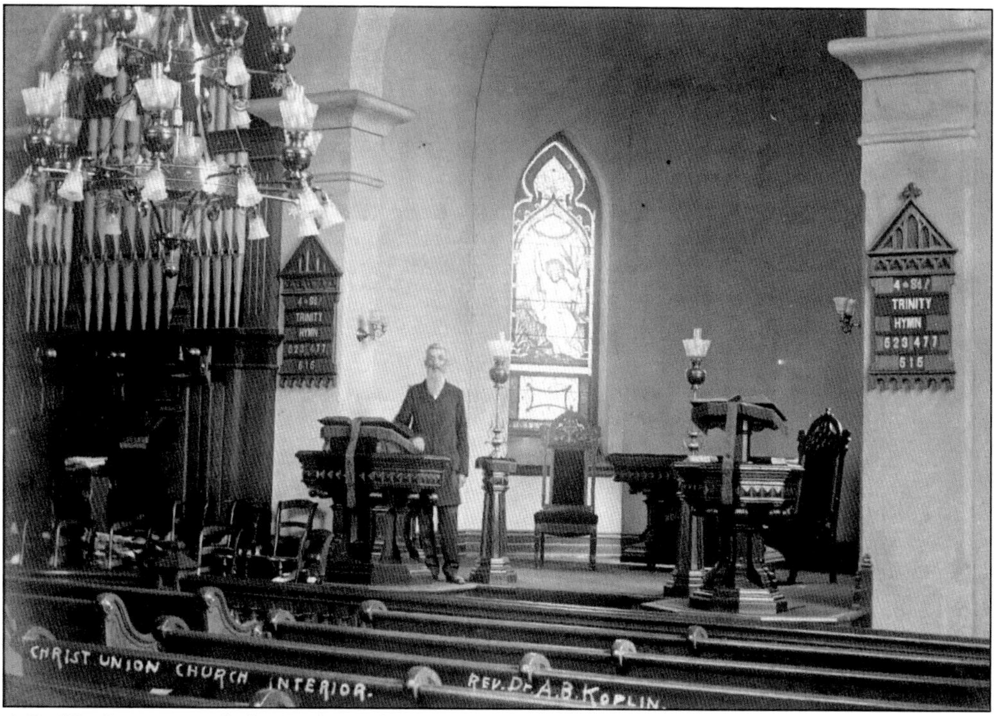

A.B. Koplin pastored the Reformed congregation at Christ Union Church, located on the southeast corner of Northampton and Saucon Streets from 1876 until 1917. This photograph is one of the few remaining interior views of the church.

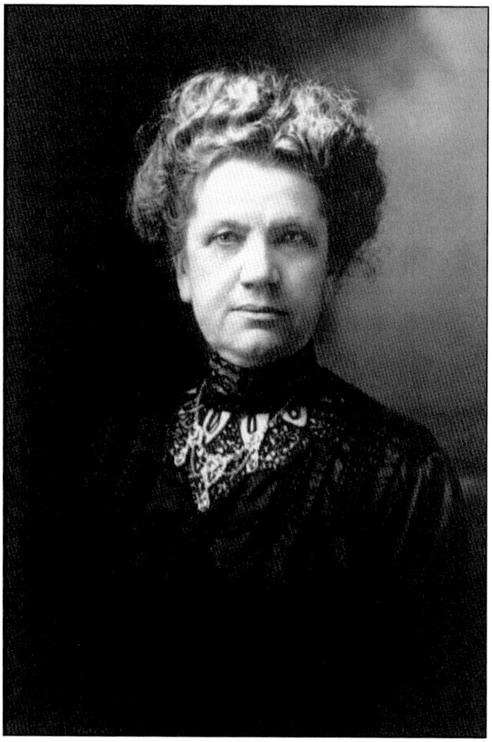

Many very old photographs found in basements and attics are unfortunately unidentified. In this case, the lady from the 1890s happens to be a relative of the author, identified as Aunt Lizzie Leidig Emery, aunt of Annie Weidner, his paternal grandmother. Photographs such as these need to be preserved. One way is to donate and file them at the historical society.

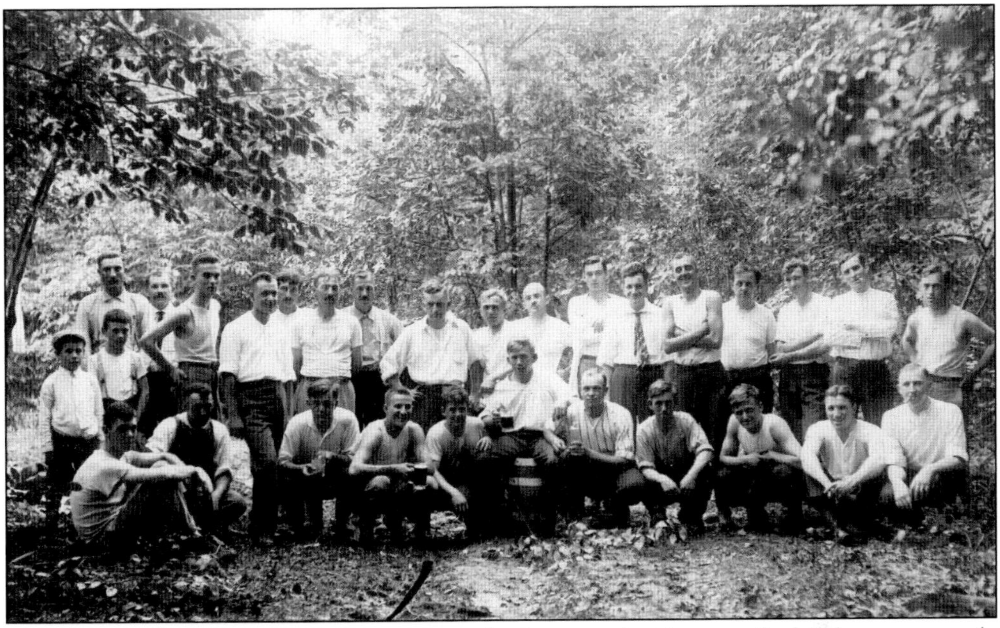

This photograph presents young men, some in the foreground with mugs of a dark brew apparently tapped from the keg in the center. Sitting second from the right is Herbert Cless, who was later active in civic duties with the borough. Standing seventh from the right is the author's maternal grandfather, Robert Weisel. It is possible that these men were involved with the boathouse on the Saucon, shown on page 75, or were members of the Eagles, a fraternal organization.

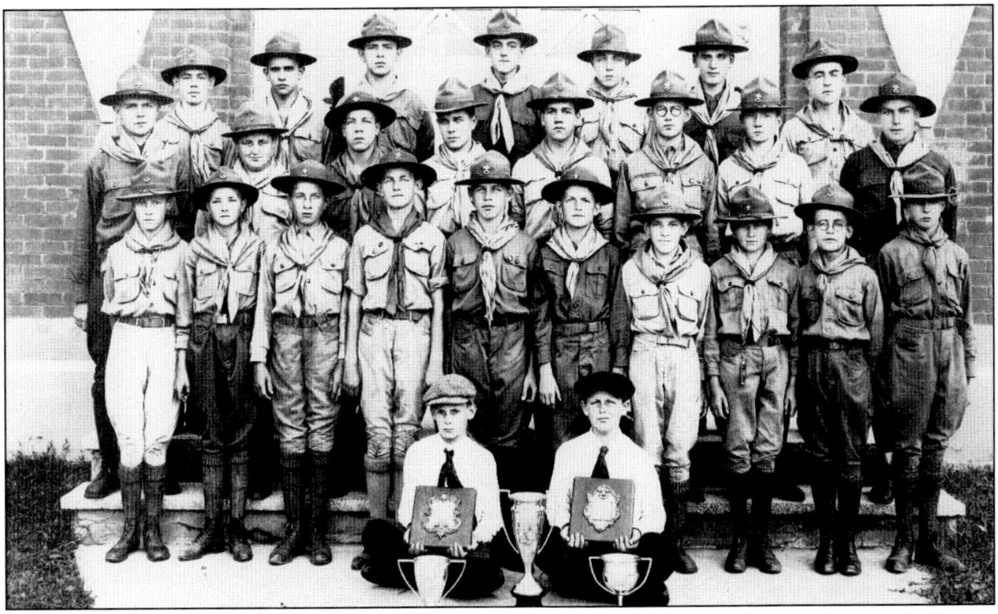

Perhaps these are boys who competed with other scout troops, since the trophies and plaques are easily seen in the front. This group most likely camped together during the first decade of the 20th century. The author's great-uncle, Lewis Kies, is seen in the middle row, third from the left.

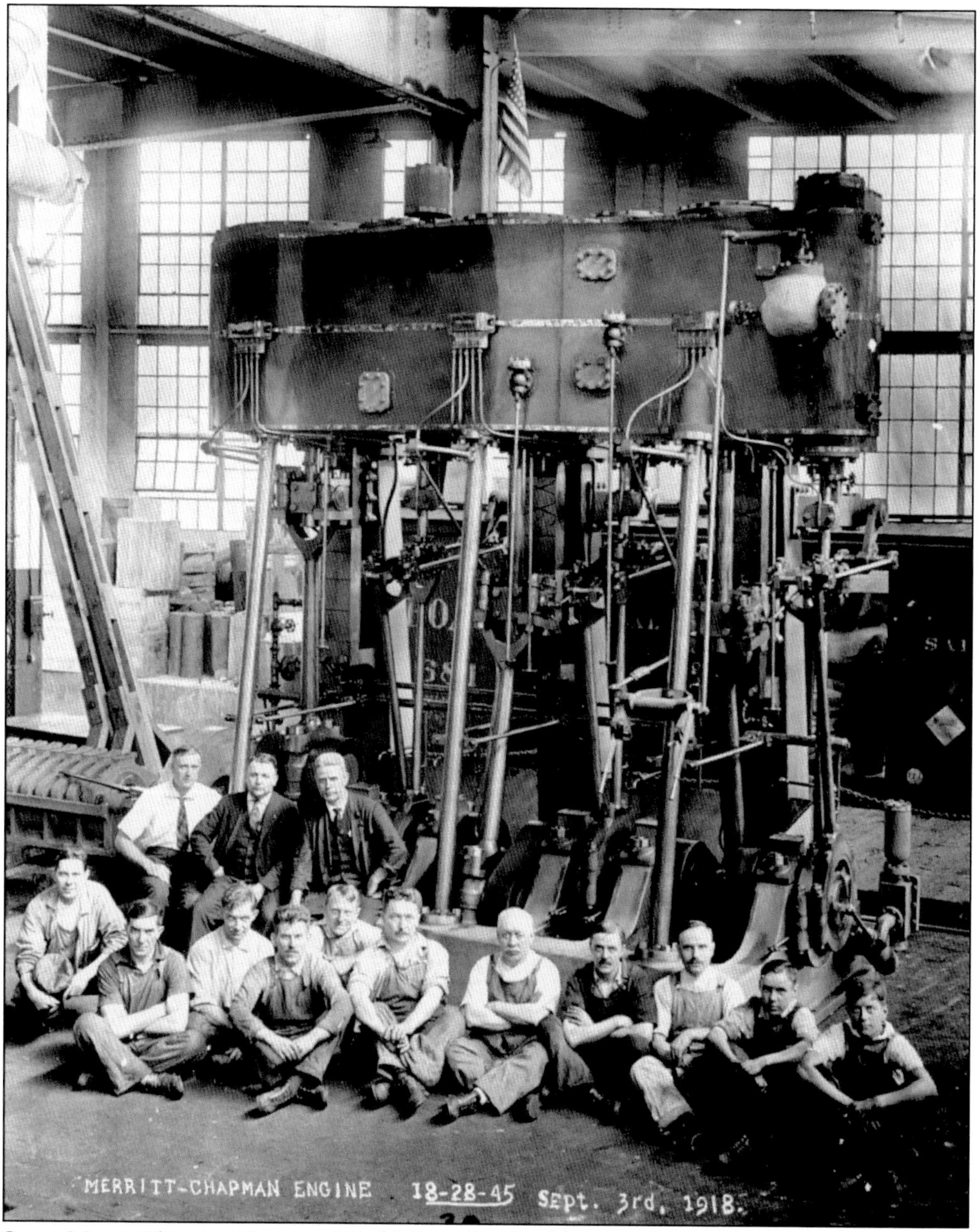

Some Moore Plant employees of Bethlehem Shipbuilding are here pictured on September 3, 1918. Hellertonian Robert Rickert was superintendent during the World War I years. He is in the back row, sitting in the center.

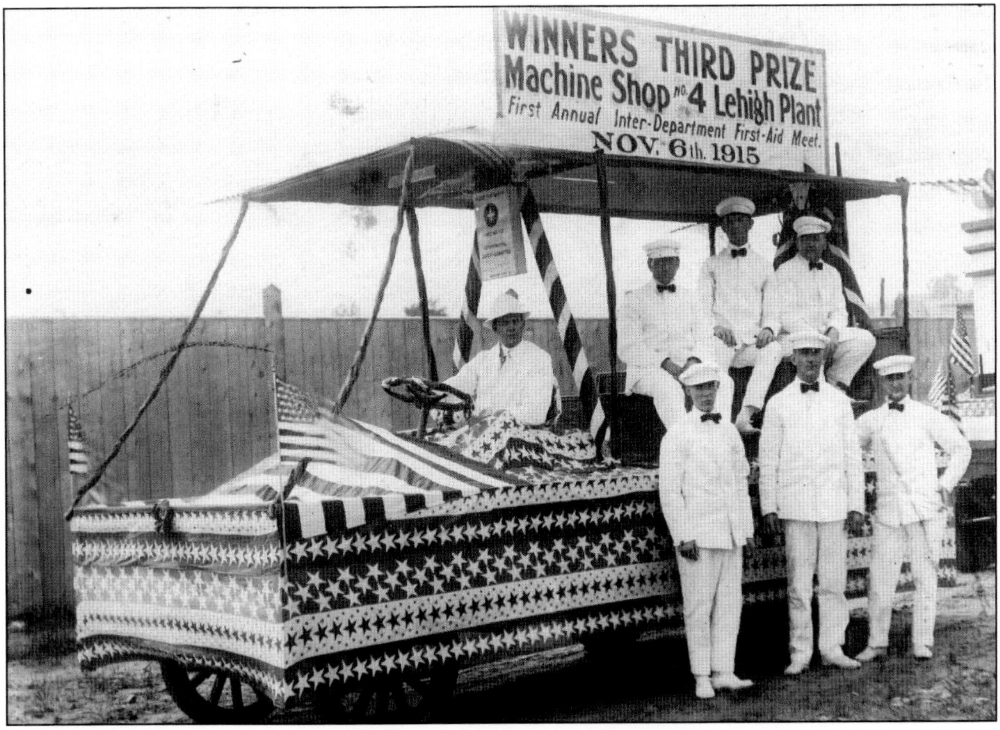

The machine shops of the Lehigh Plant of Bethlehem Shipbuilding competed on November 6, 1915. Machine Shop 4 took third prize for this float. Many Hellertonians would work here after World War I.

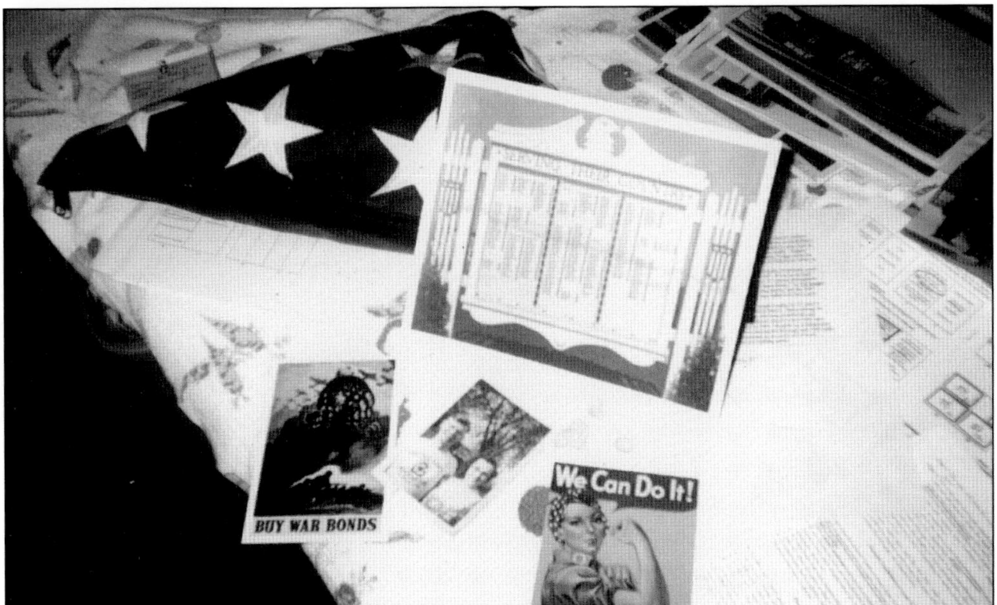

Notice Old Glory given to Beatrice Weidner to honor her husband's military service during World War II. The postcards represent posters displaying slogans of the time, "Buy War Bonds" and "We Can Do It."

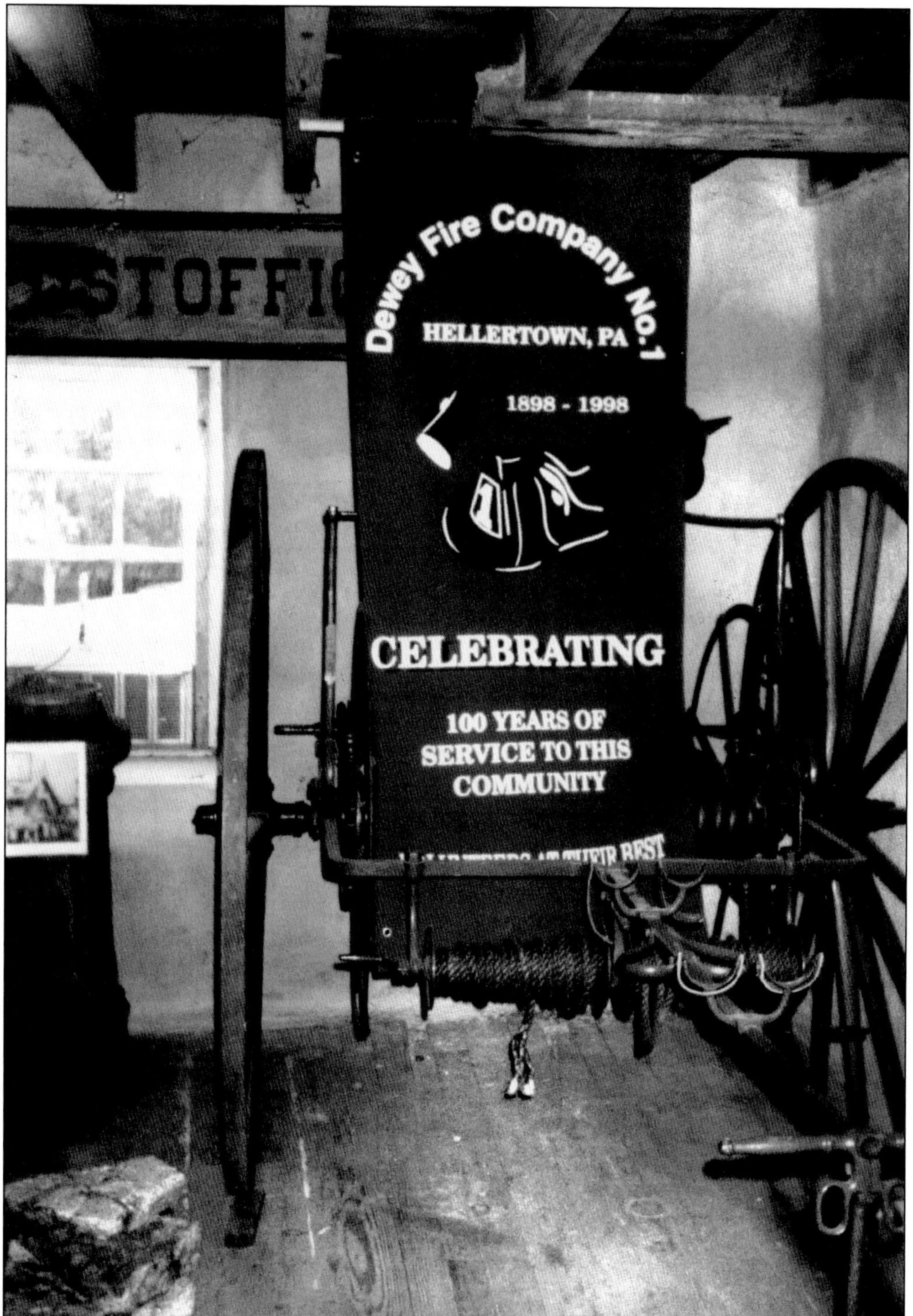

The first piece of Dewey Fire Company No. 1's apparatus is displayed in the Hellertown Historical Society Museum. It is draped with a banner commemorating the Dewey's 100 years of service.

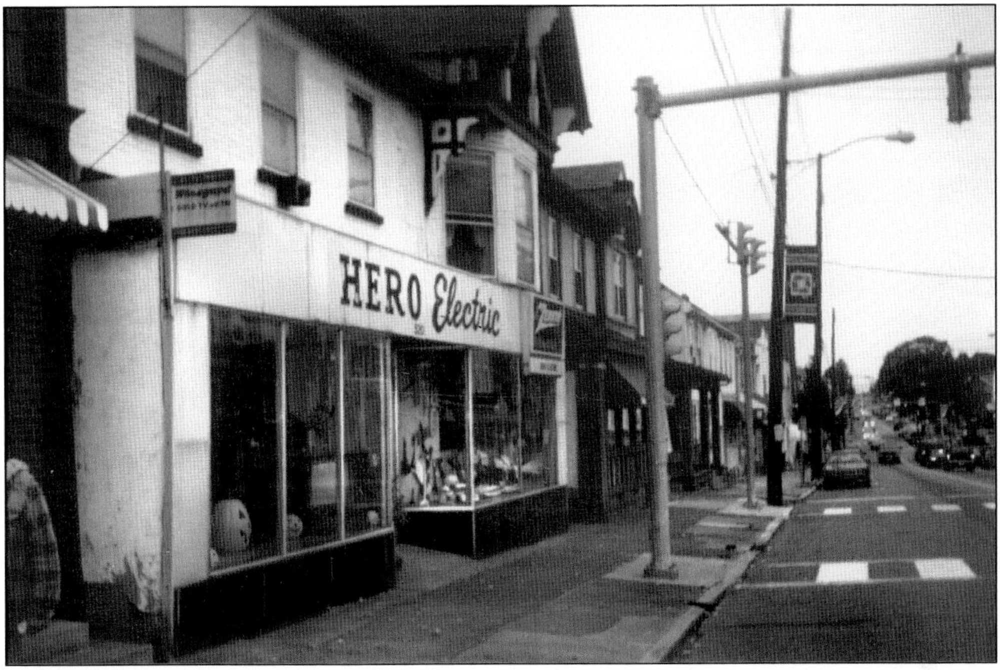

The Moll family crafted rifles in several buildings in this block of the King's Highway during the 19th century. As Nazareth was famous for the Henry firearms, so did Hellertown become noted for the production of rifles, pistols, and swords by the Molls. To learn more, you can obtain a book at the historical society, written by attorney Earl Heffner, former Hellertown resident.

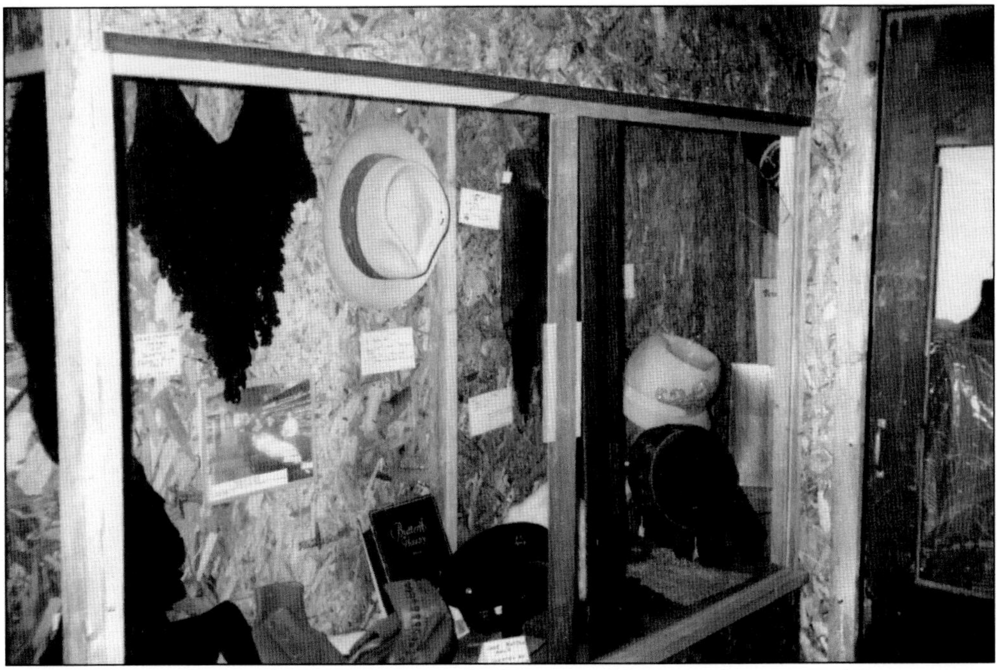

The Hellertown Historical Society Museum displays apparel from the distant past. The museum is open Tuesday and Saturday mornings from 9:00 a.m. to 11:30 a.m. or by special arrangement.

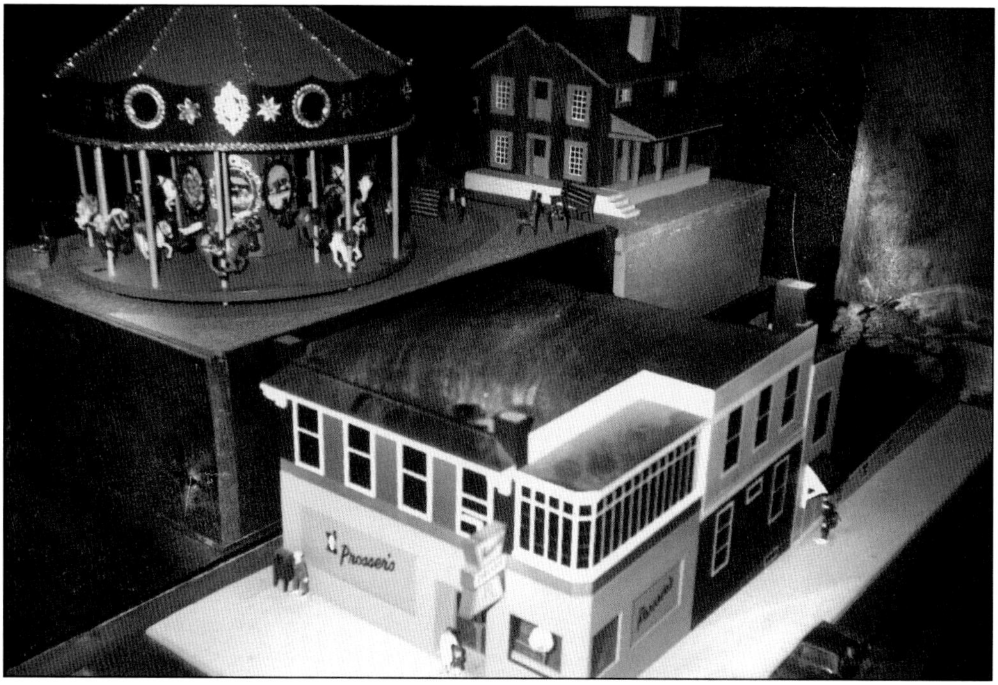

Prosser's Drugstore in miniature reminds us of the long service to the community of the Prosser family and the business that thrived on Main Street for decades. The soda fountain was one of the best in the area.

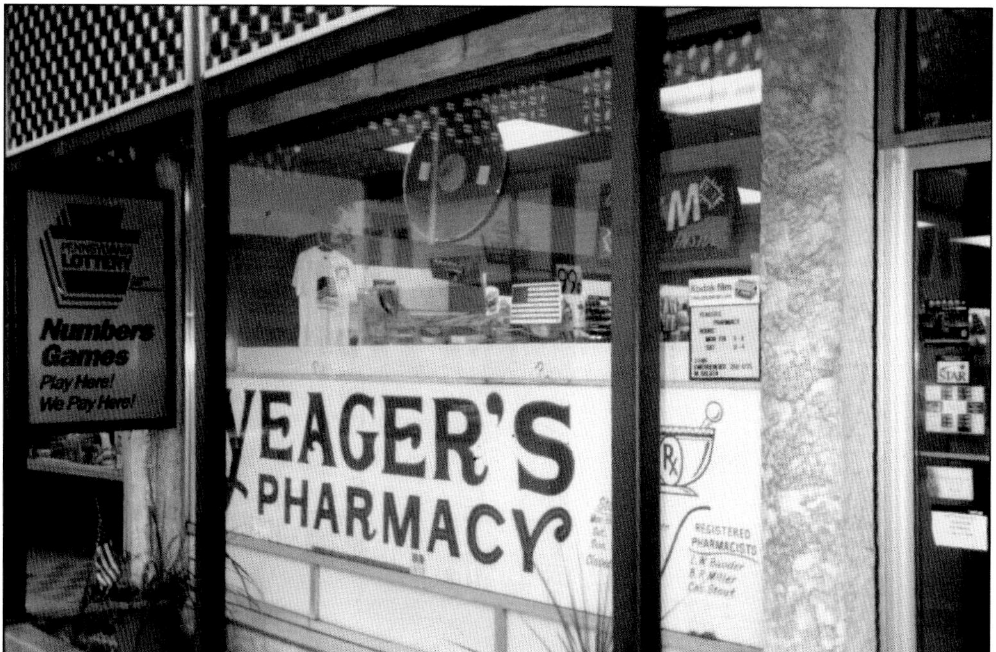

Yeager's Pharmacy moved from the Odd Fellows Hall to its present location during the early 1950s. Lindy Bauder, pharmacist, is long remembered by Hellertonians for his positive attitude and dedicated service.

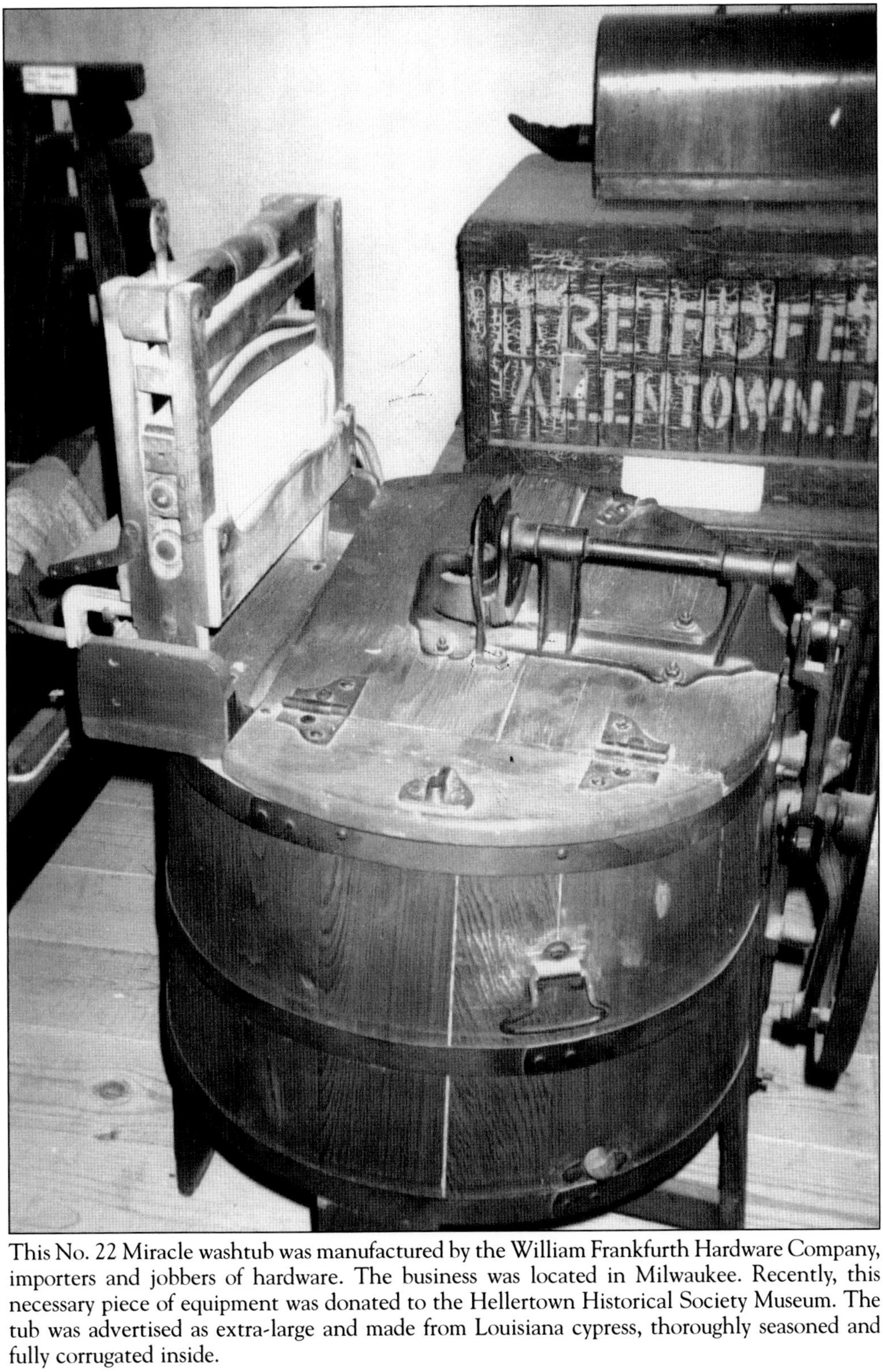

This No. 22 Miracle washtub was manufactured by the William Frankfurth Hardware Company, importers and jobbers of hardware. The business was located in Milwaukee. Recently, this necessary piece of equipment was donated to the Hellertown Historical Society Museum. The tub was advertised as extra-large and made from Louisiana cypress, thoroughly seasoned and fully corrugated inside.

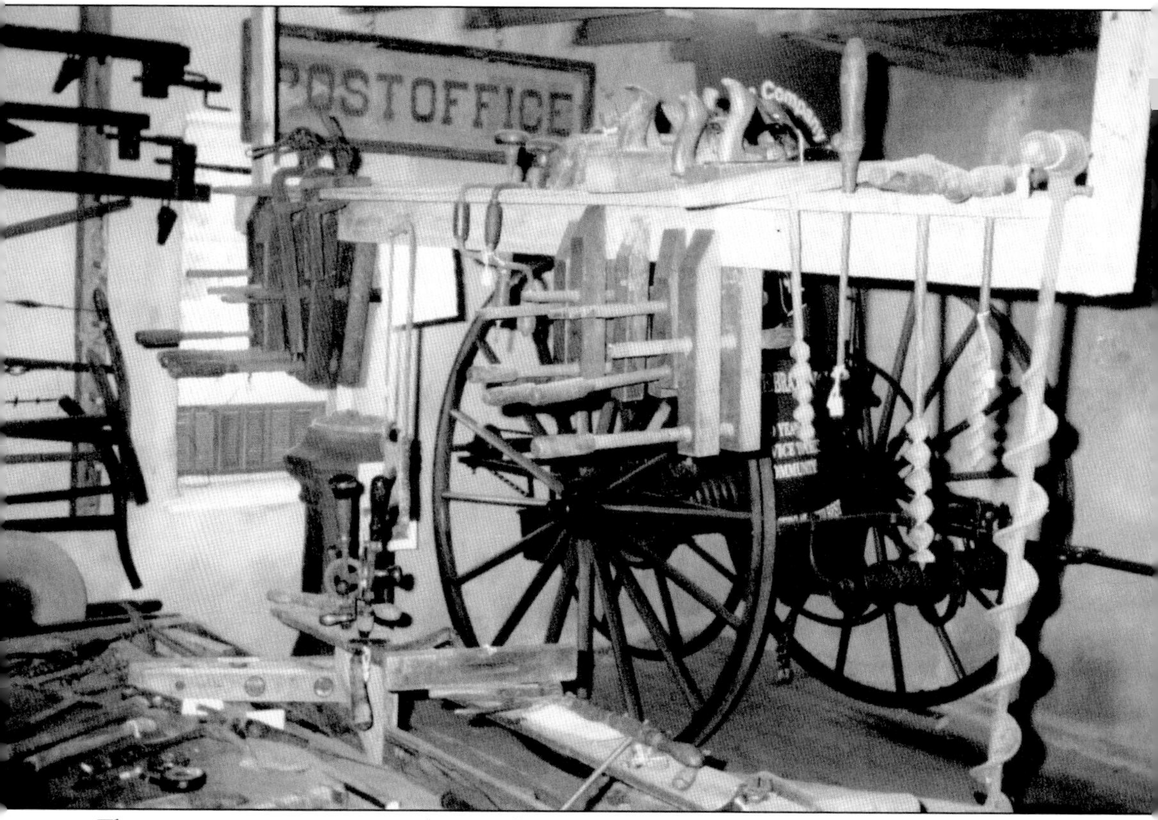

The museum contains quite a large collection of antique hand tools. The society welcomes contributions of any kind for the museum. Each item is cataloged to identify the donor. Here, you may notice several box planes and two-man saws.

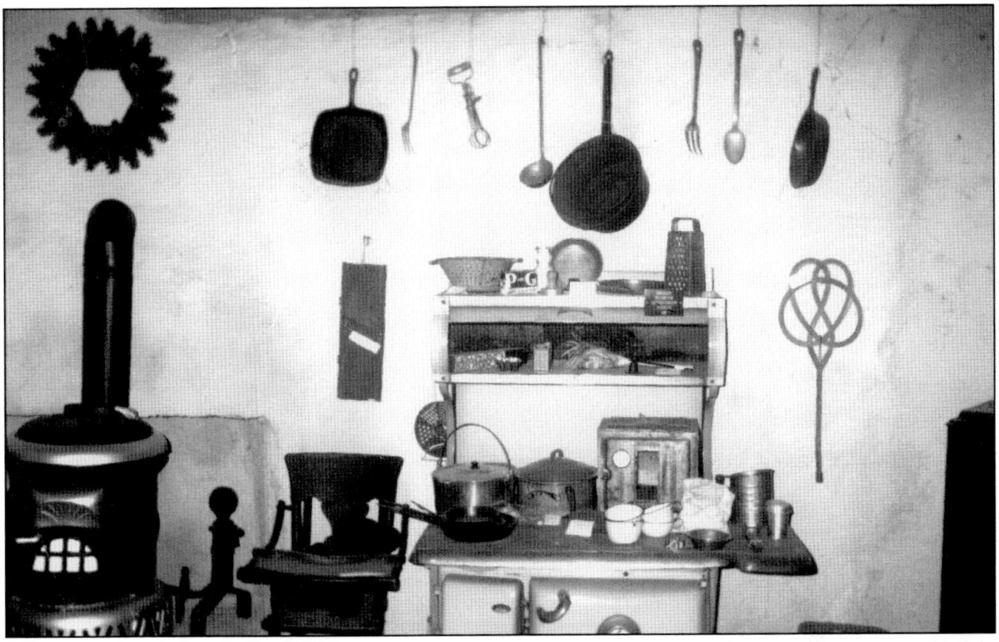

The kitchen area demonstrates cooking, baking, and warming devices that were highly thought of in their day, about a century ago. If forced to, could someone survive today with only this equipment?

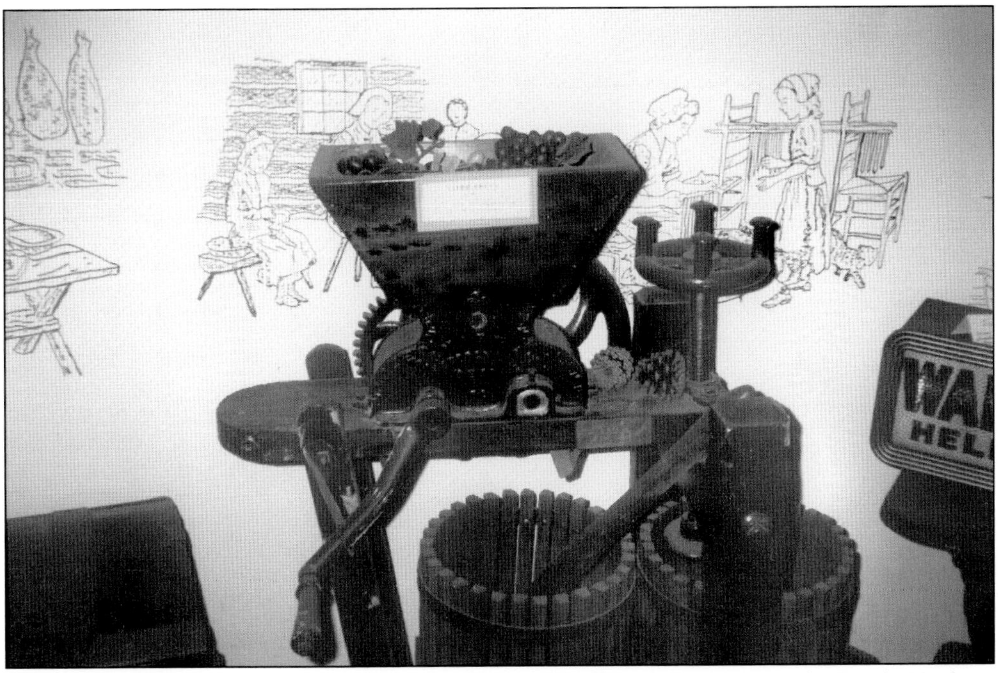

A necessity 100 years ago, the manual cider press was still in use 50 years ago by Frank Weidner. The neighborhood gang of boys would meet on a Saturday morning in fall to taste the sweet juice from just-picked apples. Sometimes, he would add grapes if he had a good crop.

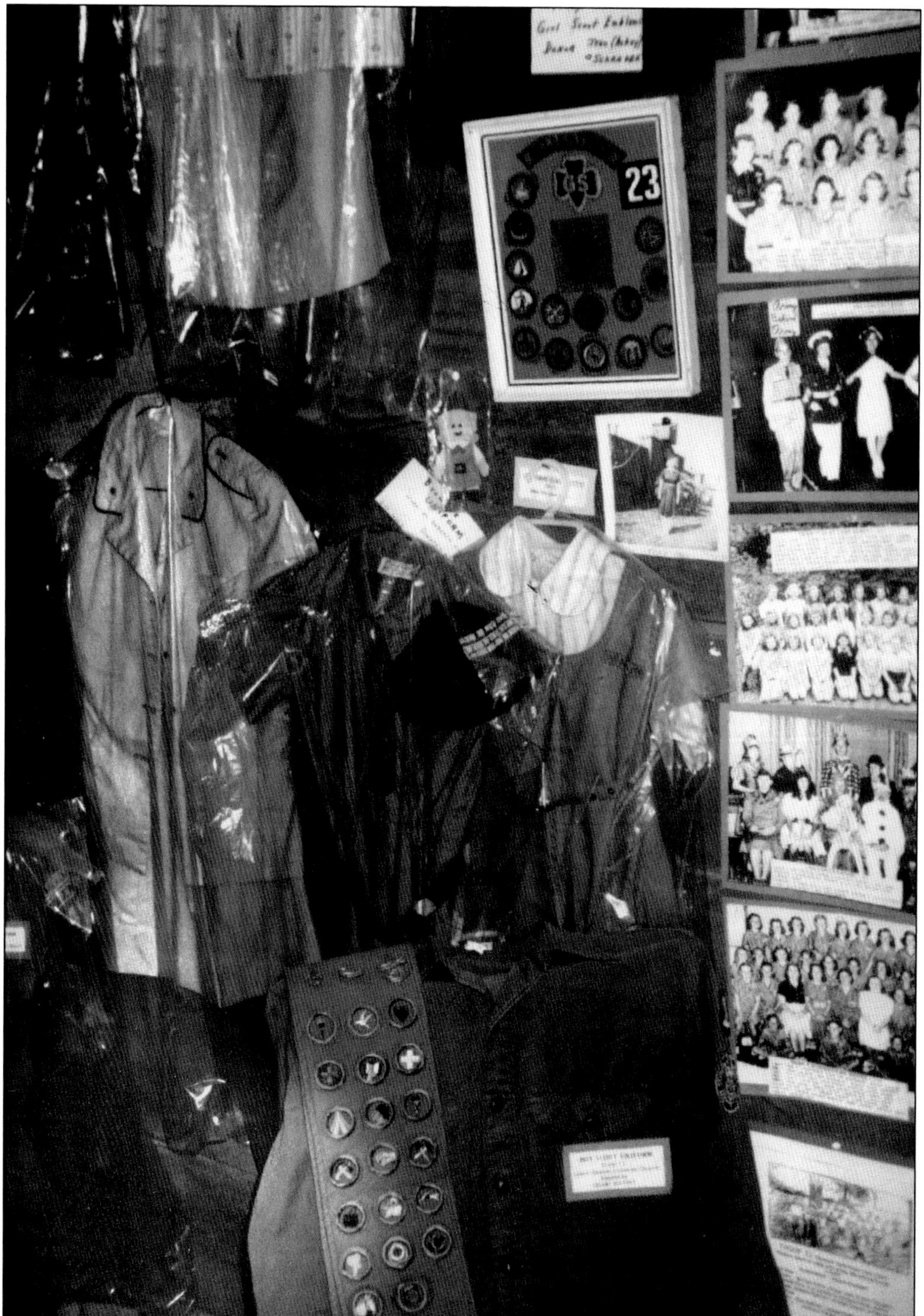

Some local Girl Scouts and Boy Scouts will fondly remember the Scout Lodge from 50 years ago and the badges and patches that could be earned. The museum contains a collection of these items, plus uniforms of an earlier area.

In the museum are preserved the hymn chart for each service and an original pew from Christ Union.

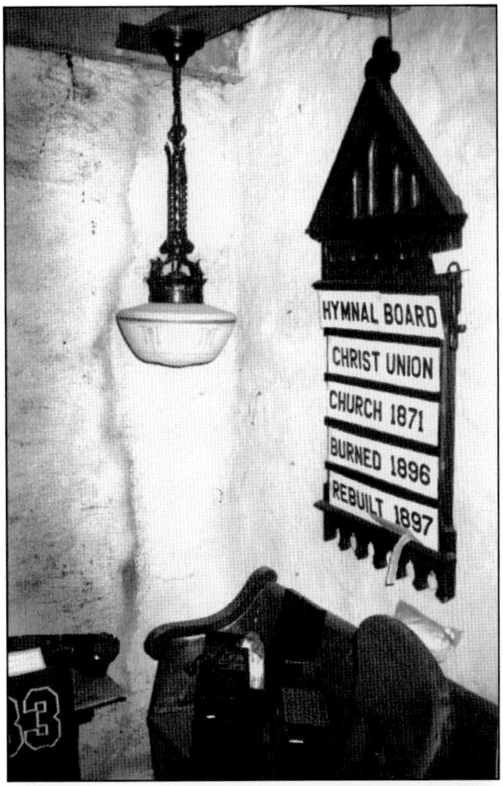

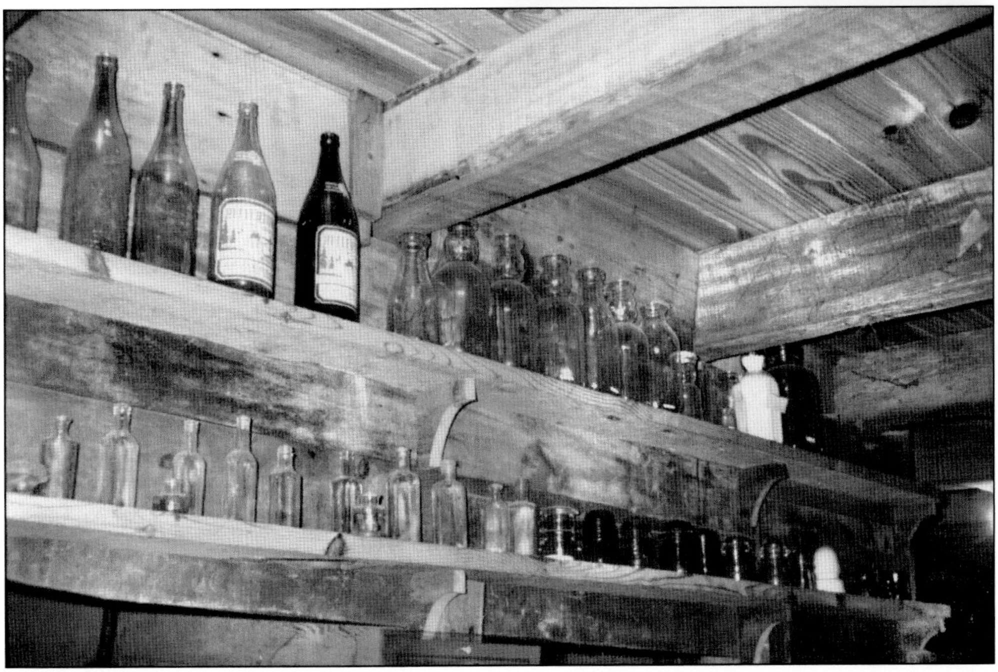

The museum has quite a large collection of bottles, including the distinctive baby-faced bottles of Brookfield Dairy and those soda bottles from the Hellertown Bottling Works, which among other flavors, produced the best chocolate soda ever.

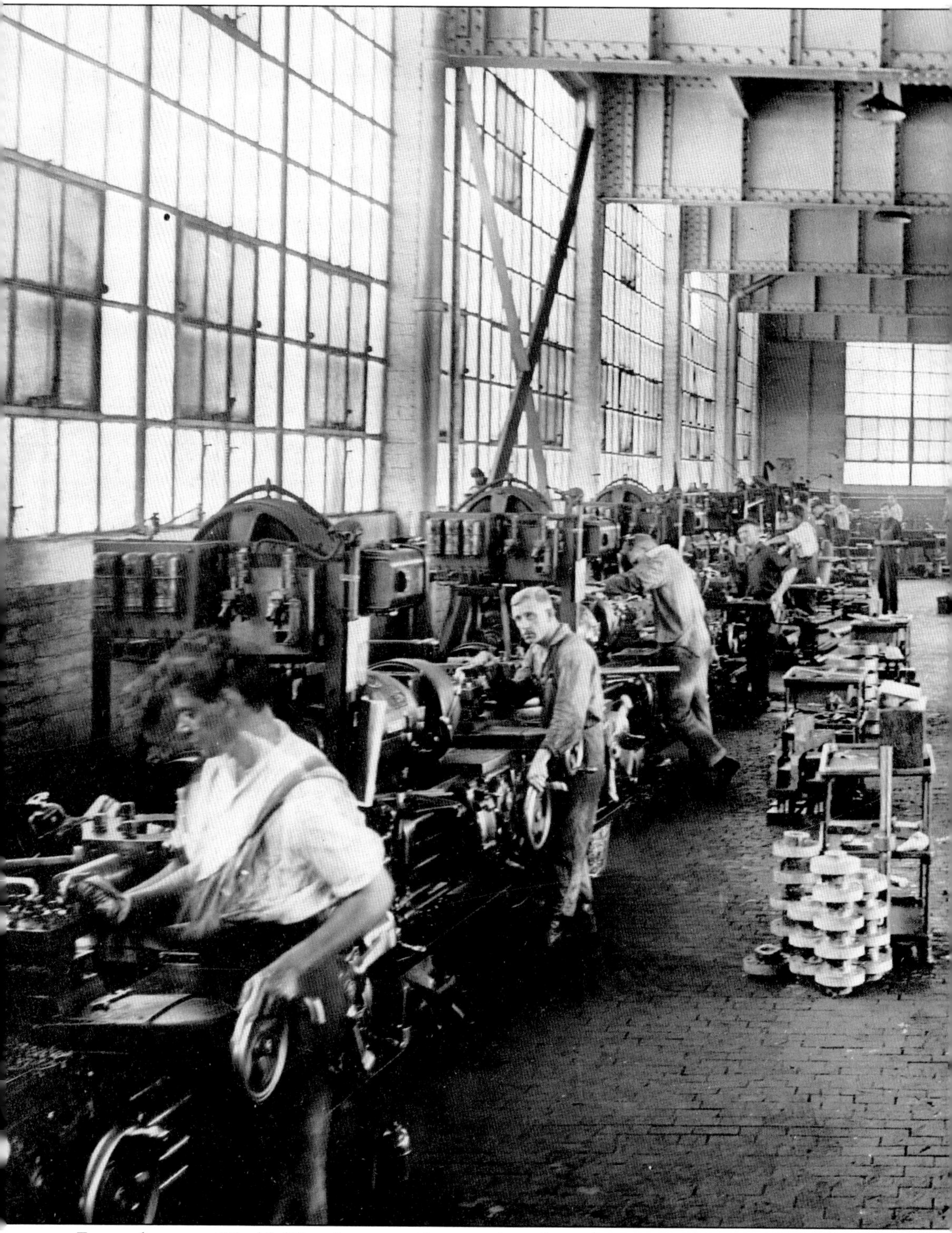

From the post–World War I era until recently, when foreign steel importing destroyed Bethlehem Steel, many Hellertonians were employed by the corporation. This photograph

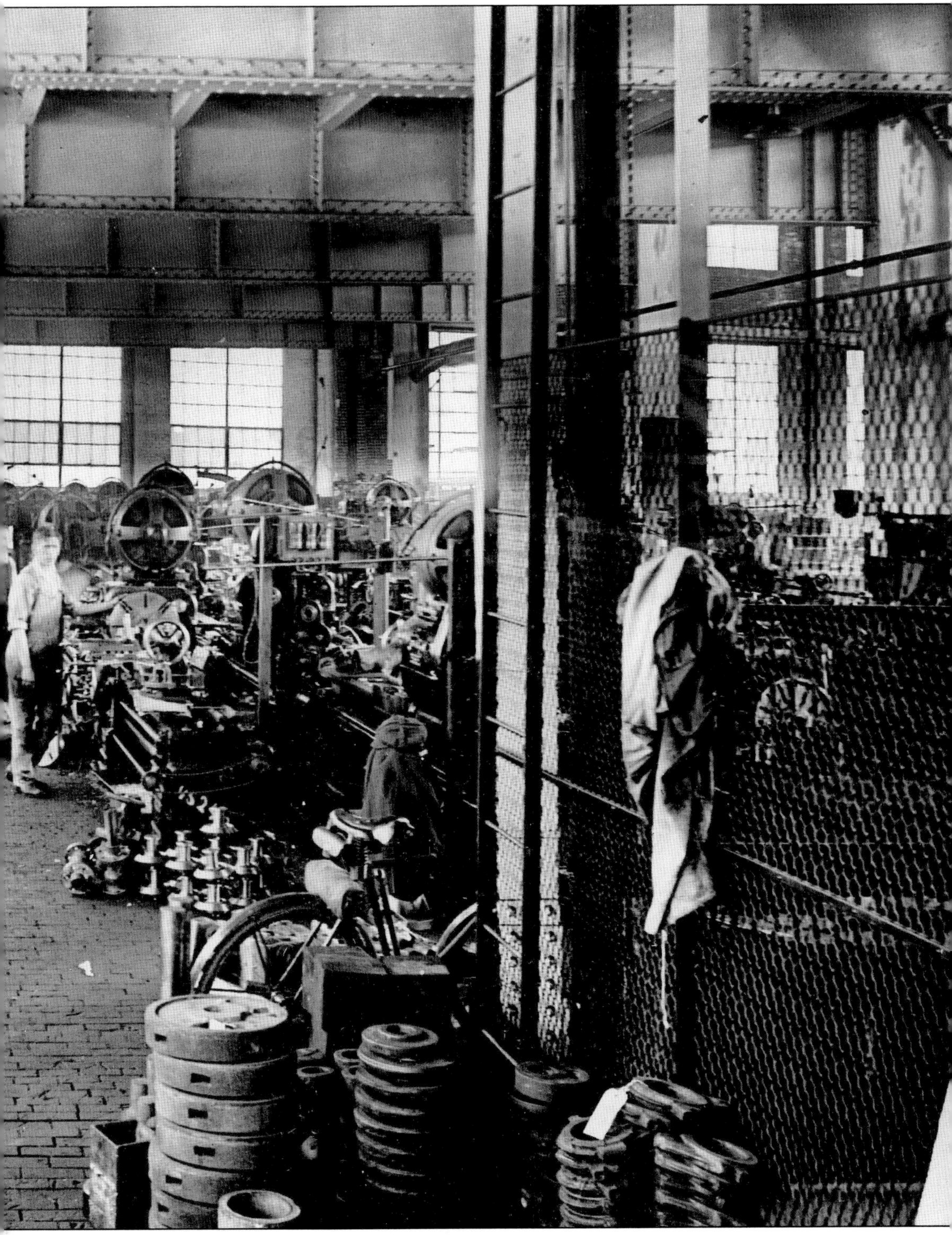

shows the machine gallery on September 3, 1918.

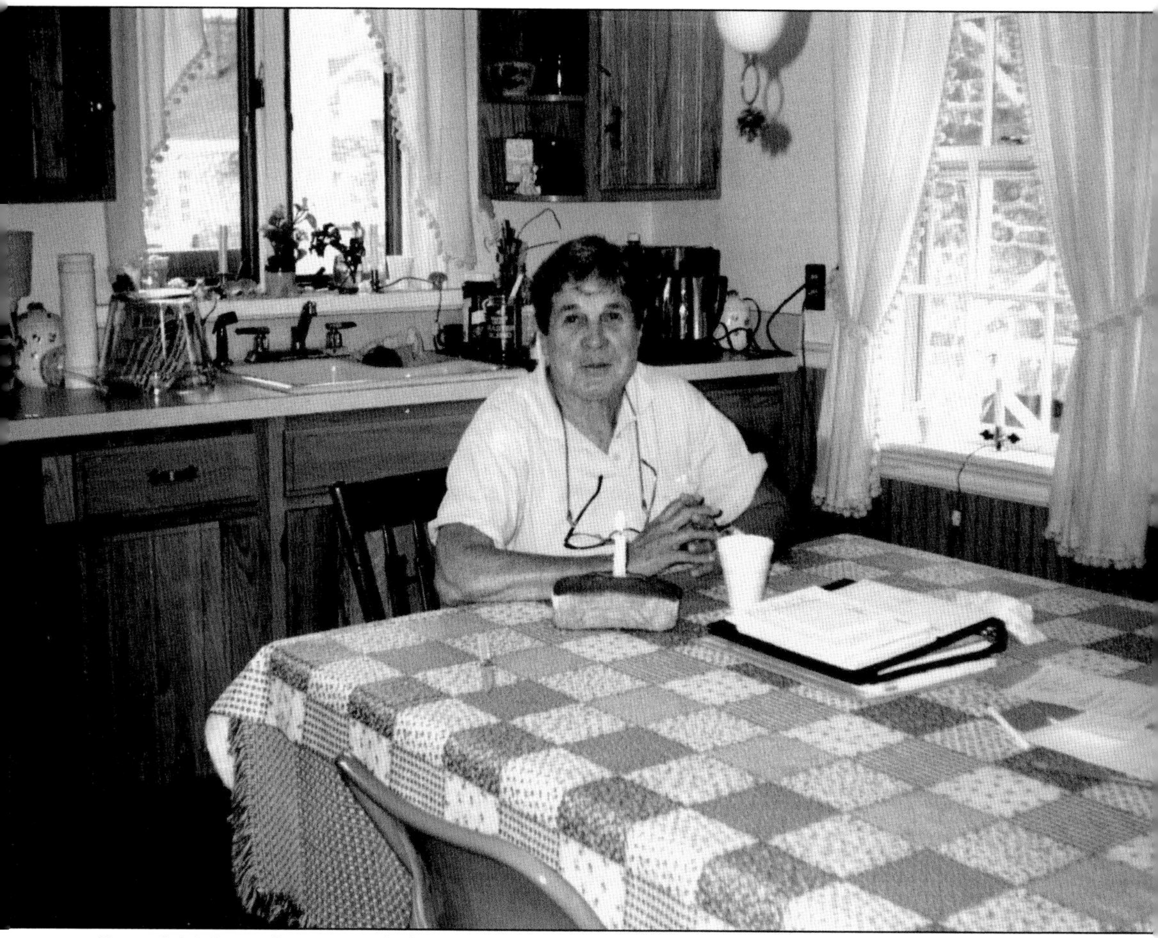

Betty McManus long served the Hellertown Historical Society in many ways. She was always there when needed. The author's first article three years ago was about her service to her country during World War II as a railroad brakeman. This book is dedicated to her memory and to all other past members who helped research and reveal Hellertown's history.